Trans *Formations*

Trans *Formations*

Grounding Theology in Trans and Non-Binary Lives

Alex Clare-Young

scm press

© Alex Clare-Young 2024

Published in 2024 by SCM Press

Editorial office
3rd Floor, Invicta House,
110 Golden Lane,
London EC1Y 0TG, UK

www.scmpress.co.uk

SCM Press is an imprint of Hymns Ancient & Modern Ltd
(a registered charity)

Hymns Ancient & Modern® is a registered trademark of
Hymns Ancient & Modern Ltd
13A Hellesdon Park Road, Norwich,
Norfolk NR6 5DR, UK

British Library Cataloguing in Publication data

A catalogue record for this book is available
from the British Library

ISBN: 978-0-334-06600-2

Typeset by Regent Typesetting
Printed and bound in Great Britain by
CPI Group (UK) Ltd

Contents

This book is dedicated to all the trans, non-binary, genderqueer, gendercreative and a-gender people of faith and people fed up with faith-based institutions who are striving to articulate their most precious and authentic understandings to those who would silence them. You are my kin. I love you, and I would not and could not speak and write as I do without you.

Acknowledgements

This book rises out of my doctoral book, which could not have come into being without the confidence and support of a number of people. I would especially like to thank:

Dr Deryn Guest for being my initial supervisor. I would not have begun this book without your confidence in me.

Professor Ben Pink Dandelion and Dr Elliot Evans for being a caring, supportive and challenging team of supervisors. I would not have finished this book without your guidance.

Chris Atkins for acting as a third-party editor for my book in accordance with the guidelines set out in the Statement on editorial help for Postgraduate Research Theses. Your proof-reading skills and enthusiasm helped me over the final hurdle.

Everyone at Westminster College Cambridge for all your compassion and colleagueship throughout my theological studies.

My dad, Sandy Young – thank you for countless conversations about theology, life and everything!

My mum, Pam Walker Young – thank you for always believing in my academic abilities, particularly when I didn't!

My sister, Abigail Young – thank you for your allyship, steadfastness and sense of humour, all of which I value more than you know.

Jo Clare-Young, my partner in 'theological' crime, for all your love and commitment, without which this would not have been possible.

Jo deserves double thanks as she has lived through me reshaping this work for you to read. So does each member of Cambridge Solidarity Hub who urge me – knowingly and unknowingly – to keep going each day.

Everyone at SCM Press, and particularly David Shervington, are due particular thanks. Their tireless commitment to publishing works that point towards justice and support of young theologians is vital, and I can't imagine this book getting out there without the commitment and support of David and the whole team.

A final word of thanks to Downing Place Church, and the United Reformed Church more widely, a church space where I am supported to belong, alongside other members of Christ's body, who give me space and time to minister, to be, to experience, to understand and to write.

God Dances With Us:
The Theology in Story

God dances with us. They leap and twirl and spin. They hold our hands gently as they follow our first tentative steps, then grip our waists firmly as they lead us in a daring twist and bend. God, you see, is neither leader nor follower, but both leader and follower, neither male nor female, but both male and female. God is gender-full and gender-less – an ambiguous flesh-less being who leaps into fleshy delight to join in our dance. God is under our skin, in our skin, gently breathing on our skin. Our God cannot be separated from us or contained within us.

Even as we feel God's embrace, we cannot define or confine them. God will not be caged. We want to keep God still so that we can understand them. Cautiously separating ourselves from God, backing off from the dance, goosebumps rising on our chilled skin, we run to our tool sheds to grab the bars that we have built out of words and theories, such as 'father', 'him', 'theocentric', 'kingdom', 'law', 'son', 'atonement', 'sanctification', 'exemplar', 'spirit', 'justification', 'eschatological realization', 'church'. These words and theories feel strong in our aching hands. God sits still as we construct arrogant theological walls and cages around them. They will not disrupt our freedom to name and confine.

When we are finished, we sit back and admire our work, occasionally pausing to throw the odd stone at the people who dare to question or live in ways that undermine our construction. We feel safe. It is easier not to dance with God. It is easier to keep them at a distance. But the people who question and deconstruct keep coming back and threatening to tear down the box. Our piles of stones dwindle, and some of our number even leave to join them. The more we shiver in fear the harder we lob our lumps of rubble and ruin.

Then, one day, some people dance up to the cage enclothed in mirrors. As they encircle it, we step away from our stones, curious, to observe them. Their dancing looks fun. We edge closer and closer, carrying a box in each hand. In one box we keep our minds, separated from our trembling bodies so that we do not risk sin. In the other box we keep our past, separated from our tenuous present so that we do not risk contamination.

As we approach the others we realize that they do not have any boxes. 'Where are your boxes?' we demand, terrified and bewildered as we stare at their empty hands. 'We do not need boxes', one of them responds. 'Our minds are swirled into our bodies, inseparable from our very selves. Our pasts are the root cells on which our present flesh grows, continuously transformed and transforming ourselves and each other. Our hands are open and empty, ready to receive and join in with the complexity and apparent contradictions of the dance.'

As we listen we remember the dance. As we watch the others dance, we catch glimpses of ourselves in the mirrors, static and staring, trembling and tenuous. Some of our feet start to tap. We want to join in. But our hands are full of boxes. We cannot dance. We feel like aliens – like there is no one here quite like us. We try to put down our boxes but we cannot do it. We are stuck, staring in incomprehension and dismay at the boxes of words that we have built to cage in our pasts, our minds and our God. We grip our boxes tighter, until they begin to dig into our flesh.

As the others dance round and round, I spot one who looks a bit like me. Fragments of who I am, of all that I have lived through and hope to become, of what I dare to believe and try to think, are mirrored not only in their clothing but also in their shining eyes. They pause in their dancing and stand in front of me. 'Kindred', they whisper kindly, and for a moment, just a moment, I feel euphoric. A wonderful realization that I am looking into the eyes of God flits into my heart. In confusion, I glance at the theological box that we build around God. 'Do not worry', my new friend laughs, making a face to draw my eyes back to them. 'We'll get to that ugly thing in the end.' Glancing at the box, and back at my friend, I realize that the walls and cages that we struggled to build are, indeed, quite ugly now. They seem misshapen, lacking something ... something essential.

I look back at my friend, their mirrors glimmering with grace and hope. 'But I cannot reach you', I murmur, dismayed. 'Let me', they suggest, confidently. They carefully uncurl each of my stiff fingers and slowly lift the boxes out of my open hands. Setting my boxes down in a fragrant bed of brightly coloured flowers, they blow on my hands, warming them. We sit down together on either side of the boxes. They take out a tool that I've never seen before and begin to prise open the boxes as I watch in awe and wonder.

Holding my past in both hands, they show me who I was, and they accept all of me. I look at the scenes with new eyes, fresh tears springing up as I realize what I have done by rejecting my very roots. They offer me my story and I take it from them reverently, and begin to rewrite my present, from the roots upwards. I smile a little. Here I am. Then they pick up my mind, struggling to hold the wisps of it as it curls around their fingers, searching for flesh. Suddenly I understand – I am held in grace. I do not need to be ashamed. I reach out for my mind, and it enters me, intertwining with each molecule of flesh, becoming me. I look in the mirrors my chosen kin holds up and I see myself as I am becoming.

As I look around, I see other people sitting in pairs and small groups, boxes discarded all around them. They are laughing and talking, playing together freely, mirrors glinting in the sunlight. The last box in the midst of us rocks slightly, as if daring us to go one step further. We have deconstructed our own boxes and embraced our authentic selves. Do not we owe God the same courtesy?

Joining hands as one diverse, messy, complex, wonderful body we approach the box and start to read the bricks and bars. Each word that once sounded so strong, each concept that once felt so right, now seems incomplete, insufficient, in the warm hands of real human bodies who matter so much more. We do not discard the words, we set them aside, ready to examine later, ready to create something new, something better, something more fitting.

As the bars are removed we begin to see more and more of God. The part of God who looks like us reaches out their wounded hands. In turn we reveal our wounds and scars. They come to join us, holding each of us in love. The part of God who looks like my mum smiles generously and walks over to a pile of bricks. Sitting down with their legs crossed, they begin to play with the bricks, laying out lots of creative new designs. The part of God who looks nothing like us swirls round our heads in bright colours and extraordinary sounds, composing a rainbow of music that tastes like sheer joy. Following its motion we begin, once more, to dance, together, mirroring each other and God. We are no longer hiding behind masks of uniformity. Instead, we wear our diversity authentically. We are no longer separated by boxes of division. Instead, we enjoy our unity together. May it be so.

Prelude

A Love That Will Not Let Me Go – Stacey

Are you familiar with that really old hymn 'Oh love that will not let me go'? I realized in recent times that however much I tried to run away from God – seeing them as this 'angry bastard with a killer surveillance system'[1] and so on – I cannot. I just cannot run away from God. I know right now that I'm angry with God and I'm shouting at them in prayer. I'm not really praying particularly reverently, I am almost shouting, 'Where are you?' But there is this something trying to put their hand on my shoulder, maybe even putting their arms around my midriff and saying, 'It's all right, it's OK, I am here, I am here with you. If you would sit still long enough you would know that.'

I have to concede that God is there in the mix of it when we are going through rubbish – I mean you've gone through things. Very often we cannot see the love of the divine expressed through those who we may not know very well. But they actually pull alongside us for a little while, even if it is not very long, and that constitutes God being alongside you just when you needed somebody.

Because of how human nature has behaved towards me and doesn't seem to want to engage with me as I am, I still struggle to truly believe that I am one of God's beloved. I have been starved of love for a long time, by human people, and it's sowed very deeply a belief that God doesn't love me either, because I believe the lies of the evil one, told to me through others.

I bet people have told you the same thing they've told me. They've told me that I was the devil's daughter, a paedo, a

5

freakin' weirdo, scum – whatever. I've had it all – and, yeah, it's got me down. But deep down I know that God does love me, and at some point – whether in the life that we are living now or something thereafter – we shall be one.

I am seeing you on the screen now – as you are seeing me on the screen now. This is how I am – and this is how you are – and God is still working away at both of us and certainly with me and helping me lose some of the chains that I bound myself up with. God is in the process of freeing me and getting me to realize that I do not have to be afraid anymore – no matter how shitty somebody is with me.

Note

1 This is a phrase commonly used by Nadia Bolz-Weber.

I

Introduction

This is not a book *about* trans and non-binary people. This is a book *by* trans and non-binary people. When I say trans I am referring to people who exist beyond the sex that was observed and correlated gender that they were assigned at birth and who self-identify with that label. When I say non-binary I am referring to people who exist beyond the binary genders of male and female and who self-identify with that label. I often write trans and/or non-binary as it is possible to be both trans and non-binary at the same time.

Let me introduce us. My name is Alex, and my pronouns are they/them. I am a transmasculine non-binary person in my late thirties. I transitioned over a decade ago. I am a minister, serving as a Special Category Minister in the Eastern Synod of the United Reformed Church, and have founded Cambridge Solidarity Hub as a core aspect of that ministry. I contribute to this book as theologian, researcher and minister, but also as a transmasculine non-binary person, sharing something of my identity and experiences. For each other person, their names and some details have been changed to protect their privacy. This wasn't the original plan, but life has changed for trans and non-binary people since I began this research, and it is not safe enough to expect folks to bare their lives in the public gaze.

Jack (he/him) is a middle-aged transmasculine, genderflux person. Jack began to transition several years ago and has just begun to take testosterone. After initially identifying as gender-fluid, Jack transitioned towards male but retains a sense of gender nonconformity. Jack has a doctorate and works in education. Jack describes his faith as gnostic and non-traditional.

He has a clear and distinctive understanding of Christian theology that draws on his own spiritual experiences, past and present multiple-religious-belonging, and wide reading from a variety of faith and theological contexts. Jack is a spiritual entrepreneur, creating safe and brave spiritual spaces for people who wish to explore their own spirituality.

Star (they/them) is a genderqueer young adult. Star has been living in transition for several years. Star identifies in a manner that is playful and that queers and challenges gender. Star is a minister in one of the four main UK denominations and identifies with the evangelical/charismatic tradition, while noting tensions between their tradition and identity. Star has a growing and distinctive understanding of Christian theology, and they frequently note the importance of continued learning. Star's theology draws on their training for Christian ministry, which included an undergraduate theology degree. Star also applies the lenses of play, genderqueering, disability-theory and experience to their theological journey.

Beth (they/them) is a non-binary young adult. Beth came out as non-binary very recently and has identified as queer for quite some time. Beth is a minister in a mainstream European denomination and has found that telling their congregation about using they/them pronouns has led to helpful pastoral and theological conversations. Beth's theology is centred around social justice and queer theory, though that wasn't their initial intention! Beth feels that, as a queer person, work around queerness and intersectional social justice is the only way to be authentic.

River (they/them) has come out very recently as non-binary and works in the leadership of a major human-rights organization. River is also discerning a call to ministry. River's passion for social justice is woven into their DNA and has always informed their vocational journey. Authenticity is very important to River and was a motivating factor in coming out. River's theology centres on God's love, and their vocation is strongly pastoral. They feel an affinity with, and vocation among, LGBTQ+ communities but can also see themselves in a rural, traditional parish.

Mike (he/him) is a young transman. Mike transitioned a few years ago and moves through the world as a man. As a Black man, Mike feels that both race and gender have informed his experiences, identity and theology. Suffering is central to Mike's theological understandings, but joy is central to his transition. He is moving towards a freer, more joy-filled understanding of God too. Mike is a writer, and his theological understandings are beautifully and poignantly poetic. As an advocate for social justice, Mike has lots of questions for God and the Church and raises the vital issue of structural injustice.

Sam (she/her) is a non-binary transwoman in her seventies, a father and a grandmother. Sam is also a playwright. Sam says that she is not a theologian but her biblically inspired plays suggest otherwise, and she believes that theatre is a missional arena. Sam has known that she was trans since childhood but only felt able to transition after the tragic loss of her wife, some years ago. Sam's theology centres around a passion for trans-formation, and extensive reading in early religious writings. She has also been strongly influenced by a family friend who taught her to meditate. Her clear resilience and creativity through, at times, very painful circumstances shine through her theology.

Ellen (she/her) describes herself as an elderly woman. Ellen transitioned socially and medically many years ago and now simply identifies as female, though her identity as a child of God is more important to her than gender. Ellen is retired, having worked in the sciences. Ellen now attends a medium-sized, inclusive local church that she started to attend when invited by a transwoman she met online. Ellen is also a lay-preacher and involved in the leadership of her church, and feels called to street evangelism and industrial chaplaincy. Ellen's deeply held and confidently expressed theology is based on tradition and experience, as well as her scientific knowledge. She feels strongly about social justice and has been known to shout about this when she preaches.

Pat (she/her) is in her forties. Although Pat identifies as female – which is also her sex assigned at birth – she also identi-fies as gender non-conforming. Pat's identity has been, in part, shaped by a single (male) parent upbringing, and a diagnosis of PCOS,[1] which she describes as an intersex condition. Pat is a minister and feels that her androgyny and gender nonconformity is a positive in ministry. Her theology centres around her belief in a loving God and her passionate understanding that the church should speak up for the marginalized. She also feels strongly that better understandings of trans and gender non-conforming identities would enable the church to understand the lives of cis people who do not conform to gender stereotypes.

Evie (she/her) is a middle-aged transwoman who transitioned socially around three years ago and takes oestrogen. Evie feels that her transition is a less important part of her identity than other factors, like being a parent and having a successful and fulfilling career. Evie is a member of a local cathedral, although her background and preferred tradition is charismatic/evangelical. Evie has a history of church planting and youth ministry and is in a process of vocational discernment alongside running her own business. Evie's theology is both practical and spiritual, biblically informed and continuing to develop. Evie says that she is still learning a lot about both gender and theology.

Stacey (she/her) is a woman in her late sixties. Stacey transitioned a while back and lost her family and her career as a result. Stacey used to work in education and has an unfilled ministry vocation. Stacey has felt very isolated since being rejected by her local church leadership and speaks with both wisdom and sorrow about her difficult experiences in professional, ecclesial and family contexts. Stacey is very spiritual and widely read and feels a particular affinity for both the mystics and the well-known Lutheran minister Revd Nadia Bolz-Weber. Stacey's theology draws on a wide variety of texts, as well as her own experiences. Suffering is central to her theological understandings.

I would like to introduce myself in more detail. My name is Alex, my personal pronouns are they/them, I am a trans-masculine[2] non-binary[3] person, and when I was a child I thought I was an alien. I felt so alienated I thought that one day I would be taken to the place where I belonged. This sense of being alien is how I often introduce myself in conferences, workshops and church services. I start with my name and pronouns to explain how a person should refer to me in the dialogues that will follow. I then go on to introduce my gender identity,[4] because my identity and correlated experiences, hermeneutics and insights are core sources that I bring into conversation with scripture, and with the identities, experiences, hermeneutics and insights of those I meet so that all parties might learn and discern together. Finally, I explain that when I was a child I thought I was an alien so that those I meet can begin to understand the alienation I have experienced as someone whose identity, experiences, hermeneutics and insights are often considered subaltern.[5]

I am also a Christian and an ordained minister in the United Reformed Church. Before beginning to explore my vocation to ministry, the lack of transmasculine and/or non-binary Christian role models contributed to the alienation I experienced. This has improved slightly over time; there are now other transmasculine and/or non-binary Christian ministers and writers. However, there are very few trans[6] and/or non-binary authored theological and theological-anthropological texts. This meant that I continued to feel alienated in theological education, confronted with reading list after reading list compiled entirely by cis[7] theologians. I only encountered trans and/or non-binary theologians in the reading list for one lecture; an ethics lecture where trans and/or non-binary identities were a matter of ethical debate and the contributions of the trans and/or non-binary writers referenced, as well as my own verbal contributions, were largely dismissed. I believe that being unable to read texts by anyone in your discipline who shares your identity characteristics is highly problematic. I found myself further alienated and lacking in personal and academic confidence. I wonder whether much 'imposter syndrome', wherein one feels lacking in the academic skill that one perceives others to have, is related to the inability to recognize oneself in the experiences and insights of others.

As well as my own experiences, I also became aware of a knowledge gap, or a dissonance in the knowledge assumed in trans-related literature, created by the lack of trans and/ or non-binary voices in Christian theology. I realized that my understandings of what it means to be human, and of what and/ or who God is, are inextricably intertwined with my experiences of being a transmasculine non-binary person. I found that trans-apologetic[8] literature assumed a distanced, if non-judgemental, God and a rupture between past and present self in transition. Further, I did not find any compelling theological challenge to the accusations of individualistic self-interest often levelled at me as a trans, non-binary Christian. I began to wonder how other trans and non-binary Christians understood their own humanity, and the God who they related to. I was desperate to know whether the dissonances I was noticing were mine alone, or whether any other trans and/or non-binary people felt, and thought, similarly. There was no cohort of trans and/or non-binary theologians whose work I could draw on to consider this question. I also wondered if theological understandings of humanity and God might be partial, or even mistaken, due to their cisnormative bias.

There was a clear need for an increase in trans and/or non-binary authored theological literature, particularly literature that is not trans-apologetic in nature, but rather grounded and/or constructive.[9] It was also obvious to me, though, that the feeling of alienation I experienced affected my ability to contribute to theological discourse in any way other than by offering trans-apologetic material. I was only ever invited to speak about being trans and non-binary, and about how I might defend myself against critics of trans and/or non-binary identities. I was never invited to speak more generally about anthropology and theology. This dilemma led me to feel called to complete research with other trans and/or non-binary Christians, to enable a group of us to contribute something authentic, confident and unapologetic to grounded theology. This book begins to address the trans–cisgender imbalance in both academic theology and church ministry. By addressing this imbalance, trans and non-binary voices will be increasingly able to contribute to understandings of God, understandings of humanity, and ecclesial understandings and praxis.

This book is grounded in my identity, experiences and insights, and in the identities, experiences and insights of trans and non-binary people who joined in interviews with me as part of my doctoral research. Our identities, experiences and insights are not manipulated to fit into a given theological framework but, rather, are stated as plainly as possible.

To ignore my own identity, experiences, insights and my interest in this work would be to assume false objectivity. I cannot claim academic distance. Rather, I am a researcher-participant, a dual role that enables me to analyse and relate participants' identities, experiences and insights faithfully while also recognizing my own personal interest and perspectives in the topics discussed. In doing so, I have not overdetermined the findings but, rather, have been able to note where I – my own identity, experiences, praxis and theoretical understandings – have been changed by them. This reflects my belief that there is no generalizable, singular objective lens and that instead, each theologian's writing is affected by their own identity, experiences and insights. When complete objectivity is claimed by an individual, the researcher pretends absolute personal disinterest in the subject of their research. This cannot be so. As such, I do not see my writing as intentionally unusual or subversive but radically honest. I refuse to lie or omit or alter in order to attend to academic convention. This would be to contribute to the marginalization of unconventional voices, including the voices considered in this book.

Feminist standpoint theory

There is no 'view from nowhere'. This is a central claim of standpoint epistemology. Standpoint epistemology, arising out of feminist theory and praxis, is positioned in opposition to the idea that the production of scientific knowledge can be objective and apolitical. Instead, standpoint epistemology suggests that all knowledge from a single or homogenous source is affected by the standpoint of the producer of that knowledge and is, therefore, both subjective and political. Further, standpoint epistemologists suggest that marginalized and/or previously accessed standpoints have particular knowledge that can provide novel and therefore essential insights to any discipline. Standpoint theory expands the relevance of voices from a particular standpoint. Whereas the contributions of marginalized people are often limited to discussions assumed to be about them, standpoint epistemology suggests they may have contributions beyond those discussions. In theology a standpoint epistemology exposes the limiting of trans and non-binary voices to the topics of sex, gender and sexuality, and highlights the ways in which a trans and/or non-binary standpoint can contribute to theology and theological anthropology more widely.

This book arose out of my understandings that:

1 All theological sources are subjective or provisional, meaning that without the subjective contributions of trans and non-binary people to Christian theology, (a) there is a clear knowledge gap and (b) trans and non-binary people are treated as objects of theological discourse, rather than participants of it.

2 The enfleshed nature of theology means that abstract theologizing that is not rooted in the lived experiences of human beings risks the God-trick.[10] Further, any claim that such abstract theologizing by cis people is not rooted in their lived experiences is inherently errant.

3 As enfleshed, subjective beings, our viewpoints are always partial. As such, no trans and/or non-binary person can be held as representative of all trans and/or non-binary people.

4 Theologies arising out of the enfleshed, subjective, partial viewpoints of particular trans and/or non-binary individuals have the capacity to be revelatory; to expose the cisnormativity inherent in theological and ecclesial assumptions and to call out unjust theory and praxis.

5 There is a need for a movement in both the discipline of theology and Christian denominations away from some people being restricted to binary debate about ethics towards all people being free to engage in fully participative dialogue about theology and anthropology.

6 These views are inherent in standpoint epistemology. Here, I explore each of them in turn, in preparation for returning to them throughout this book.

We must resist neutrality

Those who claim generalizable objectivity in their research and writing hide normativity behind a mask of false neutrality. In theology, for example, it is often assumed that the normative usage of the pronoun 'He' for God assumes that those using it do so from a neutral, objective standpoint, rather than noting the potential impact of patriarchy. The risk of a claim to generalizable objectivity is that some voices are privileged and others are marginalized. In other words, some people generally function as 'objects' of research rather than 'subjects' of research, meaning that their unique viewpoints are uncontributed. Feminist standpoint theory was a response to the understanding that the supposedly objective speaker of normative and assumed facts was usually male. This book responds to the understanding that the supposedly objective speaker of normative and assumed theological facts is usually cis. Therefore, if trans and/or non-binary individuals are unheard or marginalized in theology, there is a risk that we are seen as 'objects' to be studied rather than subjects or participants in the processes of researching and writing theology.

Knowledge is always rooted in social context and that, as such, the social context of any given researcher and/or writer affects the process of research and the resulting theory. The social context of the UK presents increasing challenges for trans and non-binary people. As such, the subaltern location of trans and non-binary people in this context affects our contributions to research and theory. This book is affected by my identity and location and the identities and locations of my research participants. By acknowledging this, we can contribute subjective understandings from our social context that differ from the equally subjective understandings contributed by cis people.

The way in which subjectively false neutrality is recognized by standpoint theorists is often criticized as being a form of 'epistemological relativism'. In other words, recognizing subjectivity risks destabilizing theory by noting that it is never absolute and always contextually limited. This critique, however, is unravelled by Sandra Harding (2004), who argues that given that all knowledge is contextually situated, it is illogical to use this reality to critique knowledge from any one theoretical perspective, standpoint or identity group. I believe that all theology prior to the eschaton – the life after life – is relative and provisional and recognizing that relativity and provisionality in this discipline is particularly essential given the power issues at play. If an ecclesial leader with substantial power and influence can claim that their theological understandings are the objective truth, the potential for abuse is disturbing.

Donna Haraway (2004, p. 95) writes:

> Situated knowledges require that the object of knowledge be pictured as an actor and agent, not a screen or a ground or a resource, never finally as slave to the master that closes off the dialectic in his unique agency and authorship of 'objective' knowledge.

As a trans, non-binary Christian, I have often felt like a 'resource', used as an object of pity, education, prayer or abuse. Even when I am granted some agency, it is often only extended to training others about my identity, answering debate or offering pastoral care to other trans and non-binary people. By writing this book I resist this objectification, claim my own agency and provide space for research participants to do likewise.

We must honour incarnation

In claiming agency, we are literally fleshing out trans-related theology. We are present in the flesh, not discussed or theorized about in absentia. Harding (2004, p. 12) points out that some feminist standpoint theorists describe the importance of theory rooted in a 'women's standpoint', whereas others describe a 'feminist standpoint'. Trans-related theologies often discuss trans and non-binary people as an 'ism' – as a homogenized class of people to be studied rather than as individual people who are trans and/or non-binary and have agency and perspectives that flow out of our own lived experiences. It is important to highlight, then, that this book is grounded in 'trans and non-binary people's standpoints' rather than in theories about the phenomenon of being trans and/or non-binary.

Harding (pp. 132–4) observes:

1 participants in standpoint theory research must be seen as human beings with bodies and social contexts; ...
2 knowledge should be formed in conversation with those embodied and situated human beings, rather than being formed in supposedly objective observation of them; ...
3 knowledge is formed in community and/or relatedness, not individually; ...
4 diverse and individual participants must not be homogenized.

The defensive corner that trans and non-binary Christians have been backed into by cisnormativity means that we are:

• often neither seen nor heard
• spoken about instead of with
• unable to find and theorize together with trans and/or non-binary Christian peers
• often subjected to accidental homogenization by allies who lift up the voices and experiences of one or two trans and/or non-binary Christians as normative, rather than seeking to hear the multiple, even conflicting, perspectives of trans and/or non-binary Christians.

Haraway (2004, p. 85) argues: 'We need the power of modern critical theories of how meanings and bodies get made, not in order to deny meaning and bodies, but in order to live in meanings and bodies that have a chance for a future.' I have often felt, in ecclesial contexts, that trans and non-binary identities and bodies are simply denied. The normativity of dimorphic,[11] binary language and theological understandings erases me and every other person who is neither male or female or who is both male and female. In order that trans and/or non-binary people may have 'a chance for a future' in the ecclesial context, the development of theological and anthropological theory that is 'rooted in our meanings and bodies' is both essential and overdue.

To achieve this groundedness, trans and non-binary theologians must:

- be seen and heard
- speak into discussions about theology and anthropology
- find and theorize together with trans and/or non-binary peers
- resist homogenization by refusing to be representative and, instead, seek to hear and to lift up the multiple perspectives of trans and/or non-binary Christians, even those with whom we disagree.

After a decade of being held up, unwittingly, as representative of trans and non-binary Christians, I have written this book as a part of my own reparative effort.

We must call for fragmentation

Contrary to the intentions above, critics of standpoint theory cite the same 'essentialism'[12] that feminist theorists critique. In other words, projects rooted in a feminist standpoint risk suggesting that all women are the same. Similarly, there is a risk that a book written from a trans and/or non-binary standpoint suggests that all trans and non-binary people have similar identities, lived experiences and insights. As such, it is vital to note that this book contains aspects of the unique identities, experiences and insights of ten individual trans and/or non-binary people. Our views are our own and are not representative of all trans and/or non-binary people. Any theology that claims that 'all trans people identify/experience/think in x way' is essentializing. Rather, I contend that these particular trans and/or non-binary individuals have insights to offer that are (a) distinctive because of their identity and location in their social context and (b) unheard in the theological discipline and/ or in the church more widely because of the lack of theological material written from a trans and/or non-binary standpoint.

Haraway (2004, p. 87) observes that any claim to 'infinite vision' is 'an illusion, a god-trick' and that, as such, 'only partial perspective promises objective vision'. Recognizing that individuals' identities, experiences and insights are not the absolute truth does not, therefore, limit their potential. Rather, standpoint epistemology recognizes that human beings are not omniscient and that each of our perspectives is limited. As such, it is epistemologically essential that any academic discipline contains multiple perspectives from multiple standpoints. I do not, therefore, propose to stop cis people from writing trans and/or non-binary related theological and anthropological literature. Rather, I argue that the addition of trans and/or non-binary voices to theological and anthropological discourse strengthens theory. Voices must continue to be multiplied until the eschaton and, until such time, we must recognize that any truth is fragmented and any truth claim is partial. Monovocal truth is partial, with polyvocal truth reaching closer to 'strong objectivity', the truth that builds on the identities, experiences and insights of all.

As such, this book must be expansive enough to create room for a variety of views, for fragmentation. Truth must always be 'stuttering', or layered, not certain. Throughout this book I, and the other participants, assert our own identities, lived experiences, and theological and anthropological insights. We cannot state that 'God is x' but only that 'We experience God as x.' This distinction is important. We also challenge individuals and institutions who speak with certainty about who and what God and humanity are, and how they function. We question overly confident assertions and queer normative generalizations. We do so not to offend or to silence, but to create space and to free potential. We seek to speak honestly about God, which we can only do by speaking provisionally.

We must be revelatory

Given that each standpoint is unique, researching any topic from new standpoints brings new insights, angles and questions to the topic. Part of my motivation for working with other trans and/or non-binary Christians was curiosity regarding the new insights, angles and questions that we might be able to bring to theology and theological anthropology. I was able to read about the theological views of countless cis people but very few trans and/or non-binary people. I wondered what revelations may arise.

Projects rooted in standpoint theory are revelatory; by virtue of their yet marginalized voices, their participants have the experience and knowledge necessary to unmask the logic of normative and/or oppressive systems. As a regular visitor to many churches, and as someone who offers pastoral care to trans and/or non-binary people, I am all too aware of the cis-normativity that dominates ecclesial discourse. This dominant system can only be fully exposed by trans and/or non-binary Christians who speak a language that is counter to the normative ecclesial language.

Revelation requires a common counter-language. Dorothy E. Smith (2004, p. 32) argues that an insider researcher is a 'native speaker' of the counter-language in which they are researching. As a trans non-binary researcher, I am a native speaker of the languages of trans and non-binary experience. As such, I can hear the revelations offered by trans and non-binary voices with clarity and empathy. This characteristic of being a 'native speaker' speaks to the importance of insider-research in curating theologies from trans and non-binary standpoints. Worryingly, there are very few trans and/or non-binary theologians.

Concerning the theoretical world of feminist standpoint epistemology, Smith (p. 21) writes: 'Men appear in this world as necessary and vital presences. It is not a women's world in the sense of excluding men. But it is a women's world in the sense that it is the relevancies of the women's place that govern.' In both academic and ecclesial contexts, the 'relevancies' of the trans and/or non-binary person's 'place' do not 'govern'.

This book does not ignore or discount the identities, experiences and/or insights of cis people, who 'appear in this world as necessary and vital presences'. Rather, I ask what is particularly relevant to the trans and/or non-binary participants of this research. This book is a world in which 'it is the relevancies of the' trans and/or non-binary people's 'place that govern'.

The idea of governing spaces is necessarily political. Standpoint epistemology's political nature is sometimes a source of controversy (Harding 2004, p. 2). However, I am reminded of the words of the Palestinian poet Marwan Makhoul (2019), who observes: 'In order for me to write poetry that is not political, / I must listen to the birds, / and in order to hear the birds, / the warplanes must be silent.' In the midst of 'culture wars' surrounding trans and non-binary identities this quote resonates with me. From the location at which I stand, it is not possible to write theology that is apolitical – there is simply too much noise. Further, any claim that majority theories and insights are apolitical is disingenuous. Speech, particularly speech that contains theoretic truth claims, is always political, given that it has material effects on the conditions in which people live.

Harding (2004, p. 5) explains that understandings gleaned from marginalized political standpoints can be 'toolboxes' that facilitate transformative theories and praxis. The political is practical. Marginalized peoples must be able to make truth claims in order to develop tools that we can use to challenge that very marginalization. If this process of toolmaking is seen as political, perhaps it needs to be.

We must be in motion

The curation of transformative tools is a motional praxis – it is a process that moves us from one position to another. Standpoint epistemology is inherently motional. Standpoint projects emerge naturally when the voices of the oppressed are heard. This book, then, is part of a motion out of silence towards multivocal utterances. This emergence, though, requires transgressive movement on the part of the speaker. It is not possible to speak out of a trans and/or non-binary standpoint without transgressing normative, binary theological and anthropological ideas. This transgressive movement is a movement that is heavy with risk.

To move transgressively is to struggle, not least when speaking from standpoints where even language is problematic, novel and/or contested. bell hooks (2004, p. 154) observes:

> We are wedded in language, have our being in words. Language is also a place of struggle. Dare I speak to oppressed and oppressor in the same voice? Dare I speak to you in a language that will move beyond the boundaries of domination – a language that will not bind you, fence you in, or hold you? Language is also a place of struggle. The oppressed struggle in language to recover ourselves, to reconcile, to reunite, to renew. Our words are not without meaning, they are an action, a resistance. Language is also a place of struggle.

This book moves transgressively by struggling with language. By daring to address both oppressed and oppressor this book risks offending everyone. By daring to transgress dominant norms this book risks freeing voices of dissent. In daring to speak with trans and non-binary peers in the process of shaping and speaking our theological and anthropological views together, we struggle, united in our diversity, to describe ourselves for ourselves, to reconcile ourselves to God, to reconnect our voices and to transform the spaces in which we move.

Standpoint projects are acts of 'resistance' from the 'margins' of society that function by curating new, transformative locations from which to speak (hooks, p. 159). Trans and/or non-binary Christians are at the margins of both church and theological discourse. As I have researched and written this book, I have moved to a new, transformative location. As you read it, I hope that you might too.

Grounding this book

Exploring the gap left by the lack of trans and non-binary voices in Christian theology, I realize that steps are gradually being taken to begin to address similar gaps in other fields, such as disability theology. In particular, Deborah Beth Creamer's early contribution to disability studies is strikingly relatable to me, and to this book. Creamer (2009, pp. 4, 115, 120) argues:

1 The field of body theology is limited by the assumption of a bodily norm.
2 Body theology leaves a vital aspect of being embodied, namely disability, underexamined and, therefore, misses the experiences of disabled people out of other aspects of discourse around embodiment.
3 Body diversity exists, and that diversity is not abnormal and does not need to be changed or corrected.
4 The prevalent models of exploring disability do not encapsulate the complete diversity of disabled people's lived experiences.
5 Disability theology 'deliberately embraces experiences of disability' and has 'great potential to benefit us all'.

Similarly, I contend:

1 The field of trans-related theology is limited by the assumption of gendered norms. These norms must be deconstructed if trans-related theology is to contribute to theology more widely. Further, there is an urgent need to find ways to talk about human identity in general and gender identity more specifically, that do not limit or marginalize people's authentic lived experiences.
2 Trans-related theology leaves vital aspects of being trans, namely the lived experiences and insights of a diverse range of trans people, underexamined and, therefore, misses the experiences of trans and non-binary people out of other aspects of discourse around gender. For example, we lack trans and non-binary theological perspectives on topics such

as, but not limited to, God's gender, feminism and patriarchy, trauma, trans people in ministry, gendered violence
and trauma.

3 Gender diversity exists, and that diversity is not abnormal
and does not need to be changed or corrected. Trans-related
theology needs to be founded on the first-person authority[13] of trans and non-binary people. It is essential that we
cease feeding a debate regarding the ethical validity of trans
and non-binary identities and, instead, accept that trans
and non-binary people exist and ask what they can teach us
about being human and about God.

4 The prevalent models of exploring gender do not encapsulate the complete diversity of trans and non-binary people's
lived experiences. Academic understandings of trans and
non-binary identities overwhelmingly rely on difficult
experiences such as dysphoria. Trans and non-binary identities are medicalized and pathologized rather than being
heard and affirmed. It is vital that trans-related theology
includes and takes seriously the self-understandings of trans
and non-binary people and not only what is written and/or
said about us.

5 Trans-related theology, and gender-related theology more
generally, should deliberately embrace diverse experiences
of trans and non-binary identities. These lived experiences,
and the arising insights, have the potential to benefit all
people, not only trans and non-binary people. Most trans
and non-binary theologians only write about being trans
and non-binary. Our contributions should extend beyond
our identities into theology more widely.

Writing in 1995, in a similarly early contribution to gender-
related theology, Elaine Graham highlights the knowledge
gap in theology that is related to gender, given changing
understandings of the latter. Further, Graham (1995, p. 222)
explores the complexities of speaking into this gap, arguing:

> Gender is a complex, dynamic and self-reflexive phenomenon;
> and a 'theology of gender' will not be a straightforward

application of selected categorical statements about empirical differences. Instead, theology itself must engage with the pluralism and complexity of interdisciplinary theories of gender at a profound level.

Graham suggests the need to hear multiple voices, so that gender is not further essentialized, limited to two binary categories that are rooted in stereotypes and assumptions. Almost three decades later, gender-related theology is still rife with simplistic understandings, both of binary sex and gender and, more recently, of what it means to be trans. The 'pluralism and complexity' that Graham notes have not yet been adequately attended to. This is a clear gap in the field of trans-related theology.

The knowledge gap that Graham points towards is the gap of not knowing how real people, across a diversity of experiences and understandings of gender, understand anthropology and theology. The part of that gap that I am particularly interested in relates specifically to trans and non-binary people. How do other trans and non-binary people understand being human? Who and/or what do other trans and non-binary people think that God is? How do God and humanity relate, in the conceptions of other trans and non-binary people?

Addressing this knowledge gap is not, however, about generalizing broad-brush ideas from the identities, experiences and insights of a sample of trans and non-binary Christians. Rather, it is necessary to attend honestly and authentically to diversity and individuality. Graham (p. 225) reminds the reader that this work will 'do nothing to dispel the fundamental limitations of using human experience to apprehend the divine, but rather remind us of the provisional and metaphorical nature of all "God-talk"'.

Attempts to talk definitively about humanity, or about God, are limiting and assume norms, such as those critiqued by both Creamer and Graham. The task is not, in other words, to fill the knowledge gap with clear answers but, rather, to question the assumptive answers that have been used to obscure the gap, by creating space for additional trans and non-binary narratives to speak into the gap. For example, where an assumptive understanding of trans identities might say that trans people are 'born in the wrong body', those hoping to create spaces for trans voices might ask the individual, 'How do you understand the connections between your identity and your body?' The answer given will be the answer of that individual, which might differ from the answer of any other individual, highlighting the diversity of knowledge that is obscured at best, erased at worst, by assuming and/or generalizing.

Outline

So what's in this book?

The book contains research data, including direct quotations, from interviews with participants and theological reflections on that data which include autoethnographical material. The chapters are punctuated by several Interludes, as well as a Prelude and Postlude, which reground the data, analysis and arising theory in the identities, experiences and insights of one of the interview participants. These Interludes are taken directly from interview transcripts and are, as such, written in participants' own words.

After considering questions of process, I move to our main findings. Chapter 4, 'Narrating our Experience', considers the narrative themes within which people's identities, experiences and insights are framed in their interviews. Each interview is framed by narratives of suffering, resilience and joy. Understandings of trans identities are often framed by the theme of suffering. The alternative theme of resilience still assumes suffering. Several folks use intentional framings of joy, exploration and play. There is a need for theological attention to narratives of trans joy. Theological reflections on trans identities are overwhelmingly framed by the theme of suffering and, in some cases, resilience. Joy is not a prevalent theme in trans-related theology. This has been the case in sociological and clinical understandings of trans identities too, until recently. There is, however, an increasing move towards euphoria[14] as a framing theme, in a reaction against dysphoria-based[15] models. Will J. Beischel et al. (2021) explain that 'gender euphoria describes a joyful feeling of rightness in one's gender/sex' and go on to argue that it is essential that clinicians and gender theorists understand and use this relatively new grassroots term. It is notable that dysphoria models focus on the past and/or incoherent self, whereas euphoria models focus on the present and/or coherent self. It fundamentally shifts the discourse of trans-related theology to move the focus from dysphoria and suffering, along with necessitated resilience, to euphoria and joy.

Chapter 5, 'Breadcrumbs of Delight', discusses our anthropological understandings, in which mirroring,[16] continuity, complexity and joy are foregrounded. Understandings of trans identities often assume past/present, mind/body disconnections. This is perhaps most clearly demonstrated by the trope of 'sex change' or 'sex swap' that is currently used in print media. Rhianna Humphrey's (2016) article regarding the harm caused by inaccurate representations of trans identities in the media highlights the prevalence of these terms, and the correlated harm. Trans-apologetic literature fails to provide a strong challenge to this trope based on assumptions of disarticulation. Conversely, continuity of identity, self, mind and body are experienced by participants. This continuity was supported by participants' anthropological and theological understandings. This shows the role that theology can play in critiquing harmful tropes.

Another trans trope is that of individualism. Perhaps the clearest example of this is found in the tragic suicide of the teacher Lucy Meadows, described as 'selfish' for transitioning by a columnist in a major UK newspaper, shortly before her death (Brown, 2013). There is also evidence that many trans people internalize this trope, believing their own actions in transitioning to be selfish (Rood et al., 2017). Further, selfishness is linked, by some, to sinfulness (Norwood, 2013). It is vital, therefore, to critique this trope from a Christian perspective. Selfishness and/or individualism was not apparent in the conversations that I had with other trans Christians.

Rather than individualistic desires, the reflexive mirroring of self, of the other and of God are key to identity formation and development. This shows that not only are we not overly individualistic, but we are also the exact opposite. Each of us actively rely on relatedness as a formative element of transition and take personal risks and/or make personal sacrifices in order to prioritize relationships, both personal and professional. This is a clear rebuttal of a pervasive trope that has caused considerable damage. Further, the theme of mirroring speaks to the church more widely about how we might better construct theological anthropologies that enable dialogue, rather than reinforcing debate.

Chapter 6, 'Dancing with God', considers our theological understandings, which are dialogical and participative in nature. I have found that trans-apologetic literature avoids any extensive reference to God, focusing instead on trans narratives, and on biblical support for trans identities. I am not dismissive of this approach – it has been necessary to work in this way in order to respond to trans-critical literature. This binary process does, however, raise particular difficulties. It is inherently androcentric whereas many feel that theology, as several of the people who are a part of this book point out, should be theocentric. The risk is that God is marginalized from, or constrained within, the very human parameters of these texts. Rather, explicitly exploring theological concepts enables participants to explore God as both intertwined with, and yet entirely distinct from, their own identities, experiences and understandings. This is a carefully navigated balance that seeks to reaffirm God's centrality in trans theology and also to recognize the inseparability of God and our lives and, therefore, of theology and anthropology.

Despite some of us highlighting the centrality of God, all of us feel strongly that God cannot be known with any certainty. This is in contrast to trans-apologetic literature which, by its very nature, attempts to assert God's definitive opinion in relation to trans identities. In doing so, trans-apologetic literature risks the same critique as trans-critical literature – claiming to definitively know the mind of God. Rather, this book attempts to multiply understandings of God, rather than to concretize any one particular understanding.

In our conversations we explored multiple ways in which God and humanity participate in action together – described by one participant as God 'dancing' with us. God, experienced as Creator, Spirit and Christ, is continually in positive action, communication and transition, working over and against forces of normativity, judgement and injustice. Again, this is distinct from trans-apologetic literature, which asserts a non-judgemental God in response to the trans-critical judgemental God. This approach risks implying a clear gap between God and humanity. Rather, our understandings of God and of humanity are inextricably intertwined. This highlights the agency of both God and humanity, freeing both God and humans from the binds of a distancing hierarchical stance. God is considered by participants to be gender-full and/or gender-less,[17] rather than merely male. This is distinct from the instinct to claim that God is simply beyond gender. This instinct is evidenced in the United Reformed Church Equal Opportunities Committee (2013, p. 3) paper on inclusive and expansive language, which asserts that 'God comes to us gender-neutral'. Such claims push God away as an abstract mystery. Instead, participants experience God in the particular, both in gender and in the lack thereof.

Finally, after the conclusion, there is a chapter that shouldn't be there ... This is the chapter that I said I would never write. But I will let you experience it, and decide what to do with it when you get there – there's a lot of work for us to do first!

As you read this book you will notice that:

- it does not fit neatly into any one theological discipline
- the participants have experienced significant marginalization
- norms and assumptions are que(e)ried[18] throughout.

The challenges presented by these three characteristics – resisting categorization, experiencing marginalization, and que(e)rying assumptions – are intentional and worth examining and re-examining as you progress through the book. I could have avoided them, but that would be to avoid the authentic realities of trans and non-binary identities, experiences and insights. Rather, then, I suggest that these challenges are integral to the comprehension of the book offered.

This book does not fit into any one theological discipline. It contains elements of ethics, biblical studies, practical theology, public theology, liberation theology, body theology and queer theologies, to name but a few. As such, this book asks essential questions of the academic pursuit of theology, particularly que(e)ring the divisions within our discipline.

This book is curated from the identities, experiences and understandings of trans and non-binary Christians, each of whom has experienced systematic and personal marginalization in theological discourse, in churches and in society. Parts of it are, therefore, painful to read, and this raises questions around the ways in which we can amplify trans and non-binary voices and more helpfully frame discussions around trans and non-binary lives. As a result of the marginalization participants already experience, I do not reference trans-critical literature. Rather, I choose to allow trans and non-binary voices, and the voices of our allies, to speak authentically, rather than in reaction to critique. As such, this book asks essential questions of the systems and structures of the academy, church and society, particularly que(e)rying hierarchies, debate of lived experiences and binaries.

It is vital that the identities, experiences and insights of interview participants are foregrounded in this research. Analysis is important, but I decided I must also give substantial space for the voices of those whose real lives are at the heart of this research. There are references throughout to the fact that theorizing about people's lives without giving space to their actual lived experiences is problematic at best and abject objectification of the individual at worst. As such, I use extensive quotes from interview transcripts, and in addition, I include extensive transcript extracts, edited minimally for readability. It would, perhaps, be more conventional to include these as appendices. However, I feel it is essential to foreground these extracts, rather than appending them.

This book que(e)ries norms and assumptions in trans-related anthropologies and theologies as well as in ecclesial praxis. Many of the identities, experiences and insights differ from or complexify those presented in trans-apologetic literature and strongly critique harmful or limiting ecclesial practices. As such, this book asks essential questions of trans-apologetic literature and of ecclesial understandings and praxis, particularly que(e)rying those conversations that occur without us, but about us. This book demands change, and asserts autonomy and respect for each participant interviewed, and for each trans and non-binary Christian who has experienced being marginalized from debates about our own lives. We are asking to be heard.

Notes

1 Polycystic Ovarian Syndrome (PCOS) refers to a clinical condition whereby cysts form on the ovaries. This is usually correlated with higher-than-average levels of testosterone.

2 Transmasculine refers to the gender identity of people who have transitioned/are transitioning towards masculine or male.

3 Non-binary refers to the gender identity of people who identify as something other than the binary gender identities of male and female.

4 Gender identity refers to a person's sense of self in relation to being female, non-binary or male. For example, my gender identity is transmasculine non-binary.

5 Subaltern refers to those who are marginalized and/or oppressed in relation to characteristics including, but not limited to, gender, sexuality, financial status and beliefs. The term is used in postcolonial studies and critical theory to refer to populations who are excluded from a social power hierarchy. It was coined by Antonio Gramsci in relation to those excluded from hegemonic institutions and systems. See Marcus E. Green, 'Rethinking the Subaltern and the Question of Censorship in Gramsci's Prison Notebooks', *Postcolonial Studies*, 14, 4 (2011) pp. 385–402.

6 Trans refers to people whose gender identity and/or presentation differs from their sex assigned at birth. Trans is an umbrella term that I also use to include non-binary.

7 Cis refers to people whose gender identity and/or presentation does not differ from their sex assigned at birth.

8 Trans-apologetic refers to theological literature that explains and/ or defends trans identities.

9 Grounded theology refers to theological material grounded in the lived experiences of particular individuals. Constructive theology, a departure from and/or re-evaluation of systematic theology, refers to theological material that allows for incoherence and does not allow any predetermined system to constrain it.

10 The 'God-trick' is the idea that a single source can observe the objective truth as if from above, as if the person claiming to tell the truth was God, and therefore removed from any particular location or perspective. It challenges the ideas of universal facts and objectivity. This term was coined by the feminist standpoint theorist Donna Haraway. See Donna Haraway, 'Situated Knowledges: The Science Question in Feminism and the Privilege of Partial Perspective', *Feminist Studies*, 14, 3 (Autumn, 1988), pp. 575–99, https://doi.org/10.2307/3178066 (accessed 12.3.23).

11 Dimorphic sex model refers to the belief that there are two distinct and separate sexes, indicated by chromosomes, reproductive organs, hormones and secondary sex characteristics.

12 Gender essentialism refers to the idea that set characteristics, including bodily and psychosocial norms, can be attributed to the respective binary genders of male and female, correlated with sex accordingly.

13 First-person authority is the philosophical idea that a person uniquely knows their own mind. For example, the way I know what I think and feel is distinct from the way that my sister knows what I think and feel. Similarly to Talia Mae Bettcher, I use this term to suggest that the individual has expert self-knowledge, and their avowals – self-declarations – should not be denied, rather than to suggest that the individual's self-knowledge is entirely inerrant. See Talia Mae Bettcher, 'Trans Identities and First-Person Authority', in Laurie Shrage (ed.), *You've Changed: Sex Reassignment and Personal Identity* (Oxford: Oxford University Press, 2009), pp. 98–120.

14 Gender euphoria refers to the joy a person may feel in relation to their body and/or the way society perceives their gender.

15 Gender dysphoria refers to the discomfort a person may feel in relation to their body and/or the way society perceives their gender.

16 Mirroring is used, herein, to refer to the ways people reflexively reflect each other and God.

17 Gender-full refers to the state of being full of/containing every possible gender identity. Gender-less refers to the state of being completely empty/outside any possible gender identity. While there has been significant discussion regarding God's gender, gender-full-ness outside the male/female binary is novel. Janet Martin Soskice speaks to the problem of a complete de-gendering of God in search for inclusive and expansive language. See Janet Martin Soskice, *The Kindness*

of God: *Metaphor, Gender, and Religious Language* (Oxford: Oxford University Press, 2008), p. 86.

18 Que(e)rying refers to a play on words, combining 'queer' and 'query' to denote the questions raised of norms by queer theories. See Gary David Comstock and Susan E. Henking, *Que(e)rying Religion* (New York: Continuum, 1997).

Interlude 1

Child of God – Ellen

If you read it carefully, God created Adam in their image, male and female. And it doesn't say a rib it says side. So you can read that as God split the hermaphrodite Adam into two and completed them and made them male and female. If God created us in the first place then God can do that. Why not? You know, if God can create the whole thing from nothing, then that's not a problem. I'm not saying that is the correct interpretation, I'm saying that it can be read that way.

So, I mean, God created humans in his – or their – image, male and female. And if you try to claim that means non-binary doesn't exist – it's like saying, 'On the third day God created the moon, he also created the stars, there are no such things as comets, asteroids or planets.' The thinking goes that they do not exist. Because they aren't mentioned in the Bible they are non-existent, and if you believe in them you're a heretic. If you're gonna take the line 'If it is not mentioned in the Bible then it doesn't exist' then you have to have no motor cars, no electricity ...

And when it comes to being the body of Christ, let's go back a step. Let's think about Jesus. Jesus was male. He had to be one or the other – I mean he might have been intersex. You know, nobody did a chromosome test, did they? And parthenogenic births do happen, they're very rare but they do happen, and the offspring is always female. So Jesus was a trans man. Alternatively Mary was XY and totally androgyne insensitive, so she was a trans woman. Now, I do not actually believe that; what I believe is that God did a miracle because God does miracles. But it is an interesting argument.

As to how God did the miracle: it was a parthenogenic pregnancy, because there was no man involved so it's possible that

Jesus was XX and presented fully male for some hormone reason or another or that Jesus was ordinary XY because if God's doing a miracle anyway then he might as well just tweak the chromosomes. Why not? I mean, it's a miracle. I think though, with any miracle, you ask how did God do it and the answer is, it doesn't matter. How did Jesus turn water into wine? Was there a little bit of yeast left in the jar somewhere? Well, probably not, but it doesn't matter. The point is that he did. The science existed then even if we didn't understand it then. Chromosomes existed.

God the Father is without gender. Jesus had to be male because if he had been female nobody would have paid any attention to what he said, you know, in that society. That's a solid reason for him being male. And that was for all of the time he had a physical body. So to me, Jesus still is male because that's the way he lived, that's the way he was incarnate.

In my church we tend to use neutral language for God. Our previous minister used expansive language, which was my first introduction to such a thing. So if she was reading a prayer in alternate lines she would address God as 'she' and 'he'. 'They' doesn't work because most people would understand 'they' to really mean 'he' but you're being politically correct. Which doesn't work. If God created mankind, humankind, male and female in their image, then they are male and female. And I would say that includes non-binary of various sorts. Our language doesn't cope. In the resurrection we will neither marry or be given in marriage but we will be like the angels who do not have gender.

Paul says in the kingdom there's neither slave nor free, Jew nor Greek, male nor female, so we're all non-binary. Earlier you asked how I identify myself and I said I identify as a woman, as a Christian and as a trans woman where that's relevant. But, of course, in the resurrection I won't be a woman. I will still have my memory and my history of being a man and being a woman, but I won't be – I will have a resurrection body, whatever that is, it's not clear exactly what that means, except it does seem to say I will have a body in which I will be able to worship or whatever. These are details.

But if we are neither male nor female then that shouldn't be an essential part of who I am. The fundamental part should be that I'm a child of God; a child of God, made in the image of God, as a spiritual being, temporarily clothed in a body. It's difficult to feel that. Because what we feel is our body; it's always with us, but I should be able to think about it as a spiritual matter. So as a child of God, and keeping the word 'child' rather than putting a gender in, in that sense we are all equal. I need to work on my self-perception that that is how I identify. As a child of God.

In so many churches you get told that men and women are of equal value but they have different roles and, in brackets, that anything important is a man's role. Particularly anything up front, standing up and speaking, anything that gains you honour is a man's role. It happens that way because that is the way we have always done it.

I said I will remember being a woman and I will remember being a man. I'm assuming that we keep all our personality even if we do not keep the physical body, because as a spirit I definitely won't have a gender or a body. But when I'm looking at the distinction between spirit and personality, it is tricky, because I do not really understand it. On the mount of transfiguration Moses and Elijah appeared and the disciples, who had never met them, immediately recognized them. They didn't recognize their bodies, they recognized their spirits, who they really were.

There are a lot of images in the Bible because people were trying to describe something that they couldn't describe. So I would see God as a warrior. Then Jesus quotes God as saying, how often would I have gathered you as a hen gathers her chicks under her wings; so now God is mother hen, or mother. God is mother in that passage. We see fragments of God.

I would say God is mischievous. I can easily see God in all those roles and more, but we cannot understand the full nature of God. We can understand the picture of a general leading an army, we can understand the picture of a mother nurturing her children, both of which are true, and are fragments. God holds multiple truths.

We should be the Church of God not the church of this building. We should change our point of view. We should preach the gospel. We should evangelize, which is an unpopular word these days, and we should do it in different places. I have been speaking with a local minister about that, about getting involved in chaplaincy, evangelism and mission out and about, but I get the impression that he doesn't really want me.

2

What is in a Name?

Stacey, Ellen, Evie, Jack, River, Star, Sam, Pat, Mike and Beth are names used to describe the trans and non-binary people I have conducted research with throughout this book. Those are not their real names, and the need to use alternative ones bothers me. Because of that, I decided to write this very short chapter, 'What is in a Name?'

When I began the process of research, like any student I had to go through an ethics review process. It was clear that it wouldn't be possible to guarantee anonymity for each person I interviewed. Despite this, I strived to protect their identities. They were therefore invited to choose another name during their interviews and, again, as I was writing up my thesis, so that their name would not be recognized. All but one refused. This surprised me but it shouldn't have. My name is precious to me; it turns out I am not alone in that.

However, that was in 2019, before the recent rise in anti-trans sentiment and action. I have thought, prayed and talked about names for the last year or so, wrestling over whether to include people's real names in this book or whether to change their names in order to add another layer of protection. I have been written about, googled and then written to countless times and I know the risks involved. Most trans and non-binary people do. It would simply not be ethical, knowing what we know, to put people's real names in this book and to open them up to scrutiny, critique and perhaps even attack.

Nevertheless, names matter in life. Many trans and non-binary people choose our names with much attention and care. Some of us feel that our names are a calling, given to us by God. The meanings of our names often speak truths for which we have no other language. Both desire and fear, joy and trauma are attached to names and naming when a name you were once called can be used as a weapon.

Names matter to God too, so much so that they are often changed. Abram and Sarah's new names mark their new identities as parents of many (Genesis 17). Israel's God-given name represents part of his journey, marking the time that he wrestled with God (Genesis 32). Peter and Paul's new names in the Gospels and Acts mark their new roles in the early life of the church. Names are so powerful that God's is hidden, their self-designation being instead simply 'I am'.

Just stop and ponder for a moment ... Imagine members of the public reacting so strongly to one aspect of who you are that you had to hide your name ... What is in a name? So you don't know their names, but will you honour their stories?

Interlude 2

Not Just Tolerated – Evie

Actually, most of my life and my faith journey is tied in with trying to not be that person who was trans. So, at the early stages I felt that being trans was a bad thing, but I actually thought that one day I would wake up female. I remember for years praying for an hour every night that I would wake up as female. I really wanted that to happen and it obviously didn't, and I didn't even know about God. I didn't go to church. I just had this instinctive kind of reaching out to try and call out to someone to kind of help me in that situation. I do think that led me onwards in my faith, even though it was very independent of formalized church, formalized religion.

I became Christian at 17, but even up to that point I had only told one or two that I was trans and they totally rejected me as a result. So that just reinforced my sense that this was shameful. I felt strongly that I need to stop feeling like this. I also along the way felt that I'm actually effectively a straight woman really. I like men better than women. But then I became a Christian at 17. Really it was in part because part of me was thinking actually that if I get involved with this stuff I will become a woman. It was interesting because I ultimately genuinely came to believe that Christianity was all true. There was then a kind of authenticity to my faith.

It gradually wasn't just about how do I not be trapped in this body, this gender. I realized, probably within the first year or two, that actually being trans was very unacceptable in that kind of environment. I did tell people about it. I told my minister at the time, the head of the kind of the ministry team, some of the elders of the church, and it was very much with the view of 'Please help me to stop feeling like this.' Because I recognized that they don't think this is right and I felt like I was sinning and I needed to resolve that. I became very active in my faith, I joined a Baptist church. It was a very active Baptist church, they were very into spiritual gifts and all of that type of stuff.

I became a member of the Christian Union and took a leadership position in the Christian Union. I was very much thinking about moving down a pathway towards doing full-time ministry. While I was a university, I came out to my girlfriend at the time, who became my wife, and she was a very strong evangelical and still is a very fundamentalist Christian. Her view was that this isn't right. The church agreed with that. I was just kind of mortified really and ashamed of myself. I just carried on trying not to do this and went through all the kind of usual stuff that you go through. People praying for you and deliverance and all that kind of stuff to try and get past it really.

Obviously that never works, but you keep going in the hope that that's gonna happen because by that stage you don't want to lose your marriage and you don't want to lose all the other things you have in your life. Really my reaction to the transgender thing was very much a kind of purge and I was repeatedly crying out to God saying, 'Help me not feel like this', but I was then left feeling ashamed because my gender dysphoria didn't stop. That was also overlayed with my sexuality, with the reality that I had married a woman but I actually much preferred men. That was a very confusing time, during and just after university.

When I left university, I was hired into the church to work as an assistant minister and that was a fulfilment of my dreams really. While I was at university I went to a conference on church planting and I realized that I had a real affinity with church planting and starting new things. I realized at that point that God was with me and that was what God wanted me to do with my life. Joining the church as their assistant minister made me feel like everything was going in the right direction, but always inside I knew there was this incongruence with what they believed about trans people and gay people. So it just was so uncomfortable. I felt like I was letting them down and really flouting what they believe. After about a year or so, I made the really difficult decision to leave because I felt that

I couldn't justify working there because I'm so at odds with what they believe.

I was lost at that point because I'd spent years thinking that's what I was going to do. And suddenly now I wasn't doing that. I drifted really in terms of work, and trying to work out what it was I wanted to do with the rest of my life. And I did carry on going to the church, just not working there, and then I fell in with a group of people who also were passionate about church planting, so I helped to start a children's church then I went on to help to plant a church in a pub. And that was brilliant. I did that for quite a few years, really. We grew up and the church, the children's church, grew frenetically. It was a really kind of great experience, but I was still really grappling with this all of the time.

Then they asked me to be an elder of the church and I did that. There is an interesting story around that because I was obviously not out as being trans and I was very much just trying to avoid it. But then one of the members of the church said that they had seen that I was trans because I had confessed it out loud in prayer circles. That elder told some people outside the church about it, and broke the confidence of the prayer room. So the church were mortified and obviously they expected me to kind of go off on one and be like, 'How dare you do that?' And I was like, 'Well, I am trans. I am.' If people find out about that, I'm not surprised because that's who I am as a person.

I think they were so surprised by how I responded to that that they then started saying that I would be fantastic in leadership of the church. I did that for a number of years. Then I went through a very difficult experience that caused me a lot of shame, and I realized that who I was living as was not who I was supposed to be. I was an elder of the church and I couldn't reconcile that with who I was. I told the church certain things about my life and they were not happy. So I got booted off of the leadership of the church.

Obviously then they wanted me to go back through a whole period of deliverance ministry stuff to try to purge myself of this sinfulness. At that point I just resigned. I just thought, 'I cannot do this anymore. I cannot face this. If that's what it means to be part of the church, then I'm not gonna be part of the church because I can't.' I've now spent, since I was seven, getting on for 20 years of pleading with God to not let me be like this and then them pushing me to do that again was just the last straw really. I just left church and kind of drifted for a while, and didn't participate in it and never really went away from my relationship with God, because that's really important to me, but I just couldn't be a part of church in any formalized way.

I've described myself in the past as almost the world's best liar because I learned how to hide being trans very effectively. It was tiring. I would think about every word I said in literally every conversation. I would constantly be worrying about whether this was the sentence that was going to give my secret away. I was terrified.

Over that period it got more and more difficult. I decided that I needed to transition because I'd got to the point where I was having panic attacks because the dysphoria was so palpable. It was around that time that the Church of England said 'We're gonna potentially hold services for trans people to confirm names' and that kind of stuff. I thought, actually maybe this is kind of a place where I could be accepted.

I looked up inclusive churches to find out my nearest church and I emailed them to ask if I was accepted. And they told me that the clergy would welcome me, but they weren't sure how the congregation would cope. Part of me thought, 'Come on, you've put yourselves on inclusive church, so surely they will be OK', but I didn't actually have a lot of confidence around that. I went along and actually found that it's just not my cup of tea at all in terms of style of worship but they also weren't calling for people to burn trans people. I can tell that they care about me and they want me there and they like having me as part of their church. That is a huge thing from my perspective, in terms of being welcomed and really embraced, not just tolerated.

3

Process

Research

Trans and non-binary voices are just beginning to be heard in Christian theology. Our voices are, however, still marginalized and often confined to ethical debates. By conducting this research and writing this book I have produced a polyphonic, grounded, trans and non-binary theology. I have enabled ten trans and non-binary voices to speak theology into being, and to share some of my own theological understandings too.

This chapter explores the way in which I have curated the theologies and theological anthropologies contained within this book. This is how I got to the stories. The aim of my research was to learn something about the identities, experiences and understandings of a variety of trans and non-binary Christians. The chapter begins with an explanation of my research paradigm, which draws on insights gleaned from grounded theory, feminist theory, particularly feminist standpoint theory and queer theory. I then explore autoethnography, the use of my own identity, experiences and understandings as research data. I attend to critiques of autoethnography, before moving to discuss queer autoethnography and going on to discuss the ways in which I have practised autoethnography as part of my fieldwork.

The attention then turns to my participants. I explain how I chose who to include in this research, and explore the importance of attention to diversity and, in particular, to unheard voices. I then discuss the practice of fieldwork, including how I found people to talk with, holding and writing up those conversations, and analysing the information that I was able to gather. This includes some discussion of changes necessitated by the Covid-19 situation.

Queer, grounded, feminist interpretation

The paradigm that I research and write within can be described as queer, grounded, feminist interpretation. But a theory is just a theory. Any theory is complexified by the lived realities of the folks that I have been having conversations with and by what has emerged in those conversations.

Grounded theory describes research and writing that draw on data that is 'grounded' from the roots up in the lived realities and testimonies of actual human beings. Grounded theory is all about interpretation, allowing me to pay attention to identities, experiences and insights that are both fluid – changing – and apparently self-contradictory. In other words, I don't need to come up with one settled view. Rather, this book is all about sharing the views of diverse individuals and honouring their individuality. Grounded theory is developed out of the insights that come up during research and arises out of a question, rather than a hypothesis. The question that I wanted to answer was 'What views about God and about being human are held by people who identify as Christian and trans or non-binary?' This was not a closed question, nor a question with a single answer. As such, any hypothesis would undoubtedly have been the product of my own identity, biases and social reality. Grounded theory allowed me to recognize these limiting factors and to seek the wisdom of other trans and non-binary Christians about this research question. It also encouraged me to follow the direction in which those other people led me, rather than rigidly controlling the research and steering it in the direction of my choice.

As I began to consider my questions I became very aware of the need for attention to individual identities and ideologies, social construction, power dynamics and intersectionality. In this work, gender identities were a clear focus. As such, I needed to explore the things I've just mentioned through the lenses of gender theory. The roots of the gender theory that I drew on in my research are feminist, with particular attention to feminist standpoint theory.

Feminist standpoint theory locates research and analysis

in women's lived oppression, locating knowledge in their life experiences. While this book is not only rooted in female experience, it is rooted thoroughly in the experiences of trans and non-conforming people who are systematically, socially and epistemically oppressed, including transfeminine people, transmasculine people and non-binary people. An example of systematic oppression is the complicated system that trans people must navigate to obtain a Gender Recognition Certificate and the fact that there is no such legal recognition for non-binary or non-conforming people. An example of social oppression is the difficulty that trans people experience accessing public toilet facilities. An example of the epistemic oppression of trans people is the relatively small proportion of published academics who identify as trans or gender non-conforming. The life experiences of those I spoke to are absolutely centralized in this book. While I anticipated that they would have experienced oppression due to their gender identity – or lack thereof – it was also vital to pay attention to privilege, which each of us has in varying amounts.

In the field of gender studies, privilege is often related to male-ness. This relation is complicated by trans experience. Trans men and transmasculine people do not necessarily experience privilege in the exact same way as cis men. Questions arise as to whether someone who was assigned male at birth retains male privilege as a trans person. Similarly, one might ask whether a transmasculine person, who has experienced life presenting as female prior to transition, gains privilege in transitioning. Although this might seem straightforward, transmasculine privilege is heavily reliant on 'passing' and non-discovery and is, therefore, a fragile privilege. There is not a singular straight-forward answer to this question. As such, I frequently had to ask questions of both myself and research participants concerning gender and power.

Asking questions about power in an interview scenario was difficult, but important. A primary concern was to ensure that I was genuinely hearing what the participant was saying, rather than merely hearing information that was limited by my own views or assumptions. To do this, I used echoing techniques, to check if I understood the person's statement. This technique is used in interviews, counselling and pastoral care, whereby the interviewer repeats back the interviewee's statement in the form of a question. For example, if a person seemed to be stating that they felt angry about a situation I might have responded, 'I'm hearing that that made you really angry, is that fair?'

When questioning gendered privilege and oppression, the individual's experiences were key. If they seemed to be expressing that they felt, or had felt, a sense of privilege or oppression because of their gender in a particular scenario, I asked if that is/was, indeed, the case. Rather than asserting my own opinion, I attempted to attend to their impressions while striving to understand the reasons for them. I did not assume that masculinity equates to privilege; nor did I assume that femininity equates to oppression. Rather, I attempted to engage in these questions in a nuanced manner. In addition, I tried to ensure that I understood the ways in which a person's identity differed from my own, including factors such as ethnicity, disability, gender and socio-economic status. When identity factors that I did not understand fully were raised by the people I was speaking with, I asked for more detail, rather than making assumptions.

It is also important to note the intersectionality of privilege and oppression. They aren't located in one identity facet alone. Feminist standpoint theory does this by offering intersectional analysis. This helps the feminist researcher to avoid flattening all female experiences into one narrative. Similarly, I gave attention to the intersections and considered whether privilege and oppression that are not directly related to trans identity contributed to my conversation partners' theological understandings. Important characteristics to consider included those noted as protected in the Equalities Act (2010), namely age, disability, gender reassignment [sic], marriage and civil partnership, pregnancy and maternity, race, religion or belief, sex and sexual orientation.

I asked each person to fill out a demographic form, which helped me to notice the intersectional identities that they held.

This is used in three ways: in choosing participants; in our conversation together; and in how I analysed that conversation. I attempted to find a group of people to work with that was at least partially reflective of the diversity of the trans community. The group contained ten participants. In interviews I used the demographics I obtained to make sure that I encouraged the participants to talk about all facets of their identities and to reflect on how particular parts of their identities intersected with their transness and their Christianity.

Feminist standpoint research is self-reflexive. In writing this book I have adamantly resisted the claim to academic objectivity, preferring to recognize that all knowledge is inseparable from the identity, experiences and biases of the knower. As I researched and wrote, I examined not only my own theological understandings but also my identity, privilege and oppression. I have attempted to be transparent about my own identity, both to the reader and, primarily, to the people I was working with.

My own identity as a feminist plays a part in my research techniques. Through transitioning, I have been able to witness the complex differences in the treatment of men, women and trans/gender non-conforming people. The masculinity that I have developed is built on female socialization and eighteen years of experiences living as female. As such, it is undoubtedly different from any masculinity built on male socialization and experiences. Further, I continue to embrace feminism as a framework for gender freedom and equality through the deconstruction of the binary gender system that is at play in patriarchy. For me, transitioning enabled me to challenge patriarchy from a different, perhaps wider, perspective.

Trans people undoubtedly challenge patriarchal systems. This challenge can be observed in our critique of medicalization, our assertion of self-determination, the lived experiences of those of us who live outside the gender binary, and arguments for safe gender-neutral facilities. The epistemic oppression of trans people is apparent in the lack of trans voices in academic disciplines. There are many reasons for this lack, not least that trans voices are small in number and our experiences are only beginning to be explored in theory. This is a clear matter of privilege and oppression, given that trans people have existed throughout time, and yet our voices are only now beginning to be heard. This book attempts to counter that very oppression by enabling and encouraging trans and non-binary people to speak into theology. Several participants identified as feminist, but they also challenged feminism where it has, in itself, become a hierarchical system.

Judith Butler's (1990, 2004) understanding of gender as performative is central to my understanding of feminist epistemology and to the application of feminist theory to trans and gender-nonconforming identities and provides a bridge into queer theory. Butler critiques gender essentialism and foundationalist understandings of gender, arguing instead that gender is performative. In *Undoing Gender*, Butler (2004, p. 4) writes:

> Sometimes a normative conception of gender can undo one's personhood, undermining the capacity to persevere in a livable life. Other times, the experience of a normative restriction becoming undone can undo a prior conception of who one is only to inaugurate a relatively newer one that has greater livability as its aim.

This critique of normativity not only supports the experiences of trans and non-conforming people, but also moves towards explaining why it is helpful for cis people to read theology written by trans and non-binary people. One reading of the above quote is that transness is a liberatory performance of gender, which can show others, whether they are trans or not, how to escape the bonds of normativity and binary thinking. Butler suggests that by exploring trans and non-binary understandings of gender, it is possible to disrupt potentially trapping gendered norms.

Building on Butler's work on both gender performance and embodied gender, I think that gender and sex are both flexible and material – intangible and real – and are intertwined in complex, to date poorly understood ways. This does not limit the usefulness of queer theory, which I rely on in this book. It does, however, highlight the importance of a repeated turn to re-engage with the lived experiences of trans and non-binary people through listening to our voices, not only theorizing about our identities.

David M. Halperin (2003, p. 340), describing the history of queer theory, notes that when the term was first used in a lecture by Teresa de Lauretis the intention was provocation. Queer theory can be described as an attempt to provoke a strong reaction to norms, enabling and enticing the listener or reader to disrupt those norms. Queer theory is, in its very definition, non-conforming. Halperin also notes the danger, therefore, of formalizing or institutionalizing queer theory. To prescribe a set of rules for queer theory would be to undermine its destabilizing intention and effects. Rather, queer theory suggests the questioning of any rule, norm or construct. I wonder what reactions this book will provoke in you. I wonder what rules, norms or constructs we – as writer and reader alike – might struggle to set aside, or even challenge.

To research and write within the world of queer theory, I needed to question, deconstruct and challenge the very concerns, questions and understandings that made me want to research and write. My interpretations had to be questioned, deconstructed and challenged when they became narrowed or single-focused or where it was too easy to find agreement between my own opinions and those of the people I spoke with. Grounded theory had to be questioned, deconstructed and challenged when developing theories began to suggest new normals. Feminist standpoint theory had to be questioned, deconstructed and challenged whenever individual voices began to be flattened and/or amalgamated, and when constructs of power and privilege threatened to silence certain voices. Even queer theory had to be questioned, deconstructed and challenged when that very queering risked becoming a norm, rather than a challenge to norms. I was repeatedly reminded of the importance of never assuming what 'queering' might look like, as ten different participants gave ten different sets of answers.

This is the inherent challenge, risk and potential of this book. By using a queer paradigm, I am allowing for, even encouraging, its destabilizing effects. This book doesn't provide a solid foundation but, rather, ever-shifting sands. The challenge has been to allow deconstruction, while curating a coherent, grounded work. The risk is that this book will be immediately rejected by readers whose own identity, biases and experiences prioritize normativity, objectivity and universal truth. The potential is that this book might queer norms; questioning, deconstructing and challenging theological understandings that flatten, limit and are used to harm.

Exploring my own identity, experiences and insights

Autoethnography is the systematic analysis of one's own personal experience that analyses oneself in context. In this book, autoethnography is the exploration of my own experiences of belonging to the identity groups 'trans', 'non-binary' and 'Christian'.

Autoethnography is not comfortable. I believe, however, that it is essential for researchers and scholars, writers and readers to be made to feel uncomfortable if we are to grow and learn. Emotive reactions to what we read, including discomfort, are important. In this book I am inviting you into my very self where both might be changed as a result of the mutual encounter. Some boundaries remain but, ultimately, those boundaries are my choice. Where I invite you in, you must make the choice whether to enter or whether to stop at the threshold.

Autoethnography did rely on a turn inwards to examine my own knowledge, experiences and emotions. It also relied, though, on a turn outwards towards others, towards social contexts and towards political realities. This is not only about me. Rather, it is also about my relationships, social context and theoretical understandings. The goals of writing about myself are not merely to tell you about myself, but also to impact wider communities and explore questions that affect many of us.

Some people might suggest that using autoethnography is a strategic mistake and might discredit my work because I write about myself as well as others. However, I do not think that reputation should be a barrier to knowledge. If I did, I would not be writing this. If exploring my own identity, experiences and insights can advance understandings of trans and non-binary people, then the risk to reputation is a necessary one. This is a calling, not a choice. Further, this has changed me; I have not been left untouched by researching and writing this book.

In my life I have faced countless arguments against being trans and non-binary that are very similar to some of the arguments often made against writers exploring their own identities, experiences and insights. I have been told that being trans and non-binary is 'self-obsessed' and that I 'just think too much about myself'. I have been told that 'There is no scientific proof that people like you [sic] exist.' I have been told that my identity is 'too much information', that who I am is too emotive or personal to discuss. Time and time again I have experienced a loss of reputation due to coming out as trans. Many of my trans friends and colleagues have reported similar experiences. These similarities led me to wonder whether there is a link between queerness and self-exploration.

The use of 'I' in this book links me, as writer, to those I am writing about. Rather than a debate between 'them' and 'us', the process of research and writing became a process shared between 'you' and 'I' through which we found experiences that we shared and we found our own experiences reframed in a way that held the potential to be transformative for all of us. I also hope that it might be transformative, in some small way, for each reader.

In researching my own identity, insights and experiences, I was constantly considering the balance between being analytical enough – really exploring my thoughts in some depth rather than just sharing them – and evocative enough – actually enabling you as the reader to feel what I am feeling, to understand what I have understood, to experience my lived experiences alongside me. It is possible to analyse in ways that are evocative. For example, to state that 'I am trans' is neither analytic nor evocative; it is simply a fact. To explain that 'I am trans. This means that I was identified as biologically female at birth based on the appearance of my genitals as assessed by a midwife. I felt a strong sense of dysphoria throughout my childhood and later transitioned towards male. As a feminist, I disagree with the assignation of gender based on genitalia', is an analysis, albeit overly simplistic, of that fact. To observe that 'Gendered as a child, I was haunted by pain, anger and fear leading me through transition to love and light' is an evocative rendering of that fact. I find it incomprehensible that just because as a tiny little baby my genitals were a certain shape and size, I was condemned to a prison of gender that was neither accurate nor chosen. Kate Bornstein (2013) writes of a life both desired and impossible. 'That is my life, my pain. Surely that, in and of itself, is a feminist issue', combines both analysis and evocation. This combination is, I believe, both compelling and educational.

As a transmasculine non-binary Christian, I have my own tentative answers to the questions I was asking when I began the process of research and writing, the questions I attempt to explore in this book. Maggie Nelson (2015, pp. 39–40) writes, 'I told you I wanted to live in a world in which the antidote to shame is not honor but honesty.' Honesty, by which I also mean integrity and authenticity, is an ethical norm by which I seek to live. In many ways this book attempts to reveal or create an antidote to the shame that many trans people are made to feel by Christian theology and churches. Personally, I have found that honesty is an incredibly powerful tool when dismantling shame, both privately and publicly. I have attempted to recount my life experiences and theological understandings in a way that embodies honesty, rather than honour. Honour is not irredeemably bad. It often, however, intends to produce pride or shame in the self or the other. Conversely, honesty is truth without the intentional production of pride and/or shame; a simple – or, indeed, complex – statement of what is, rather than what ought to be or might have been.

My own understandings and experiences as a trans and non-binary Christian were not only the foundation for my academic interest in this work, they have also been a part of why I've felt the deep personal need to find out more about other trans and non-binary people's understandings. To ignore my own understandings and experiences would have been to claim false objectivity. As a trans person, a Christian and a minister I have vested interests in this project, though not any particular theological emphasis, which I do not wish to ignore or downplay. By using autoethnography I hoped to not only create additional data, but also to record how my own theological views developed as I worked. My autoethnographical process helped me to examine my own biases and reactions and served as a clear marker as to where my views and experiences intersected with, or diverged from, the views and experiences of my conversation partners. Additionally, I have learned how the views of other trans and non-binary people can affect the theological understandings that I hold as a theologian and minister. I can no longer fathom how I functioned in these roles before having a cohort of other trans and non-binary Christians to talk with about theology and our lives.

Exploring other people's own identity, experiences and insights

Which leads me on to discuss how I worked with ten other trans and non-binary Christians to conduct the research that I now share with you. The exploration of my own identity, experiences and insights is, undoubtedly, secondary here to the identities, experiences and insights of the conversation partners who joined me on my research journey. It was crucial to work with a wide range of folks, to avoid flattening or marginalizing voices, and to work together to move towards grounded trans and non-binary theologizing.

Rather than reaching a singular consensus in this book, I strive for polyvocality by allowing differing trans theological voices to be heard and to queer the field by focusing on gender nonconformity among trans and non-binary identities, rather than binary gender conformity.

I didn't define 'Christian', 'trans' and 'non-binary' in potentially limiting ways when researching. I could, for example, have defined 'Christian' as referring to someone who believes in key tenets of the Christian faith or who attends church regularly. I could have defined 'trans' as referring to someone who has transitioned from male to female or from female to male. I could have defined 'non-binary' as referring to someone who lives as neither male nor female. It is also necessary to stress that the definitions of these categories included those who choose not to conform to any label or definition regarding their gender identity or faith identity, but who still recognized themselves as belonging to the identity groupings being researched.

To assert precise definitions would, however, have contradicted the things I care about. I discerned that my way of doing this work should prioritize the self-determined identity of the individual and should queer conventional systems and norms. To apply rigid definitions to the identity labels of 'Christian', 'trans' and 'non-binary' would have narrowed the group of folks I could talk to, to those who identified within the boundaries of those definitions or who were willing to mask their genuine identities in order to conform with my system. Further, there are observed the positive effects of enabling participants to self-define, rather than relying on the clinical definitions that, for some, have been controlling.

As such, I decided to rely on self-definition. This may mean that some readers will not recognize some of the people whose stories are shared in this book as 'Christian' or as 'trans' according to their own biases and definitions. However, the benefits outweigh the risks. Allowing for self-definition enhances the diversity of voices shared, queers perceived norms and allows folks to be open about their own genuine self-identification. Additionally, this allowed for a questioning of those very definitions: 'What does it mean to be Christian if one is also trans or non-binary, and vice versa?' Links between each person's definitions of their faith identity and gender identity were one compelling type of information that I was able to gather.

People under the age of 18 were excluded from this book. This exclusion criteria was both ethical and practical. Those under the age of 18 are likely to be in the process of forming their religious and gender identities and it would have been unethical to subject them to research that may overly inform or disturb those processes. Further, inclusion of people under the age of eighteen would require parental consent and possible accompaniment. At best, this could have skewed data collected, given that participants may have altered what they said in an interview if their parents were present. At worst, this could have led to a young person disclosing information to or in front of a parent or guardian that they were not yet ready or willing to disclose. I do believe, however, that the voices of trans and non-binary children and young people need to be heard, and I explore this topic later.

Gender is socially relational. As such, it was vital to pay attention to the ways in which the experiences and opinions of those with trans and non-binary identities are also shaped by other identities and cultural/societal factors. I attempted to speak with as diverse a selection of trans and non-binary folks as possible. Diversity in trans and non-binary theological discourse, as well as in trans and non-binary visibility more generally, is still limited. The voices of trans women, trans people who identify with a binary gender, trans people over 45, able-bodied trans people and white trans people are still predominant. As such, I particularly welcomed hearing from trans-masculine people, non-binary or non-conforming people, those under 45, those who are disabled and those who are Black.

I also attempted to gather data from participants with differing levels of education and theological education, and in varying levels and types of employment. It would have been possible to only speak with trans and non-binary theological students or graduates. However, I believe that all trans Christians have valuable theological insights to share.

An open and flexible style of interviewing was used to enable all people to share their views, regardless of education or background. The use of individual interviews, as opposed to focus groups, allowed for more diversity. Christina Beardsley and Michelle O'Brien (2016, pp. 5–6), who wrote *This is My Body*, note the difficulty that they found in reaching trans men, given that the group they chose to conduct their research with did not attract transmasculine people. It is logical that most groups will encourage participation based on similarity rather than difference. By interviewing individuals, I was able to focus on diversity rather than similarity.

Apart from gender diversity, the other demographics that I gathered data about were age, education, theological qualifications, marital status, occupation, ethnicity, denomination and disability. The one area where I was unable to reach a diverse sample of trans/non-binary people was ethnicity. Only one of my ten participants was Black, and I did not find any Asian participants, despite contacting a wide range of organizations and individuals. There is a clear need for research into the ethnic diversity (or lack thereof) in LGBTQ+ Christian communities in the UK.

Out of the ten folks I interviewed, three were aged 25–44, four were 45–64 and three were 65+. Educational diversity was slightly less balanced. Half the people I interviewed had a graduate degree. Of the remaining five, three had undergraduate degrees, one had an undergraduate certificate and one had GCSEs. Eight participants had no theology qualifications; I believe it is positive to be able to hear the theology of those whose voices are not already heard in theological institutions. Of the remaining two, one had an undergraduate degree in theology and one had a doctoral degree in theology. There was no tangible difference in the interviews of those who had degrees in theology, compared to those with similar, non-theological qualifications. Seven were single at the time of interview. There were a wide range of occupations, from unemployment to senior management. Three were in ordained ministry. Four identified as 'other' than the four main UK church denominations. One described their faith identity as 'gnostic' and 'heretical'; another was dechurched at the time of interview and a third was questioning their denominational identity. Three identified as members or adherents of the Church of England, two of the United Reformed Church and one as a dechurched former member of the Baptist Union. Half the participants identified as disabled, with four mentioning mental health difficulties, four mentioning learning disabilities and/or neurodiversity and one mentioning physical disability. The intersections between neurodiversity and being trans/non-binary were raised several times.

The concept of 'acceptable faces' of being trans, wherein some trans voices, identities, experiences and/or narratives are deemed acceptable and others unacceptable, is a risk to academic integrity. There are multiple layers to this construct of 'acceptability'. One such layer is the acceptable binary; the idea that transitioning to a binary gender is more acceptable than living in the spaces between or outside binary genders. Those spaces are, however, increasingly recognized by the trans community. In an analysis of resources by trans individuals and groups that seek to teach about trans identities, Laurel Westbrook (2010, p. 26) highlights the breadth of diversity in the trans community, noting that gender is taught as 'a continuum', as 'diverse' and/or 'fluid'. Each of these terms explicitly includes more than the binary male and female. Further, Jeffrey Alan Johnson (2015, pp. 160–1) notes that 'the stigmatization of gender nonconformity ... comes from being outside the valid data states.' This means that those whose identities are not contained within the 'data states' 'male' and 'female' could be overlooked. As such, attention to non-conforming and non-binary identities is particularly important.

Westbrook (2010, p. 52) also critiques 'teaching transgender' articles, noting that there is a tendency to naturalize trans identities. It is understandable that trans people may defend our existence by attempting to prove the scientific truths or binary norms of trans identities. Naturalizing in this way, however, risks flattening trans identities to the most societally acceptable version of transness and erasing those who do not fit the profile, propagating a problematic form of respectability politics. Much of the theology that defends the possibility of trans identities, is written from a binary perspective. In these accounts, transness is sometimes treated as a medical condition or anomaly that can be cured, enabling the individual to live as male or female, as if they are cisgender, effectively erasing their identity as trans.

While it is, of course, valid for an individual to identify in these terms, the theological anthropology of trans and non-binary identities should not be limited to binary accounts. It is vital that the voices of non-conforming and non-binary people are heard, so that our theological understandings of what it means to be human are widened. In addition, it is important to pay attention to the effects of the 'acceptable faces' phenomenon on non-binary/non-conforming people's identities, experiences and understandings. My concern about unheard voices led me to prioritize non-binary identities in finding people to speak to. I also considered the effects of the 'acceptable faces' phenomenon when interviewing and writing up my research.

Gathering and analysing demographics regarding gender identity is complex, partly for the reasons above. I chose to invite people to write down how they identify in relation to gender, rather than offering tick-boxes. This allowed each person to answer authentically, rather than having to choose a best-fit option. It offered them the open space for a narrative description, doing more justice to the complexity of identity, and created richer data. It also decentralized the normative gender binary. Six identified under the umbrella category non-binary, with four identifying with a more binary gender identity. Similarly, six identified as transfeminine or female, while only two identified as transmasculine or male. Two participants did not identify at all with male or female identities. The following words were used by participants to describe their gender identities:

> Agender, androgynous, genderflux, genderqueer non-binary, genderqueer, living full time as female, male, man, mtf, non-binary transmasculine, non-binary, simply female, trans guy, trans, transgender female, transgender, transmasculine, woman.

It was also important for me to bring my own genderqueer, non-binary, transmasculine identity to this research, analysis and writing. During this process I have reconsidered my own identity countless times and been challenged to further

deconstruct the binary norms that I use to mask my own queerness in the public eye.

I used word of mouth, snowballing and contacts to recruit
conversation partners. I have a wide network of connections
within both LGBTQ+ and Christian communities, as well as
a good reputation as a minister working with trans and non-
binary people. I used a plain text advert in order to attract
those genuinely interested in participation, rather than using
colourful and incentivizing adverts to attract the maximum
number of potential participants. The LGBTQ+ community is
sometimes distrustful of researchers, as many LGBTQ+ people
have had experiences of research being done to them, rather
than with them. I felt that my personal and low-key approach
would help me to build up trust, rather than suspicion.

In addition to personal networks I also contacted churches
and other Christian organizations that work with LGBTQ+
people, such as the Metropolitan Community Church. This
allowed me to recruit more participants of differing demographics. I only contacted churches and organizations that
were explicitly affirming of, and welcoming to, those who hold
trans identities so that I did not perpetuate harm. Further, I
asked contacts to recommend that potential participants contact me, rather than asking the contacts for personal details.
This discouraged contacts from outing trans and non-binary
people to me without their permission. These further contacts
helped me to recruit a relatively diverse set of people.

Potential participants were sent a participant information
sheet and a demographics questionnaire, which they were asked
to complete if they would like to participate in the research. The
demographics questionnaire enabled me to assess the accumu-
lating diversity of the sample and use targeted advertising to
further diversify where necessary. Initially, participants were
then asked if they could travel to the University of Birmingham
or, alternatively, to identify a public space with a private room,
such as a church or community centre, where it was safe and
convenient to meet.

I had completed my first two interviews when, in 2020, the
Covid-19 pandemic interrupted all our lives, including neces-

sitating changes to my ministry, which moved online, and my fieldwork process, which would either have to change or wait until the lockdowns finally ended. For all qualitative researchers who relied on in-person interviews, there was a clear need for a change in practice.

I sought advice from my supervisors and the university ethics committee before deciding if, and how, to continue. They agreed to a change in my interview process, so I contacted everyone who had previously been sent a participant information sheet and a demographics questionnaire, and asked whether they would be comfortable meeting online. A significant majority were happy to do so, some happier than meeting in person, so the following eight interviews of the total of ten were held on Zoom. After briefly introducing myself and giving the participant an opportunity to ask questions, I asked them for permission to begin recording. I then recorded the interview on Zoom. I was conscious of the risk of Zoom fatigue and took care to try to avoid that.

At the start of each interview I told the participant a little bit about myself. This broke the ice and built trust and openness. I focused on my trans and Christian identities and also explained something about my ministry and my motivations in this research.

I began by asking the participant to tell me about themselves, and then moved to topics of identity and theology. Rooke (2010, p. 67), when conducting research with trans young people, found that telling one's own story is incredibly important to trans people and that there is a lack of spaces where one can do so. As such, giving adequate time for personal testimony not only created rich data, but also had the potential to benefit participants. I asked non-leading questions in ordinary language, avoiding any technical language unless my conversation partner used it first. Where possible I limited interjections and interruptions, allowing folks to talk freely and at length when they were able to do so.

At the end of the interview I thanked the person and explained that I would contact them when I had completed their transcript and asked if it was OK to email them if I had any subsequent questions. I also provided the participant with a list of local support organizations. In her research, Rooke found that participating in research implicitly involved each participant doing personal work on their own identities. As well as supporting this personal work during the research process, signposting to other resources allowed participants to reflect on and, where appropriate, continue this work. Several participants mentioned already having knowledge of local and national support groups, highlighting the fact that they were adept at managing their own self-care.

Moving to Zoom resulted in shorter transcripts. Having said that, the data gathered was fuller, with most sentences full of meaning. Several people reflected that they had been able to speak more openly over video conferencing, whereas two shared that they would have valued meeting face to face. As such, the move to video conferencing interviews was neither entirely helpful nor entirely unhelpful. It is notable, though, that it did impact on people's responses, enabling fuller responses from some, and being a source of disappointment for others. I have not found any correlated difference between the richness of the interviews of those who found video conferencing helpful and those who did not.

Each of the trans and non-binary people I spoke with has, in the data they provided, contributed something unique and important to Christian theology. I have been and continue to be inspired by them, their stories and their understandings. In and among and through and around the complexities of paradigms and theories, methods and analysis, their voices are heard. It was necessary to pay careful attention to how I did this work, so that their voices are amplified, not flattened or diminished. It is also necessary to note, though, that human lives defy rigid codification, academic norms and theological orthodoxy. Such is the nature of a grounded, feminist, queer theological work.

Theological method

Throughout my training for ministry, I was taught that attention to Albert C. Outler's (1985) Wesleyan Quadrilateral was the foundation of good theological method. During my research, however, I became increasingly aware of the ways in which the marginalization of experience in the use of this quadrilateral of scripture, reason, tradition and experience does harm to those whose lives are adversely affected by the traditions, theories and scriptural interpretations of those who hold power. In July 2020, I wrote the following in my theological journal:

> One of my fears when I started this research project was that it would be criticized as overly focused on 'experience', rather than all of the sources from which theology is drawn. Because of this, I have had the Wesleyan Quadrilateral (WQ) in mind as I have been interviewing participants and coding their interviews. The WQ is scripture, experience, reason and tradition.
>
> As it happens, I needn't have worried, as my participants have had really intricate and well-articulated theological understandings that draw on scripture, reason and tradition as well as their experiences. I wonder if sometimes we forget that experience is inextricably woven into the other three sources. They have repeatedly reminded me that by focusing on reason and tradition, the church ignores their theological insights and revelations and uses dispassionate theory to control and wound them. Each individual who articulates theological understandings does so as a human being, with their own experiences, understandings and perspectives. Our study of scripture and ecclesial tradition is a series of experiences, as is our use of reason, and reception and examination of the reason of others.
>
> Sometimes we experience scripture, tradition and reason as things that are done to us. I have experienced scripture as done to me time and time again when people have told me that I have to be either a man or a woman. I have experienced tradition as done to me when someone in the hierarchy of

my tradition questioned whether I was living a holy life, as a queer person. I have experienced reason as done to me when I have read each of the countless articles written by theologians in which they rationalize their opposition to trans people's identities.

I have been moved, and often horrified, by the ways in which my interview participants have experienced scripture, tradition and reason as done to them, which has caused real harm in terms of faith, church belonging, spirituality, mental health, physical health, financial well-being and relatedness. When will those with power stop hurting us? I love, though, the way in which we can actively engage in doing scripture, tradition and reason for ourselves and in relationship with others.

Reflecting on my journal entry, I realize that my discomfort was related to the marginalization of experience in theological method, and the fallacy that it is possible to separate reason, tradition and scripture from experience. The problem is that objectivity is an illusion, which misleads us to believe that one objective theory can inform universal practice without doing harm. Nuanced, reflexive treatments of tradition, reason/theory and scripture must acknowledge the experiences out of which they arise. In this way, prioritizing experience can diversify praxis, critique and correct harm, and enable new insights.

Unfortunately, the prioritization of tradition, reason/theory and scripture has created a divide between philosophical/theoretical and practical theologies. At a recent conference regarding theological methodologies, Heather Walton (2021) highlighted the theoretical turn towards relational ontologies and suggested that, in the discipline of theology, relational ways of working should include a blurring of the boundaries between the theoretical and the practical. In order to have continued relevance, theologians must move beyond our differences to create and curate theologies that speak into the academy, churches and society.

Moving beyond the difficulties of marginalization and the problematic distinction between philosophical and practical theologies has, for me, meant moving away from traditional or systematic theological method towards a nuanced method that draws insights from grounded theory and from queer, embodied, indecent and practical theologies. Chris Greenough (2020, p. 34) notes that it 'is more helpful to consider what queer theologies do, rather than what they are'. The slipperiness, or indefinability, of queer theologies requires and enables me to define my theological method by what I do – and avoid doing – rather than by normative labels.

Grounding trans theology

I explored grounded theory, and the way in which it informed my research, earlier in this book. By drawing on grounded theory this thesis not only prioritizes, but centralizes trans voices. As a corrective to the silencing and/or absence of trans voices in trans theologies, the theology that follows draws exclusively on trans voices. It is not a trans-inclusive theology; it is a cis-exclusive theology. This is not exclusion for its own sake; rather, this method correlates directly to the trans exclusion in dominant theologies from biblical times to the present. It is essential that trans voices are allowed to speak for ourselves, by ourselves, as well as alongside cis voices. In other words, if the majority of theologies are written entirely by cis people, at least one theology should be written entirely by trans people. This is not a criticism of cis-authored trans theologies. Rather, I offer a trans-authored trans theology in order to further a trajectory towards the hearing of all voices in this complex dialogue. As well as the importance of hearing trans voices, I am motivated by the potential theological insights of trans people. Trans voices have the potential to challenge and undo some of the theological binaries that have trapped many people – trans and cis – for a long time.

It is important to note here that not all queer theologies are grounded in the experiences of queer people. As Greenough (2020, pp. 4–33) explains, while LGBTQ+ contextual theologies – which are rooted in LGBTQ+ experience – might seem a direct antecedent of queer theologies, the latter move beyond sexuality to the critique and disruption of norms more generally, and are often theoretically complex. Nevertheless, queer theologies are not monolithic, and their extensive variety includes experience-based theologies. Several theologians highlight the importance of a continued strand of queer theologies that centralize LGBTQ+ experience. This book is part of that strand.

Interrupting kyriarchy

To curate a queer theology that is grounded in trans experiences it is essential to consider the effect of cisnormative power on trans and non-binary identities, experiences and theological understandings. Trans and non-binary theologians, writers and readers must encounter and counter cisnormativity and transphobia. Further, if our work is to be intersectional we must challenge all kyriarchal norms, difficult though this task might be.

Isherwood and Stuart (1998, pp. 18–19) argue that the problem of theological power imbalances has functioned since the early church, highlighting the legislative control of embodiment enacted by the Church Fathers. Greenough (2020, pp. 4–34) highlights the disruptive nature of queer theologies, in particular the disruption of unjust power. This prompts me to consider how I might ensure that this trans theology disrupts unjust theological and ecclesial power systems that seek to control trans identities, bodies and people.

The key to this disruption, for me, is found in whose theology is brought into dialogue within the chapters of this book. Gerard Loughlin (2007, p. 8) highlights queer as 'the insult turned', noting the turn from shame to pride. It is vital to consider how trans and non-binary theologians might enter into theological discourse without the manipulation, power, control and shame that we have experienced being repeated in the creating of theology. Unequal power dynamics arise when trans and non-binary people are invited to discuss or debate our identities, experiences and arising theological understandings with cis people who seek to invalidate them. It is important to me that, in this theology, trans and non-binary voices be allowed to speak for themselves. As such, no cis theologians are brought into dialogue in the main chapters of this book. This means that I do not compare and contrast the theology herein with the insights of other theologians, with the exception of occasional reference to the limited field of trans-authored theological literature. Instead, I bring my participants' and my own identities, experiences and understandings into dialogue with each other, enabling me to highlight the breadth, depth and diversity of trans and non-binary people and our theological understandings, and allowing a more equitable dialogue. In doing so it is not my intention to suggest that cis people cannot critique or come into dialogue with this book and the voices and ideas shared in it. Nor am I arguing that cis people should not write trans-related theological texts. Rather, I encourage that dialogue to follow, after careful listening that prioritizes trans and non-binary voices. In order to be heard, we must be allowed spaces – or take them – where we do not have to shout over others with more power and less lived experience of what it means to be trans and non-binary.

Freeing bodies

To listen well to trans and non-binary voices it is necessary to engage with the trans and non-binary bodies that our voices speak out of. Some trans-apologetic accounts marginalize elements of trans embodiment by resorting to medicalization and problematization. Each of the people I have spoken with has experienced similar erasure, as have I. Theologians who write body theology highlight the importance of reclaiming the body in our theologies. Their prioritization of the body is rooted in their understandings of incarnation and its inextricable entwinement with liberation. The incarnational embodied methodology that they argue for prioritizes the connections between embodiment, emotion and reason. As trans and non-binary people we reclaim our bodies every day from theories and norms that seek to marginalize them. In this book I centralize trans and non-binary embodiment and ask what it reveals about incarnation. I also consider the ways in which both the marginalization and reclaiming of trans and non-binary bodies are active in the identities, experiences and insights shared.

Marcella Althaus-Reid (2001, p. 24) locates theology in the body, suggesting that only transgressive embodiment can transform regressive norms. She also argues that the body, particularly its suffering, is objectified by systematic theology. In the theology that follows, trans people speak for ourselves out of and about our bodies. I avoid medicalizing the identities, experiences and bodies that are a part of this theology and do not compare the insights shared to cis understandings of trans embodiment. I refuse to analyse or deconstruct other trans people's understandings of their own bodies. Nor do I prioritize any one form of trans embodiment. Where suffering arises as a theme, I strive to allow the individual to tell their own story and to theorize for themselves. This allows their suffering to speak out as a precious strand in dialogue, rather than being an object, used and manipulated by others.

Ideas that marginalize and erase trans and non-binary are persistent and persuasive in both trans-critical and some trans-supportive theologies and ecclesial statements. By creating space for trans and non-binary people to speak openly about our own experiences of embodiment, this theology seeks not only to 'lift' but also to deconstruct these injunctions, in the hope that negative understandings of the trans and non-binary body might ultimately be resected from this field and replaced with celebration of authenticity.

Informing praxis

This book queers the philosophical/practical theological divide. It is my belief that theory should inform praxis and that praxis should be informed by theory. The separation of theory from praxis is an illusion. Rather, supposedly orthodox, traditional theory informs contemporary ecclesial, political and civic praxis. Living in Love and Faith, the most recent substantial UK denominational response to LGBTQ+ identities, was largely constructed by cis people and relies heavily on traditional understandings of theological anthropology. The binary categories of male and female are treated as the norm throughout. The UK Government has failed to address the inadequacy of the Gender Recognition Act (2004), which prioritizes the cisnormative binary categories of male and female. Transphobic hate crime is still under-reported, under-charged and under-convicted.

Cisnormative understandings of sexual-dimorphism and related gender theory are foundational to all of the above ecclesial, political and civic limitations on trans theory, trans voices, trans lived experiences, trans bodies and trans lives. There is a need to expose the link between limited theory and limited praxis. Further there is a need to suggest the ways in which trans-authored trans theory can enable better praxis. As such, this book links theory to praxis throughout. Further, it avoids complex theoretical language that might create barriers to a wide range of practitioners in the relevant fields.

Turning the church inside out

Relating theory to praxis requires a mobile stance in relation to the church. It is not possible to engage with grounded trans and non-binary theological literature unless the listener/reader is willing to stand outside churches and critique their unjust power. Conversely, it is also necessary to engage with trans people inside churches and to consider what the hope of new life means for us. This necessary mobility also functions for each research participant and for me, as researcher.

This mobility is not straightforward for trans Christians, particularly those engaged in church ministry, lay or ordained. The voices brought into dialogue in this theology have complex relationships to churches. Each self-identifies as Christian. Each experiences religious belonging differently. Further, each is critical of particular aspects of Christian theology and praxis. Some of those whose stories and understandings are represented are actively considering leaving their churches. But while we remain, we are unafraid of offering strong critique. This introduces an element of risk into this theological project. This risk is, however, essential to the curation of grounded trans theologies. I have had to balance steps to protect those I have been speaking with, with the risks that they have voluntarily taken throughout the process of research and writing. I take care to represent their identities, experiences and understandings accurately and sensitively. But I do not soften their critiques of churches or their disclosures of the harm done within them. While I cannot determine your answer, I ask you, the reader, to 'do no harm' as you engage with the selves that we lay bare.

Indecent incoherence

Before beginning research it was my intention to create a theology that spoke to most, perhaps all, of the key topics raised in systematic theology. I also intended to limit content to philosophical/theoretic theology, to the exclusion of practical theology. I now realize these intentions were rooted in a fear of being found incoherent. Althaus-Reid (2009, pp. 105–16) suggests that 'Decent theologians struggle for coherence ... Yet, we may ask, what is wrong with being incoherent theologically?' The radical authenticity and honesty of my research participants, as well as the increasingly hostile religious, political and societal context in which trans and non-binary people in the UK find ourselves, have challenged me to deconstruct my own biases and to take a methodological hammer to my own imposter syndrome. I have experienced the expectation of theological coherence as a kyriarchal insistence on appealing to normative systems. Althaus-Reid conversely, suggests that 'queer in-betweenness' and disarticulations are the sites at which God might break in.

The disruption to normative systems that trans and non-binary people enact in the facts of our very existence has the power to enable change. The striking testimonies of those I have interviewed impels me to be indecently incoherent, to allow trans and non-binary voices and the topics that matter to us to speak out, interrupting and deconstructing theological norms, including the idol of coherent systems. By doing so, it is my hope and belief that this theology can be a part of enabling real change.

And so my theological method is grounded, is positioned against kyriarchy, is located in the body, is both practical and academic, does not hesitate to critique the church and is intentionally incoherent, rather than in any way systematic. My theological method, which I have been developing over many years, has been impacted immensely by the call to an unpicking of the anthropological and theological norms that restrain us, so that we might centre truth and justice. This unpicking is necessarily incoherent, as norms are claimed to be coherent. It is unflinchingly critical of the church, where norms may be reinforced. It is specifically located in the body, as our bodies testify to the lies of binarism. Finally, it is anti-kyriarchal, seeking to tear down the panopticons – prisons – that reinscribe and reinforce normative, hierarchical values.

Interlude 3

Desire for Connection – Jack

The category of trans and non-binary is so broad. For me it mostly means not identifying with traditional gender categories, playing around with them, adapting bits and pieces. Also being creative with gender expression and changing over time. And just challenging people on their assumptions on what gender means, what it should be.

In my late twenties I worked out that I wasn't a cis woman and that just wasn't a category that I ... I had felt uncomfortable with parts of that for a long time, but I think I only became explicit about it or was out about that later. Exploring ... what else is there? Thinking that transitioning would be the right step for me. But then I decided against that. Just realized it, for me, where I am at the moment, it feels more authentic or better to basically be an atypical woman not a transman. I'm being perceived as such by most of society anyway. As an atypical woman. So I'm non-binary anyway in how others see me not only how I see myself.

In my first parish I was not out as non-binary because in that parish, I was their first non-male priest and I was just ordained a month before I started there. Which was also a challenge for some people. I think I was about 30 years younger than all their previous priests. They had a lot of challenges. Non-binary was just that one additional level that I felt I could not bring up. Within my church, I've only been openly out for the past couple of months. Recently, I realized that it would be a good time to be more explicit about preferred pronouns. So when I wrote a short introduction blurb I used they pronouns and I sent it to my boss first and she asked me if I could avoid the pronouns and just use she, since it would cause too much trouble. That was a bit of a surprise for me.

Eventually, it got sorted out and I could use they pronouns and with the actual members it hasn't been a problem. Ever since, people have been incredibly supportive, even the older people just ask questions but try to respect me; people self-correct when they slip up.

It's much less of a problem than those with authority thought it would be. Quite the opposite. People are curious, people ask questions. I already gave a teaching session on it. There are a couple of older people who probably just decide not to worry, not to think about, not to notice which ... I'm glad that a lot of people started thinking, not everybody will and that's OK too.

I've been excluded a lot in the church for ticking several of those 'different' boxes. It was an experience of, 'Oh, you just don't quite fit in. We can't pin it down, but there's something that's not quite right. We don't think it would be a good fit.' That's the sinful expression of church. That's not a church that God intended. In a way that's part of my task to fight the good fight and keep going. I mean, sometimes it was also just necessity to get through and find a job. Because once you are on that pathway, it's also not that easy to kind of just drop everything, go back into a secular employment, because you invested so much time, so much one way or another ... money. Some have to take on the battle of whether you want to or not. I wasn't aware of how much of a struggle it would be, actually. I never saw myself as much of a queer theologian, or I didn't see that as my main battle. It's more like something that just came along with other battles or other experiences and just being myself.

I do believe that God calls us as who God created us to be. And that includes all parts. I mean, all the experiences we bring, all the different aspects, and I think being queer is just so much at the centre of somebody that it's hard to leave that aside or ignore that in ministry. Being queer, but also just the experience of being part of any kind of marginalized group, means that more and more I am moving away from main-stream hermeneutics to hermeneutics of social justice in all its aspects, becoming more and more aware of the intersectional elements of theology, which I think is really growing on the edge and for me queer theology is part of that. Being queer is part of the wider picture and is also moving into me looking into social justice advocacy and chaplaincy.

Marginalization ... I think that is where the centre of queerness is. There is always that element of having to fight, experiencing suffering, experiencing being othered. That's not how I would define queerness but it is how I would understand it. It is linked to suffering in a way, even though that suffering is probably experienced on a different level for each person.

I sum God up as love and holiness as growing in discipleship, in fellowship. Holiness is growing in love and compassion for other people, but also in a way for the wider creation, and just experiencing more and more of that universal desire for love and shared heart. A desire to be a shared being, a desire for connection.

I understand the Trinity, or the church's teaching on the Trinity, as being about God's desire for relationship. Also that movement, that kind of dancing God. I think there's a very strong sense of love, but also connection, community within that. God's gender is actually something I've been thinking about in the last couple of weeks because my boss here very much insists on calling God 'mother' wherever possible. Using that kind of slightly more seventies, very gendered language. I'm realizing that I never found it helpful. I notice a lot of people do and I'm willing to do it, but I like the idea of using more provocative images, provocative gender imagery around that. In a way I prefer calling Jesus 'sister' to feeling very progressive by calling God 'mother' because in a way it's already so obvious that it almost doesn't ... it doesn't add much for me. God is beyond gender almost, and it's good to use images and to kind of stretch our understanding, but just traditional gendered language for God I don't find particularly helpful. Language does matter. For me we understand God only inasmuch as we try to move beyond binary language, and I think theologically as well as, socially, we haven't arrived there, we're not at the point where gender doesn't matter for language, we do need to be attuned and aware, but I think there is a bit of a danger of overemphasizing binary gendered language as a kind of theological meme. In my experience gendered language in theology or biblical studies is just often very binary. For me personally, it doesn't really help a lot. It can just emphasize the binary.

I think that what God asks of us is about growing into that love, but also in a way joining into that dance, that trinitarian dance, but also that kind of becoming more and more aware of the traces of God and of God's spirit in our life. There is that more horizontal level of just growing as disciples and growing in compassion and love for each other. And there's also that more spiritual, vertical level of also growing in wonder and just realizing where the divine is present in our lives. That is about playing. Both in a light sense but also in a serious sense of entering a certain realm and just exploring without knowing what the outcome will be.

As it is for us, it is also for the church. The church needs to be both a place where people grow in love and to use its power and its voice in society to speak out for those who experience marginalization or any kind of suffering, but also needs to be a place where people can explore and are allowed to play and be creative and experience that divine aspect of their lives.

4

Narrating Our Experience

Before considering the theological insights of trans and non-binary Christians, it is vital to explore our experiences and the narrative themes, or lenses, through which we understand God, ourselves and others. Narrative identity is the unfolding story that a person creates in order to understand themselves and others. It is not static but, rather, continually transformed by our experiences and evolving understandings (McAdams, 2011). Trans narrative identities are formed in relation to, but not necessarily limited by, embodiment, lived experiences, and communication with others (Nagoshi et al., 2014, pp. 195–6).

Although narrative identity formation is relational, and affected by social context and communications, there should be an element of autonomy – everyone should be free to construct their own narrative identity, selecting the themes or lenses through which they understand themselves, their lives, those they connect with, and the world. Talia Mae Bettcher (2009, p. 98) argues that 'trans politics ought to proceed with the principle that trans people have first person authority (FPA) over their own gender'. In other words, trans people should be able to form their own narrative identity; to tell their own authentic gender story without question or disbelief.

However, trans people's autonomous narratives are often denied; said to be false by others who claim expertise in regard to trans people's lives and identities. Graham Mayeda (2009, p. 195) suggests that this denial means that the trans person 'is treated as a child who must justify [their] actions rather than as an adult who is simply asserting [their] identity'. I believe this denial of autonomous narrative and the subsequent need to justify our identities and actions, rather than simply asserting them, is one of the key reasons for the prevalence of trans-apologetic literature in the field of trans theology. I have certainly often felt the need to explain and defend who I am, and why I have transitioned, rather than being able to simply share my identity, experiences and insights without justification.

Dan P. McAdams (2011, p. 99) observes that in constructive narratives, 'people draw heavily on prevailing cultural norms and the images, metaphors and themes that run through the many narratives they encounter in social life.' In the UK, a study of 256 trans and non-binary people found that 95 per cent of participants felt that the media did not care about their perceptions of self and 70 per cent felt that media representations of their identities were negative or very negative. Under 5 per cent felt that they were positive (Trans Media Watch, 2010). More recently, in the USA, a study of 545 trans and non-binary adults showed that 97.6 per cent had experienced negative media coverage of trans identities (Hughto et al., 2021, p. 36). It is inevitable that these negative media perceptions of trans identities help to create and support tropes that affect trans people's narrative identity formation and must be considered when exploring trans identities, insights and experiences.

In the following chapters I describe our experiences and arising theological insights. Before moving to theology and theological anthropology, though, let's explore which of the key narrative themes of suffering, resilience and joy that arose in each person's interviews. This will enable me to consider, in what follows, how these themes impact, and are impacted by, our lived experiences and arising theological and anthropological insights. It is important to note that these are the themes I perceived in one conversation and are not necessarily representative of a person's whole narrative identity. I suggest that narratives of joy are necessarily dependent on narratives of suffering and resilience, which are not necessarily problematic in and of themselves, but argue that there is a need for an increase of trans theology and theological anthropology that utilizes joy as a narrative frame.

Suffering

One clear narrative theme shown in the media in relation to trans identities is the theme of suffering/pathologization. Jaydi Funk, Steven S. Funk and Sylvia Whelan (2019, p. 124) show that pathologization of trans and non-binary people is the norm in media produced in the USA. It is worth noting that USA-produced media is widely viewed in the UK, particularly since the advent of content streaming. Craig McLean (2021, pp. 481–2) concludes that both mainstream and social media in the UK push a narrative of trans people as being unsafe. These limiting narratives observably impact the lives of trans and non-binary people.

For three people, Stacey, Ellen and Beth, experiences of suffering have contributed to the narratives of identity that they shared with me, and suffering was a key theme throughout our conversations. This does not mean that suffering is the key theme of their narrative identity formation. Nor does it suggest that they view their selves, others and trans/non-binary identities in a negative light. However, it is notable that their experiences of suffering informed the narrative course of our conversations together and have been influential in their theological development.

Stacey

Stacey (she/her) is a woman in her late sixties. Stacey transitioned a few years ago and lost her family and career as a result. Stacey used to work in education and has an unfilled ministry vocation. Stacey has felt very isolated since being rejected by her local church leadership and speaks with both wisdom and sorrow about her difficult experiences in professional, ecclesial and family contexts. Stacey is widely read and feels a particular affinity for both the mystics and the well-known Lutheran minister Nadia Bolz-Weber. Stacey's theology draws on a wide variety of texts, as well as her own experiences. Suffering was a key narrative theme throughout Stacey's interview.

Stacey's transition itself has been very positive. Despite the joy of transition, however, Stacey suffers greatly due to the reactions of other people, specifically other Christians, to her identity and transition. Stacey explains:

> It's hard to know where to begin as there's so much I could say about a life of neglect, an absence of genuine love. A life of betrayal, denial, abandonment and what feels like a complete absence of justice with total rejection of me either in a life completely void of professional or vocational fulfilment, pre- or post-transition. I have no problem with being transgender in and of itself and my GRS[1] was both necessary and an unqualified success. Since then, I'm happy in my own skin having only ever presented as female once my 25-year marriage broke down. What I wasn't prepared for was the total rejection of me as a female, in professional and church circles. It's this which has caused and still causes me the most grief in life, leaving me hideously unfulfilled professionally, vocationally.

It is striking that Stacey's suffering is not internal but, rather, related to society, family, church and vocation. She does not suffer because she is trans, she suffers because of how other people respond to her being trans. Stacey's familial relationships have been a cause of difficulty since young adulthood. Stacey reflected that societal pressure to live as 'a normal young man' was central to her marriage and subsequent divorce. She felt a strong sense of guilt in relation to her marriage, believing that she should not have married, given her own uncertainty, at the time, as to her identity. When Stacey went on to transition, as an older adult, she was outed to her children, which led to her relationship with them ending. This led Stacey to feel that coming out has 'cost me everything'.

Stacey described experiences of spiritual abuse in churches and faith-based settings. To define spiritual abuse I draw on the observation in Oakley et al. (2018, pp. 144–5) that spiritual abuse is experienced as 'the employment of belief leading [directly or indirectly] to harm of another', which may include 'coercion and control', 'manipulation and pressuring of individuals', 'control through the use of religious texts and scripture' and 'divine rationale' for the mistreatment of others. Herein, therefore, I define spiritual abuse as using beliefs, scripture and God as rationales and tools for harm including, but not limited to, coercion, control, manipulation, pressuring and mistreating others. In the case of the trans and non-binary people interviewed, this included control or attempted control of identity and presentation, including attempted conversion, control or attempted control of religious belonging, including exclusion from church communities, and financial, emotional, verbal, physical and sexual abuse in a religious setting and/or with religion as rationale.

Stacey's experiences of spiritual abuse included attempted conversion, which included 'counselling' and being accompanied to her home to 'get rid of female presentation tools'. In the so-called 'counselling' that Stacey experienced, being trans was 'linked to the devil'. Stacey also described receiving 'no pastoral contact' when she was seriously ill for months and unable to attend church. Stacey explained that a change in church leadership meant an 'instant change' from inclusion to exclusion, including losing her job as floor manager. This led Stacey to feel that she was 'ostracized just for being myself'. Stacey says, 'I've felt about as isolated as I think it's possible for anybody to feel.'

Stacey uses the word 'insincerity' to describe her experiences of church, having encountered both a bishop and a priest who claimed to support inclusivity but then made all LGBTQ+ employees redundant. Stacey also witnessed a degree of secrecy in church discussions around LGBTQ+ identities, which compounded the sense of duplicity.

Stacey's experiences in church led to what she describes as 'a complete mental breakdown' and the continuing feeling that 'people are messing with my life', as well as the loss of her job plunging her into poverty. Stacey struggles to forgive the church for its 'false welcome and empowerment followed by utter exclusion'. Over time, Stacey has come to feel that all churches 'reject me as female' and describes this as causing 'real grief' as well as a feeling of 'being broken'. This has led to doubt and confusion around concepts of forgiveness, reconciliation and redemption.

Despite these painful experiences, Stacey described having 'tried to walk away from church over and over again', but finding it too hard to leave entirely due, in part, to a sense of vocation towards ordained ministry. As in her attempts to connect with others, when seeking vocational fulfilment Stacey found herself rejected and isolated. Stacey is not alone in these experiences. Four out of my ten participants were single at the time of interview, and eight out of ten have experienced difficulties in significant relationships in reaction to their identity or transition. Similarly, eight out of ten have experienced vocational delays or difficulties in relation to their identity or transition.

For Stacey, then, suffering is a lived reality and, rather than avoiding suffering in her theological understandings, Stacey embraces it. In particular, Stacey relates to theological reflections on suffering by Nadia Bolz-Weber, Julian of Norwich and St John of the Cross. Empathy – shared reflections on suffering – seems to have spiritual value to Stacey and means that she feels drawn to the suffering experienced by the mystics. Both her own suffering, and her reading of theology, impact her understandings of God and humanity.

Nadia Bolz-Weber (2014), who Stacey mentioned regularly throughout her interview, writes:

> The image of God I was raised with was this: God is an angry bastard with a killer surveillance system who had to send his little boy (and he only had one) to suffer and die because I was bad. But the good news was that if I believed this story and then tried really hard to be good, when I died I would go to heaven, where I would live in a golden gated community with God and all the other people who believed and did the same things as I did ... this type of thinking portrays God as just as mean and selfish as we are, which feels like it has a lot more to do with our own greed and spite than it has to do with God. (Kindle, 1030 of 2297)

Stacey explained that Nadia Bolz-Weber

> talks about the 'angry despot' from a 'killer surveillance
> system', and that's the God that I've come to see because
> of my experiences of human nature, basically, that's robbed
> me of everything and the life I might still have had but seems
> further away with each passing day. And so, I live with that
> frustration, that pain, what did I do wrong?

In other words, Stacey's negative experiences of human beings
affect her intuitive understandings of God, leading her to feel
that God, like the humans who have hurt or abandoned her, is
a judgemental, negative force.

The theology that Bolz-Weber describes could be understood as relating to a relatively traditional understanding of
atonement; the idea that Jesus suffered and died because of our
sins, and that his death is a necessary step in our redemption.
Stacey's testimony is a stark reminder of the dangers of sin-
and-punishment-based understandings of God. She struggles
to glimpse any redeeming factors of humanity, because the
humans that she has encountered have not been hospitable to
her. Her negative experiences of humanity are projected on
to God, meaning that she experiences God as her judge and
punisher. This has a strikingly negative effect on Stacey's sense
of self-worth.

The eschatological reach of Bolz-Weber's religious upbringing is also a part of Stacey's understandings. Like Bolz-Weber,
Stacey believes that, after she dies, she will meet God in heaven.
Stacey, despite her pain, ultimately understands that 'God does
love me' and believes that 'at some point ... we shall be one',
describing the day of her death as 'a great day as far as I'm concerned', and asking, 'Why do you not take me back now?' This
suggests that, for Stacey, life is negative compared with the
eschatological future. While this may be seen as theologically
orthodox, it is concerning in terms of pastoral and psychosocial well-being and leaves me wondering whether there is
adequate pastoral support for people whose experiences are
similar to Stacey's. Since the time of her interview, Stacey's life

has improved significantly, and she has appropriate support in place. Nevertheless, it is clear that Stacey's lived experiences and theological understandings challenge her well-being and resilience.

Although the comments expressed above echo atonement theories that rely on personal belief, Stacey goes on to explain that her reading of Bolz-Weber has 'really helped me to rethink this whole business of sin and grace'. Stacey believes that we are 'all fallen' and 'all reconciled' and that in reality God is not an 'angry despot' but is, rather, a gracious host. In expressing this understanding, Stacey transforms her own suffering into grace for the people who have inflicted it. This brings to mind the reported words of Jesus from the midst of his own suffering, 'Father, forgive them, for they do not know what they are doing' (Luke 23.34). Jesus' words, spoken on the cross, suggest that he does not blame the people who have called for his crucifixion. For me, this speaks to a critique of the system that both glorifies and enables human suffering, in this case crucifixion, instead of a critique of the people who enact the warped mechanisms of that system.

Ellen

Ellen (she/her) describes herself as an 'elderly woman'. Ellen transitioned socially and medically many years ago and now simply identifies as female, though her identity as a child of God is more important to her than gender. Ellen is retired, having worked in the sciences. Ellen now attends a medium-sized, inclusive local church that she started to attend when invited by a transwoman she met online. Ellen is also a lay-preacher and treasurer at her church and feels called to street evangelism and industrial chaplaincy. Ellen's deeply held and confidently expressed theology is based on tradition and experience, as well as her scientific knowledge. She feels strongly about social justice and has been known to shout about this when she preaches. The narrative themes of struggle and injustice were clear throughout Ellen's interview.

Like Stacey, Ellen struggled with 'feeling lost' as a young adult, transitioning in later life, and losing all her family and friends when coming out as trans. Ellen said, 'My wife divorced me before I came to the point of deciding to transition but that did mean that when I made the decision to transition I had already lost everything you are liable to lose when doing so; I'd lost my family, my friends, my job, everything.' Further, Ellen was 'kicked out' of the church that she attended due, in part, to the minister's misunderstanding that being trans is a form of cross-dressing and cross-dressing is a form of homosexuality. Ellen explained that being forced to leave her church at the time of coming out meant that, alongside the difficulties of repeatedly coming out and losing family and friends, she lost her entire church-based support network. She said, 'All of my friends were members of that church and none of them ever spoke to me again, so I was completely alone.'

Ellen felt that the effect of her previous church's exclusionary teaching is 'universal hatred'. She suggested that when a person is taught to hate their sin, they are also taught to hate themselves. For Ellen, this brought to mind Jesus' commandment to 'Love your neighbour as yourself' (Matthew 22.39). Jesus says that the greatest commandment is to love God, and that the second greatest commandment is to love your neighbour as you love yourself. For Ellen, the 'love yourself' clause must function. Ellen explains that if we love our neighbour as we love ourselves, then when we hate ourselves, we inherently hate our neighbour. Ellen's church-inspired self-loathing was amplified by the fact that her minister felt that homosexuality is 'the most serious sin of all'. Ellen's experiences and insights hint at the negative psychosocial effects of damaging understandings of sin. Ellen feels that being taught to hate sin leads people to hate themselves and, therefore, disobey Jesus' command to love.

One effect of the anti-trans views of the minister of the church she was attending was that Ellen's transition was delayed while she deconstructed and reconstructed her own theological understandings. This delay had serious effects on Ellen's well-being and faith. Ellen felt that she was 'living a false life. Whatever it was, I wasn't living the truth. I lost my faith and my relationship with God.' Ellen felt that she experienced this 'false life' as 'hypocrisy' and as a 'sin', for which she had to 'repent'. Ellen's delayed authenticity was worsened by a two-year wait for hormone therapy due to the three-year Gender Identity Clinic waiting list. Ellen noted that many people obtain hormones via unofficial channels due to these lengthy waiting times.

Ellen is not alone in experiencing and critiquing long waiting times for trans-identity-related support from the UK National Health Service. In a 'letter before action', the Good Law Project (2020) notes that 'the NHS has a legal obligation to see those referred to GIDS (Gender Identity Development Services) within 18 weeks. But the average waiting time is 18 months' and goes on to report that some people have waited up to four years for an initial appointment. This letter, and the intention to pursue action that it indicates, highlights that these long waiting times are not only painful, but also arguably unlawful.

Given these difficulties, for Ellen, it was trans peer support that enabled resilience and led to a gradual return to faith. Ellen explained:

> I asked for help on a trans support forum and was invited to church with someone. The church was down this little back alley and, when I got there, I found that the person was the visiting preacher and I thought, 'the visiting preacher is a trans woman. This is my church!' A few months later, I transitioned. Then I regained my faith and my relationship with God. My understanding is that hypocrisy is quite unacceptable to God. And that is my testimony on that. And I'm now in a very supportive church.

Despite this positive turn in Ellen's faith story, the narrative theme of suffering has continued to affect her understandings of her trans identity. Ellen identifies 'more as a woman than a trans woman' but does consider her identity as 'very relevant' on Trans Day of Remembrance.[2] This highlights the correlation of trans identities, for Ellen, with oppression, violence and grief.

Further, Ellen suggested that she understands her identity as inherently problematic for others. For Ellen, 'history' is the cause of transphobia. She explained:

When we were young, we were taught that God was exclusively male which is why men are more important than women. So if you challenge that, men in particular are going to feel unstable, they feel threatened. So are many women because it's much easier for a woman to know that a man is in charge and men run the church. I mean, that is a nice stable, understandable set-up. You know where you are. And so, if you say, 'No, it's much more fluid than that', you upset the status quo. You take away stability. And anybody can be upset about that.

Ellen's understandings of trans problematization and transphobia are strongly based on a binary gendered privilege model, which she went on to suggest means that she lost her male privilege by transitioning. Ellen explained, 'I never understood anything about privilege, until I lost it because I had all the privilege. I gave up male privilege and cisgender privilege and as an elderly woman I've lost the privilege of being the right age.' Ellen's understanding of herself as oppressed, and her concern for other people who may be oppressed, was apparent throughout her interview. Despite her suffering, Ellen sees herself primarily as a beloved 'child of God' and sees her vocation to care for others and work for social justice as being core to her identity.

Beth

Beth (they/them) is a non-binary young adult. Beth came out as non-binary very recently and has identified as queer for quite some time. Beth is a minister in a mainstream European denomination and has found that telling their congregation about using they/them pronouns has led to helpful pastoral and theological conversations. Beth's theology is centred around social justice and queer theory, though that wasn't their initial intention! Beth feels that, as a queer person, work around queerness and intersectional social justice is the only way to be authentic. Queer identities and their links to experiences of oppression and marginalization were clear narrative themes throughout Beth's interview.

Similar to Stacey and Ellen, Beth's family was also affected by their identity, as well as the fact that their partner was also trans. These difficulties were, again, related to churches. Beth and their fiancé experienced considerable difficulty gaining their bishop's permission to marry despite the fact that when colleagues asked for the same permission, the response was immediate and was 'Like congratulations, go ahead. May God bless your union.' As such, Beth understandably believes that transphobia was at the root of the delay.

As well as a delayed marriage, Beth experienced a transition delay as a result of ecclesial transphobia. Beth was not initially able to come out in the parish in which they worked, as multiple meetings were required in order to agree that this was permissible. Once technically out, Beth still experienced barriers, as their supervisor suggested that they should not tell people about their pronouns, as this would be 'too difficult'. Since being ordained, Beth has experienced increasing difficulty, reflecting that 'Within the church it is a struggle. And I'm learning more and more how much of a struggle it is.' Beth's care for others led them to accept that 'People tend to use "she". I'm kind of trying to move away from that but I'm fairly open. Some people will not get there.' Although this attitude demonstrates resilience, I feel that this level of resilience should not be necessary, particularly in churches. Beth, themselves, admits that 'it is not an easy path'.

Similar to Ellen, Beth's experiences of suffering led to vocational and theological emphases on social justice. Beth correlated 'queerness' with 'marginalization' and explained that their marginalization as a queer person impelled a hermeneutic lens of 'intersectional social justice' when interpreting scripture. While Beth did describe queer hermeneutics as related to marginalization and suffering, they also highlighted the richness of queer theology, explaining that 'For my theology and my own spiritual development and practice, it's so enriching being non-binary and embodying a queer way of reading scripture.' Beth also described a practice of embodying each of the persons of the Trinity when reading scripture, a playful practice of 'just trying to shift between aspects of it'. Beth spoke about 'playing with scripture, in a sense of entering a certain realm and just exploring without knowing what the outcome will be'.

Stacey, Ellen and Beth

Stacey, Ellen and Beth have each experienced significant suffering which has contributed to their identity formation. For Stacey, this meant that suffering was a key theme in our conversation, and also contributed to her theological understanding. Ellen has also experienced suffering, particularly in relation to church, which was referred to frequently throughout our conversation. Ellen understood her suffering as injustice and, as such, the narrative themes of struggle and injustice were key themes. Beth has also experienced suffering, which they have codified as a theme of queer theory. As such, the interrelatedness of queerness and suffering were clear themes throughout our conversation.

In each case, themes of suffering were related specifically to the action, or inaction, of churches. Teresa Caprioglio (2021) argues that the theme of queer trauma is overused in society and the media as a trope that has negative effects on queer people and may be partially responsible for the lack of any appropriate response to anti-queer violence. Following Caprioglio's argument, perhaps the common themes of suffering and apologetics in trans-related theological literature have negatively impacted churches' understanding of, and responses to, trans people. It is vital to challenge the trope of trauma, without ignoring people's suffering, in order that individuals and institutions recognize the need for change.

Resilience

The media trope of trans suffering, as well as the negative experiences that participants have had, suggests that trans resilience is necessary. Like the participants considered above, Evie, Jack, River and Sam have also experienced suffering. However, resilience was a more notable narrative theme in their interviews.

Evie

Evie (she/her) is a middle-aged transwoman who transitioned socially around three years ago and takes oestrogen. Evie feels that her transition is a less important part of her identity than other factors, like being a parent and having a successful and fulfilling career. Evie is a member of a local cathedral, although her background and preferred tradition is charismatic/evangelical. Evie has a history of church planting and youth ministry and is in a process of vocational discernment. She works in talent management and is an entrepreneur, co-managing her own organization. Evie's theology is both practical and spiritual, biblically informed and continuing to develop. Evie says that she is still learning a lot about both gender and theology. Developing resilience both before and during transition was a clear narrative theme throughout Evie's interview.

Evie's resilience prior to transition was evidenced by repeated attempts to change her identity, as well as remaining in church contexts that were hostile to her identity for a prolonged period of time. Evie described life pre-transition as 'a resistance against the inevitable'. She spent years in a church where 'being trans was very unacceptable' and continued to attend due to 'internalized transphobia'. Evie described being outed at a prayer meeting and reflected that 'When I wasn't careful about who I felt to be inside people latched on immediately. And I was terrified.' Evie went on to explain:

I'd confessed to being trans in prayerful situations. They told some people outside the church about it and broke the kind of confidence of the kind of prayer room. So the church were mortified and obviously they expected me to kind of go off on one and be like, 'How dare you do that?' And my reaction was more, 'Well, I am trans. I am. If people find out about that, I'm not surprised because that's who I am as a person.'

This nonchalant response to being outed against her will highlights Evie's resilience in an unsafe context. Evie was eventually asked to undergo 'deliverance ministry' by church leaders and reflected that 'After 20 years of pleading with God to not let me be like this, pushing me to do that again was just the last straw.' For Evie, it was this attempt at converting her gender that led her to leave her church and begin the journey towards transition.

Despite the spiritual abuse that Evie experienced in her church, she continued to sense a vocation towards ministry. She explained, though, that 'The church wouldn't let me do that.' Evie turned to entrepreneurship in order to fulfil her vocation elsewhere, explaining:

I do for the work world what I think I should be doing for the church. I love helping people to move on in their development and in their capability, all that type of stuff. The church wouldn't let me do that really, so I turned to the world of work and did it there. Ironically, I talk about a lot of Christian principles in the work that I do. I stand out in the field because I'm a huge believer in inclusive talent management. And that's exactly what the church should do. Church should just say, 'We've got a phenomenal group of amazing members who we want to be the best they can possibly be in their relationship with God, with their ministry and contribution to the world', and enable that.

Instead of shaping her narrative around the suffering of being hurt and having her vocation rejected by the church, Evie has shaped her narrative around how she can take the gifts and theological insights that she has and use them in secular contexts.

Both family and friendship were key to Evie's resilience. Evie highlighted how important was the acceptance of her female friends, which she explains 'really meant the world, really mattered to me'. She also mentioned her children throughout her interview, explaining that both their positive reaction to her transition and spending time with them is 'just amazing. It's everything.' This shows that the narrative theme of resilience, for Evie, is not constructed in isolation but, rather, is supported by collaboration from those around her.

Jack

Jack (he/him) is a middle-aged transmasculine, genderflux person. Jack began to transition several years ago and has just begun to take testosterone. After initially identifying as genderfluid, Jack transitioned towards male but retains a sense of gender nonconformity. Jack has a doctorate and works in education. Jack describes his faith as gnostic and non-traditional. He has a clear and distinctive understanding of Christian theology that draws on his own spiritual experiences, past and present multiple-religious-belonging, and wide reading from a variety of faith and theological contexts. Jack is a spiritual entrepreneur, creating safe spiritual spaces for people who wish to explore their own spirituality. Jack's creative practices of resilience were a narrative theme throughout Jack's interview.

Similar to Evie, Jack has experienced explicit attempts at conversion, which he describes as attempts to 'pray the gay away', and attempted 'exorcisms'. He also experienced attempted conversion through prayer. It is notable that he was married to a man, and living as female, at the time of these attempts, and he felt that the religious community in which he was situated interpreted his gender nonconformity as homosexuality. Jack has also experienced difficulty mirroring gender norms and regular misgendering as well as being forcibly dechurched and made homeless when he transitioned.

Jack curates resilience in light of these difficulties by think-ing creatively and engaging in creative practices. Jack argued, 'I wouldn't be alive if it weren't for art', explaining:

> I was in a very, very bad place mentally and I went to a spiritual counsellor, and she was the one that got me back into painting and I think painting really did save me. Going on pilgrimage was the other thing that she got me into and also song-work. I sometimes meditate through painting or through writing but also through walking the land and what I find is when I'm doing that, songs and prayers come up naturally.

For Jack, painting, writing, walking and singing are creative practices that support resilience. It is notable that these are also highly embodied and tactile practices. Jack is connected with both the inner and outer world through intentional creativity.

Jack's creativity has not only supported his resilience, but also his understandings of identity and spirituality. Jack explained:

> I'm transmasculine genderflux. Sometimes I identify as fully male, sometimes more kind of demi-guy/trans-masculine. Mostly I just introduce myself as a trans guy. If I get forms with male or non-binary or female I always go for male and I present male, but spiritually I'm more non-binary if that makes sense. The way I present and the way I live my daily life and go into the practicalities and the logistics is a bit different from where I see myself on a more spiritual level.

Jack later suggested that it was difficult for others to under-stand his most authentic identity, hence the use of multiple descriptors. This suggests an ability to manage complexity for the sake of others and/or of recognition.

Jack also used creative thought to explore how he might best reflect his spiritual ideal of 'balance' in his gender iden-tity and presentation. He explained, 'When I first came out I experimented with half and half. I have some photos with my hair down on one side and short on the other, wearing a suit jacket on one side and flowery sparkly stuff on the other.' This creative experimentation, as well as the willingness to stand out, is striking.

Like Evie, Jack's resilience was not formed in isolation. For Jack, it was on social media that people first used his correct name and pronoun, enabling him to continue to transition. He described living in a 'visibly LGBTQ+ community' as a foundational element of his transition and explained that he met his partner at an 'LGBTQ+ faith group'. Jack spoke warmly about the 'supportive relationship' between trans people, his membership of ftm (female-to-male) groups, and the importance of members of LGBTQ+ groups using his pronouns correctly. Jack experienced mutual support in the LGBTQ+ community when he was able to swap gendered items with his differently gendered friend, who went on to become his partner. In this way, as well as through creating and leading spiritual practices for trans and non-binary people, Jack has used his own resilience to support the resilience of others.

River

River (they/them) has come out very recently as non-binary and works in the leadership of a major human-rights organization. River is also discerning a call to ministry. River's passion for social justice is woven into their DNA and has always informed their vocational journey. Authenticity is very important to River and was a motivating factor in coming out. River's theology centres on God's love, and their vocation is strongly pastoral. They feel an affinity with, and vocation among, LGBTQ+ communities but can also see themselves in a rural, traditional parish. The narrative theme of developing resilience was significant throughout River's interview.

As with Evie, River waited a long time to transition. River explained, 'I'm not comfortable in my femaleness at all', and described their pre-coming-out life as a 'gender struggle', which they related to norms around being a mother and being assumed to be/labelled as lesbian. Despite this struggle, River shared the experience of waiting to transition until a partner is ready. River described the experience of another person putting 'boundaries around my gender'. For River's partner, this reaction was due, in part, to the ways in which River's trans identity affected her own lesbian identity.

River explained that being a parent delayed their transition, as they felt comfortable with their mothering role, despite discomfort and incongruence with gender more generally and, further, that it was difficult to be trans and/or non-binary 'in the 90s', and that the societal 'cost of transition' would have been too high. However, River also described not being out as a kind of 'self-restriction' or limitation that is enacted for the comfort of others and explained that they experienced micro-aggressions at work, where people didn't always know 'the right way to speak about' trans identities.

River prioritized resilience by ceasing to attend church as a young adult due, in part, to a feeling that life was very difficult for LGBTQ+ people in church. They have recently started to be a part of LGBTQ+ specific churches, where they reflect that coming out was 'easy'. River is an ordinand and, when I interviewed them, they had not yet told church leadership about their non-binary identity and were nervous about doing so. This nervousness is not surprising, given the difficult experiences that many participants have had in church contexts and River's own pause in church membership due to those difficulties. River was determined to continue to explore their vocation, however, repeatedly reminding me that 'It's not about me, it's about everyone who is more vulnerable than me'.

Similar to Jack, the LGBTQ+ community was essential for River. River suggested that correct naming and use of pronouns within LGBTQ+ spaces was a vital practice in supporting resilience. They also expressed a sense of belonging to and prioritizing a 'queer tribe' as they transition and begin to explore ministry, explaining that encountering other non-binary people in the LGBTQ+ community 'contributed to my sense of belonging'. Drawing on my own lived experiences, I suspect that River's sense of belonging and resilience will both increase, and be challenged, as they continue their vocational journey.

Sam

Sam (she/her) is a non-binary transwoman in her seventies, a father and a grandmother. Sam is also a playwright. Sam says that she is not a theologian but her biblically inspired plays suggest otherwise, and she believes that theatre is a missional arena. Sam has known that she was trans since childhood but only felt able to transition after the tragic loss of her wife some years ago. Sam's theology centres around a passion for transformation, and extensive reading in early religious writings. She has also been strongly influenced by a family friend who taught her to meditate. Her clear resilience and creativity through, at times, very painful circumstances shine through her theology. The narrative theme of resilience was perhaps most clearly represented by Sam, who exclaimed that, 'I did have resilience, or I'd be dead.'

Out of all my participants, Sam waited the longest to transition, only beginning her journey after her wife tragically died. Sam described 'life as male', which had been her life for the past five decades, as 'unliveable' at that point. Sam's wife had suggested that they would have to separate in order for Sam to transition, but Sam felt that they may have found a way forward together, given more time. Sam described living for her children at her most difficult times and referred to herself as a 'father and grandmother', highlighting her ability to hold facts that may sometimes be seen as contradictory in tension.

Similar to Jack, Sam's resilience was supported by creativity. Sam described her career in theatre as 'a safe vocational space where I could be myself' and highlighted that this was an essential foundation to her process of identity discernment, coming out and transition, and also her well-being more generally. For Sam, 'reading', 'learning' and 'imagination', as well as her vocation as a writer, were experienced as a 'refuge' from the lack of understanding that she experienced in society.

It was reading about the ways in which some of the indigenous peoples of America 'honoured' people who they described as 'two-spirit', as expressing gender in diverse ways, that gave Sam 'some comfort', and instigated her journey of understanding regarding her own gender. For Sam, this journey led to writing, which became of primary importance in supporting her resilience. Sam spoke of 'staying alive' for her vocation as a playwright and actor.

Sam developed a lens of storytelling and explained that telling God's story was foundational to learning to tell her own story and that, in the process, she 'discovered the stories that I didn't know'. Interestingly, Sam also felt a connection with God not, initially, as a supreme being, but as a biblical character. Reading about God in the Hebrew Scriptures and supplementary interpretive texts, Sam developed a sense that God might be 'unhappy about being confined' to the gender binary and explained that in the Hebrew Scriptures 'Female G/gods[3] are being denied and told that they are abominations and I held the Bible as responsible for binary understandings of God, as corrupted.' This sense of empathy with God is important to Sam, widening her understandings of both God and herself.

Sam referenced a range of biblical passages, from the Hebrew Scriptures, through the Gospels to the Letters. As well as her understandings of God's gender, readings from the Pentateuch helped Sam to discern her own gender identity, explaining that she 'discovered' herself in the Bible when she realized that the second creation narrative, found in Genesis chapter 2, mirrored the androgynes of Plato's (385–370 BC) creation narrative. Plato describes the initial creation of human beings as two-faced, eight-limbed androgynous creatures who were then split apart by a vengeful god, who could not tolerate their cooperative power. They were then destined to go through life searching for their other half.

Sam found the Gospels to be an essential tool of resilience, noting that 'Jesus says, "Love your enemies, bless those who persecute you", so I had to treat my enemies that way.' For Sam, this understanding of scripture enabled a gracious, and even thankful, response to anti-trans protestors who picketed the initial release of her ground-breaking play. Sam also mentioned the narrative of the Ethiopian eunuch in Acts, explaining that her initial reaction was, 'Wow, salvation really does encompass me.' This narrative describes a disciple, Philip, meeting a person from Ethiopia who was a court official and a eunuch – someone who was sex-and/or-gender diverse – who is reading scripture that they ask Philip to explain to them. The encounter ends with the person asking Philip what there is to stop them being baptized. They are then baptized. For Sam, it was not a particular understanding of salvation, or the story of Jesus' resurrection, that enabled her own resilience, but this less well-known story of a disciple whose story connects with Sam's own.

Evie, Jack, River and Sam

Evie, Jack, River and Sam have each formed attitudes and practices of resilience, in response to suffering, which have become central to their narrative identities. These attitudes and practices are born out of necessity and informed by vocation, creativity and supportive social and familial relationships. There is clear potential for learning around the ways in which vocation, creativity and support can be used to support the resilience of anyone who has experienced suffering.

It was impossible to avoid being impressed by the participants' resilience. Nevertheless, I was struck by the way in which resilience is a direct result of suffering. This does not elevate suffering but, rather, highlights the limitations of any over-arching narrative of trans identities that relies on resilience with contingent suffering. This risks suggesting that suffering is a good thing, whereas the suffering of trans people is a painful reality rooted in unjust systems and practices. The theme of suffering underlies the theme of resilience. If resilience is seen as a virtue of trans identities, that means that our suffering is seen as a virtue too. The implied glorification of suffering is intensely problematic. I am concerned about the ways in which negative societal attitudes towards trans people have impacted participants' well-being and impelled them to find ways to manage and respond to pain.

Joy

Trans resilience is directly correlated to trans suffering. Perhaps a move is needed from discussing trans suffering and resilience to noticing trans joy – from a voyeuristic focus on pain and survival to a participative practice of new life. Trans people are initiating this move through practices and narratives of trans euphoria (see Beischel et al., 2021). It would be wrong to suggest that this is in any way a critique of the participants described above. Rather, I suggest that the resilience developed in light of suffering enables the euphoria lens. Suffering is perhaps inevitable for trans and non-binary people in the UK at present, whether or not we believe that this should be so. When resilience is developed, however, it is possible to reframe experiences of suffering in the light of joy or euphoria. For example, considerations of bodily suffering may be balanced with considerations of bodily transition and congruence. In conversations with cis people, I often note that the questions asked, and statements of support made, assume great suffering, and focus thereon. The idea that I might experience bodily congruence or pleasure, euphoria, does not seem to occur to many conversation partners. Similar to each other participant, including myself, Pat, Star and Mike have experienced considerable suffering and developed striking resilience. Their narratives, however, are framed around the concept of joy in both implicit and explicit defiance to cultural and ecclesial tropes of trans suffering and pathology.

Pat

Pat (she/her) is in her forties. Although Pat identifies as female – which is also her sex assigned at birth – she also identifies as gender non-conforming. Pat's identity has been, in part, shaped by a single (male) parent upbringing, and a diagnosis of PCOS (Polycystic Ovary Syndrome), which she describes as an intersex condition. Pat is a minister and feels that her androgyny and gender non-conformity is a positive in ministry. Her theology centres around her belief in a loving God and her passionate understanding that the church should speak up for the marginalized. She also feels strongly that better understandings of trans and gender non-conforming identities would enable the church to understand the lives of cis people who do not conform to gender stereotypes. Narrative themes of suffering and resilience were apparent in Pat's interview, but a narrative theme of joy was also clear throughout.

Like Sam, reading, learning and engagement with scripture has informed, and is informed by, Pat's narrative of joy. For Pat, learning a 'new language' has enabled her to better understand herself and, accordingly, to develop a greater sense of self-worth. That sense of self-understanding went on to mean that Pat's sense of faith has 'grown' and 'expanded' since she began to recognize herself as non-binary. In particular, Pat has developed a sense that 'God doesn't judge' and explains that sin is universal, that we cancel each other out and that, therefore, the concept is irrelevant. Rather than developing a theory of redemption in order to counter a theory of sin, Pat suggested that we are redeemed simply because we exist and are loved. Likewise, Pat responded to her lived experiences of suffering by choosing to focus on life and love.

Pat found 'reading the Bible for myself' important and has valued broadening her reading to extra theological disciplines, suggesting that the Bible is a 'teaching document', but not the only important text. For Pat, female biblical characters were of key importance. She related to Mary Magdalene, Hagar and Rahab, who she described as 'strong women' who 'queer gender' and 'challenge biblical and the church's gender stereotypes'. She suggested that these 'strong women' were not referenced enough in mainstream churches, highlighting the problem of a suffering/marginalization theological lens.

For Pat, it was Jesus' words about what it means to be human that inspired joy. Pat explained:

Jesus talks about eunuchs being blessed and you can easily rewrite the beatitudes in relation to that; to say that blessed are non-binary people, trans people, people who just refuse to fit in a box, women in jeans and men in skirts. Blessed are those of us who defy sex and gender norms because Jesus said so.

For Pat, gender and sex are material, but that materiality does not contradict trans and non-binary freedom and blessing. Rather, for Pat, it is as the embodied and clothed fleshy beings that we are that Jesus blesses us. It is in our daily lived experiences that we can encounter unapologetic joy.

Star

Star (they/them) is a genderqueer young adult. Star has been living in transition for several years. Star identifies in a manner that is playful and that queers and challenges gender. Star is a minister in one of the four main UK denominations and identifies with the evangelical/charismatic tradition, while noting tensions between their tradition and identity. Star has a growing and distinctive understanding of Christian theology, and they frequently note the importance of continued learning. Star's theology draws on their training for Christian ministry, which included an undergraduate theology degree. Star also applies the lenses of play, genderqueering, disability-theory and experience to their theological journey. Star's playful hermeneutics were a narrative theme that was evident throughout Star's interview. Star's sense of joy is a gritty one, rooted in protest. Star told me that they sometimes experience their ministry as a kind of 'rebellion against oppressors'. This leads me to wonder what a euphoric rebellion against gender-based religious oppression might look like.

For Star, listening to and sharing music that mirrors their experiences and/or identity is a vital element of self-expression. They centre their vocational practice of leading retreats for trans people around creative practices including music and visual arts. This creativity spills over into Star's biblical hermeneutics of play and 'genderfluid hermeneutics', highlighting the ways in which trans and non-binary resilience can influence theological practices and understandings. Star explained that they used the term 'genderfluid hermeneutics' and 'biblical play' to describe a process of experimenting with the genders of biblical characters, not as a definitive practice but as a playful one, through which new resonances might develop.

Drawing comparisons between themselves and 'fleshy' biblical characters was important to Star, who explained that 'lived experience' was an essential element of connection. Star referred to a number of biblical characters, highlighting Joseph and Samson. Regarding the latter, they described their interpretation: 'Proper headcanons,[4] Samson is transgender, and I need it to be fleshy. I need it to be about the way they dress, the things that they do with their hair.' Star's use of the term 'headcanons' shows the way popular culture has influenced their practice of 'biblical play', enabling Star to experiment with the biblical characters and interpretations that resonate with them.

Star found the Genesis creation narratives to be revelatory texts. Star related:

> The first thing that [online anti-trans commenters] tend to do is throw Genesis 1.27 at me, 'male and female he created them', and it was through prayer and study of that very scripture that I believe that God revealed to me who I am and my identity as a trans person. I was writing an essay on Genesis 1.23 and I had this powerful spiritual experience, and it was like in John 4.39 when the woman says he told me everything that I was, so even from the very beginning it was a spiritual as much as it was an emotional journey.

Star went on to explain, 'I felt like God saying that I could live in the "and" of male *and* female (Genesis 1.27), it wasn't like two sides of a team that I needed to pick.' For Star, God's affirmation in Genesis 1.27 was strengthened by what they interpreted as God's condemnation of the gender binary in Genesis 3. Star explained:

I had to play around with the fall, and I really like the idea that binary understandings of sex and gender are the result of the fall and the curse that Eve and Adam experience in Genesis 3 is basically gendered lives. God effectively says, 'Adam you're a man and this is your job, and that's what men do, and Eve you're a woman and this is what women do.' A lot of people say that being trans is the result of the fall, and I want to flip it the other way round, and actually say that binary understandings of gender and gender roles are the actual result of the fall.

While 'the fall' is not a key part of my own theological understandings, I found this explanation fascinating and helpful. It is certainly worth noting that gender roles do seem to be introduced in the biblical narrative immediately after Adam and Eve discover their own nakedness. This could be used to argue for correlated sex and gender. However, it is just as possible to see gender differentiation as the result of knowing too much. It is also clear that Star's interpretation of 'the fall' is strongly related to the interpretations that have been used against them. Star has developed a creative understanding of this difficult text that enables resilience, rather than shame.

Star also referenced the transfiguration (Matthew 17.1; Mark 9.2; Luke 9.28), relating it to trans lives by suggesting that 'In all our coming outs and transitions and things we're revealing that which is hidden to the rest of the world but is known to God and is blessed by God.' In the transfiguration, Jesus' divinity is revealed to three of his disciples, enabling them to see him as he truly is. Similarly, Star suggests that, in coming out and transition, trans people reveal their hidden identities to those close to them. Star has used this idea to help other trans people, leading a retreat with transfiguration as the theme, showing how practices of joyful revelation can positively impact the trans community.

Mike

Mike (he/him) is a young trans man. Mike transitioned a few years ago and moves through the world as a man. As a Black man, Mike feels that both race and gender have informed his experiences, identity and theology. Suffering is central to Mike's theological understandings, but joy is central to his transition. He is moving towards a freer, more joy-filled understanding of God too. Mike is a writer, and his theological understandings are beautifully and poignantly poetic. As an advocate for social justice, Mike has lots of questions for God and the church and raises the vital issue of structural injustice. These questions arise out of Mike's experiences of gender euphoria[5] and his correlated strong sense that euphoria can and should be a framing narrative theme for exploring trans and non-binary identities and lives.

For Mike, experiences of suffering were inversely correlated with joy. Mike explored the danger of narrow/exclusive theological understandings, explaining that 'bad evangelical theology' caused him severe anxiety, and led him to 'repress my desires and needs'. Mike further noted the resilience needed to manage 'not conforming to people's notions of gender in public which was very hard' and expressed that it was difficult to navigate life during a time of physical and social dysphoria. Despite this, Mike's focus is not on dysphoria but, rather, on 'euphoria'. Mike explained that 'My transition is about noticing what brings me joy and following those breadcrumbs of delight.' This attitude is in direct challenge to the trope of trans suffering and suggests that an intentional focus on joy cannot only resource trans people, but also those who have the privilege of dialogue with trans people.

Mike described having held 'narrow' and 'authoritarian' theological understandings prior to coming out, which 'broadened in my twenties', enabling his transition. Contextualization of scripture and reading for oneself were essential components of transformation. Over time, Mike has come to notice and see the importance of 'certain themes and motifs' through scripture, rather than 'specific passages'.

As with Star, Mike has grown into a hermeneutic of contextual questioning, noting that he has questions to ask of the Bible
'as a queer person' and 'as a Black person'. He expressed that
he was 'trying to decide whether there is still something valuable here or whether it all needs to go'. In this decision-making
process Mike was able to prioritize his own value over 'harmful interpretations' of scripture. This process has led to a lens
of social justice, through which Mike assesses the potential of
biblical narratives and interpretations.

Pat, Star and Mike

Pat, Star and Mike all expressed themes of joy, exploration,
play and euphoria in their interviews, which were often in contrast to their experiences of suffering, and which contributed to
their theological understandings as well as their own identity
narratives. Mike in particular showed a way in which trans
euphoria can be an intentional framing choice, encompass-
ing experiences of suffering and resilience but refusing to be
defined by those experiences. This was a poignant reflection,
which affected my own understandings.

Reflection

There is a cultural and clinical assumption of trans pathology
and/or suffering. There are clear indications in the data
explored above that some participants' lived experiences
are correlated with similar narratives of trans suffering. For
some participants, these experiences shape their narratives
and hermeneutical lenses. There is also evidence, however,
that some participants choose narratives of resilience and joy
regardless of, or perhaps in light of, their experiences of suffering. These choices are evident in how participants frame their
stories, in their tools and practices of resilience, and in their
ways of reading and interpreting scripture. These narratives
are significantly under-represented in the trans-related theological texts and deserve renewed attention.

My own experiences of suffering as a trans Christian were never far from my mind as I listened to, transcribed, coded and wrote about other trans people's experiences. Because of my experiences and empathy with them, this process of research has been an emotional experience in itself. It has been important for me to take time to rest and reflect regularly. This element of being a researcher with a similar identity to my participants has been far more difficult than I had appreciated. However, I also believe that being a trans researcher has enabled me to empathize with, understand, analyse and respond to their experiences and insights more effectively. This chapter, where I have explored suffering, resilience and joy, has been particularly emotive, considering my own experiences.

I experienced suffering related to dysphoria, coming out and transition in the early parts of my transition. Much of my childhood was clouded by feelings of alienation, both from my body and from other children. As a teenager, that alienation morphed into severe depression and anxiety. I experienced difficulties with self-harm and eating. I also experienced spiritual abuse, including attempted conversion of my perceived sexuality by prayer. In my early transition I was isolated from my family and friends and experienced several hate crimes as a result of my visible gender non-conformity. Trans-related suffering has lessened as my transition has progressed and I have gained 'passing privilege'.[6] I have written more about my experiences in childhood and in transition in *Transgender. Christian. Human* (Clare-Young, 2019).

Nevertheless, I continue to experience suffering related to the intersections of my trans and Christian identities. In churches I am often encouraged to hide or marginalize the trans/non-binary aspects of my identity in order to avoid conflict and support normativity. I refuse to do so, as I highly value authenticity and openness. This often leads to hostile media and social media attention, hate mail and threats. I have had to seek aid from the police on several occasions due to this. I have developed a 'thick skin' through necessity, and practise resilience daily. Until interviewing Mike, I had never considered my own identity through the lens of euphoria.

Many of the participants' experiences, as well as my own, can be categorized as experiences of suffering, abuse, marginalization and isolation. Some experiences are extreme and shocking. All of them were painful to hear. I have a strong sense of empathy with each participant, and care about their lives. Painful experiences should not be minimized. Nor should a person be judged for an identity framed by suffering. However, trans suffering should also not be overstated or used as an overarching narrative of trans experience. Each participant also shared their tools of resilience and some shared experiences of euphoria and joy. This led me to wonder if more work is needed to highlight narratives of euphoria in trans theology.

Stacey drew on Nadia Bolz-Weber's (2014) *Pastrix* to theologically reflect on her experiences of suffering. Despite Bolz-Weber's own suffering, she goes on to explore the lifelong difficulties of being enculturated into a suffering-based belief system and the ways in which she has been able to expand her theological understandings. Bolz-Weber's (2019) later text, *Shameless*, is particularly helpful here. In this text, Bolz-Weber unpicks, piece by piece, narratives of shame and suffering and offers, in response, narratives, theological insights and ecclesial practices of embodied euphoria. In her concluding 'Benediction', Bolz-Weber (pp. 185–200) reminds readers of the positive theological tenets of 'incarnation', 'abundance', 'radical welcome and dialogue', 'forgiveness', 'connection', 'holiness' and 'shamelessness'. These are euphoric principles that are inextricably related to suffering and resilience and yet draw the reader's attention to joy and thanksgiving. Bolz-Weber's reflections move me from suffering to joy.

Marcella Althaus-Reid's writing, however, helps me to take a further step, given her challenge to a theological focus on suffering, which she suggests is inevitable in systematic theologies. In her seminal text, *Indecent Theology*, Althaus-Reid (2001, p. 25) calls out the dangerous practice of 'sacralis[ing] oppression'. In other words, it is risky, both theologically and practically, to make oppression into an idol and, thereby, excuse ecclesial inaction. Althaus-Reid (p. 27) suggests that 'Systematic theological production has traditionally made reflection on human suffering its object of exchange', her theory being that 'incoherence' is the only appropriate mitigation. Reflecting on the participants' experiences and insights and Althaus-Reid's clear rebuke, I am compelled to:

• actively consider a lens of euphoria when creating the theological and anthropological insights presented in the following two chapters
• avoid glorifying suffering, oppression or marginalization
• risk 'incoherence' where a 'coherent' or 'systematic' presentation of theological themes would contradict the former two considerations.

This process of interviewing, coding, writing about and reflecting on participants' experiences, lenses and narratives of suffering, resilience and joy has affected me personally and theologically. I have tended to dwell on my own experiences of suffering and have focused on a narrative of suffering when writing and speaking about my identity and trans identities more widely. Participants' experiences of suffering were intensely painful to hear about and explore, precisely because they so closely mirrored my own and those that I hear and read about from other trans and non-binary people every single day. Mike's comments regarding trans euphoria encouraged me to consider my transition and identity in a new light. This has led me to explore how it might feel to use practices and narratives of joy in my own daily life, writing and speaking.

Further, Star's playful hermeneutics have affected my own theology, leading me to consider how foci on affirmation, resilience and mirroring in the Bible might become a helpful addition to my historic foci on suffering and justice. I have begun to play more with the Genesis creation narratives, and to focus on affirmation, resilience and mirroring in my reading, writing and ministry practices. This is an ongoing journey, which I am finding both helpful and fun! I am keen to ensure that my changing experiences, narratives and lenses are communicated to others, recognizing the ways in which participants' descriptions of their own experiences and understandings have affected me. Althaus-Reid (p. 25) reminds me of the harm that a theologian can do by focusing overly much on suffering. Rather, I hope that a progressive focus on joy can extend the tools of resilience and experiences of euphoria to more trans and non-binary people.

Notes

1 GRS refers to Gender Reassignment Surgery or Gender Confirmation Surgery, surgeries that a trans person may have as a part of their transition.

2 Trans Day of Remembrance (TDOR) refers to the events held annually on 20 November to remember those trans people who have been killed during the previous year.

3 I use G/gods to note that Sam was referring both to female aspects of God and to other gods outside the Christian tradition.

4 Headcanons is a term used in popular culture to describe a personal interpretation that is relatable but is not used in the 'universe' of a particular series or story.

5 Gender euphoria is a feeling of joy related to the correlation of gender identity, expression and perception. It can be described as the opposite of dysphoria.

6 Passing privilege is the idea that a trans person gains privilege, their life becomes easier, when they look like the gender that they are.

Interlude 4

It's Important – River

I'm still working a lot of stuff out about myself. I am a female-bodied person, non-binary, sometimes also OK with being called a 'woman' but sometimes really not. I am 'out' as not-cis in some parts of my life but not all. I have a female partner and have considered most of my relationships to be in some way lesbian even though I'm not comfortable in my femaleness at all. I have teenagers. In my twenties I thought for a while I could be a trans man but when I worked out I am actually non-binary, not a man, I gave up thoughts of transitioning because of the difficulty of identifying that way in the 1990s. Now I am increasingly open about my gender 'struggle' and will have top surgery finally this year, if lockdown permits.

I turn 50 this year and for the first time I feel as if my life, faith and identity are coming together and making me feel whole. I have led a compartmentalized and fragmented existence in some ways – and very boundaried and closed-in – but I am starting to break down those walls and bring parts of myself together. I have always known that I am non-binary genderqueer, and I've had that self-identification in my head for 25 years or more but generally speaking, I haven't lived in the words. I haven't owned that identity or that label and over the last 18 months I actively started to think about it and realized that it's been a really limiting thing for me to not be fully open about that, and out in the world. And, of course, the world's a very different place now from what it was like in the mid-90s in terms of the ability to even explain what that means and expect any kind of understanding around that. And I just got to the stage where it's no longer worth restricting or limiting who I am for the benefit of other people's comfort. I thought, 'Actually this time it's not impossible, and I can do it and it will make my life better, and it's important.'

One of the ways I coped with not being out in relation to my gender identity was to create a performance of a kind of gender that took me just as far as I needed to go for me to be just slightly more comfortable in my skin. I needed people to see in some way that I'm gender-non-conforming at least. I was creating an image of myself to allow just a tiny bit of visibility; visibility that wouldn't necessarily be labelled as trans but would signal something other than conventional feminine, womanly gender.

So if I can signal that in much more straightforward ways like, 'This is my name and these are my pronouns', then I no longer have to do all of that. I can wear what I like. A lot of what I do around my presentation has been a kind of code for, 'Try not to see me as this thing but see me as that thing', but if I'm much more open about who I am then I do not have to do that. I do not have to play this game with myself and with the world. I do not have to create coded ways of being in the world that aren't quite what I'm trying to say, but are a sort of vague approximation towards it, in a very restricted or limiting way. I can just say, 'This is who I am', and then people can just know that. I do not have to create other signifiers.

All my life there has been this stuff I know about who I am and where my sense of self is and how I think I'm finding my identity, and part of that is my gender and who I am in Christ needs to acknowledge that. And I've effectively been hiding that part of myself and that's been such a big tension; trying to be open about that quest, if you like, but at the same time not actually living. It is so freeing to not have to hide this huge part of who I am.

There was definitely a time when I thought the most important thing for me was just to have top surgery, that I didn't actually care that much about my name, but the thing I couldn't bear was being so uncomfortable in my body and in my skin, and if I could change that thing then other things wouldn't matter, and I've definitely pulled away from that thought that modifying my body would or could be a sort of adequate substitute for being myself in the world. It's like wearing men's underwear or using boys toiletries – OK, it's great, it does make me feel better – those are things I've done all my life, not just in my latest phase, but it's no substitute for the actual openness and honesty that comes in being just out and I think, for me, my name and pronouns are the things that will make the difference, because they're the things that everybody sees. That's really just about visibility. So I'm really pleased that I will get surgery as soon as the Covid crisis is over. It's not that that's gone away, it's just that it's not the answer, it's just part of the journey.

5

Breadcrumbs of Delight:
Theological Anthropology

In the previous chapter I highlighted which of the three themes of suffering, resilience and joy largely framed each person's narrative during our conversations. It is also the case, however, that each person experienced and touched on all three of these themes. In the following explorations I highlight the ways in which themes of suffering, resilience and joy shaped each of our understandings of being human.

I introduce our experiences of, and insights about, being human by considering the themes of createdness, mirroring and the personal qualities that became apparent during interviews. Many of these themes are explicitly related to gender identity, non-binary identity and/or transition. They also, however, have implications for how we might understand theological anthropology more widely. In particular, they point towards an anthropology rooted in resilience and joy, in a sense of inherent human goodness, rather than in suffering or sinfulness.

Continuing createdness

The idea that we are created by God is a core element of theological anthropology.[1] Several people expressed clear views about how that createdness presents. In particular, they suggested that createdness is related to processes of growth and transformation/becoming, and to identity and embodiment. Congruent inter-relationality between, rather than a disarticulation of, identity and embodiment was found to be an essential characteristic of human createdness. This congruence suggests resilience and enables joy. Disarticulation is, conversely, described as an element of suffering.

Processes of creation

We experience createdness/being created as a process. Rather than experiencing creation as an initial and finite historic event, which is now over, createdness is repeated and/or continuous. For some, these ongoing processes of creation and recreation include moments of revelation. These moments are often connected to coming out to oneself, coming out to others, and daily curation of presentation and embodiment in dialogue with identity. For several, processes of 'becoming' are central to what it means to be human. These are processes of transformation. Transition is a process of transformation in which authenticity, in response to God's call, is one aim. This process requires resilience and consists of moves towards joy.

Some of us experience changes in identity over time or experience identity as a journey. River noted that they were 'still working a lot of stuff out about myself', later explaining that they initially felt that they were a 'trans man', but at the time of interview, identified as non-binary. Conversely, Jack began his transition 'thinking initially that I was genderfluid and expecting that I was going to have femme days and masc. days', but at the time of interview, identified as transmasculine, after noticing that they 'just felt so much more comfortable and so much more myself presenting as masculine'. Beth suggested that gender is 'a nice category to play with because it is an aspect in which many people express themselves. It's so much more fluid and creative than people think.' For Stacey, the journey was a liberative one, wherein God was 'in the process of freeing' her.

These experiences of journey suggest a continued process of God's creation and highlight the ways in which individuals can notice and/or participate in that ongoing process. Both Star and Beth highlighted growth as part of the process of createdness.

Star explained that 'God doesn't create us to stand still, God creates us to become, God creates us to change, God creates us to grow.' Further, as previously noted, Star cited transition as a process of revelation. I am struck by the ways in which Star and Beth's understandings resonate with observations of the natural world, wherein both plants and creatures grow from a place of hiddenness and, in time, reveal themselves to the world.

Identity and embodiment in transition

Identity and embodiment are distinct and yet intertwined elements of our created selves. They are sometimes separated in anthropological understandings. An example of separation of identity and embodiment that is related to trans identities is the trope that trans people are 'born in the wrong body'. Ulrica Engdahl (2014) highlights that this is an essentialist trope that leads to the over-regulation of trans bodies and identities by others. This trope asserts the correlation of 'femaleness' with a vulva and 'maleness' with a phallus. It implies that particular clinical treatments are required in order for transition to be valid and reduces trans and non-binary people to sexed aspects of our embodiment, thereby objectifying us.

We have much to contribute on the connections, and disarticulations, of identity and embodiment. Several participants suggested that authenticity is key. Several participants had, however, experienced separations or fracturing of body from identity, and of identity from presentation. In particular, fracturing was experienced prior to transition. Many described transition as a journey from limitation towards fullness of life. All participants transition as a necessity. When explaining the need to transition, while some described experiences of dysphoria, euphoria was also described as a motivator.

Prior to transition, several of us experienced suffering as a fracturing of body from identity in something akin to a Cartesian split. River explained, 'I've always felt massively disconnected from my physical self' and hoped that 'if I have surgery, I might feel less disconnected'. Similarly, Ellen, who had undergone gender-affirming surgery, felt that this was an essential part of her transition, providing 'a sense of rightness'. There was also, however, a sense in which embodiment and identity are spiritually disconnected for Ellen, who suggested that as 'a child of God', each of us is primarily non-binary. For some participants, personal and social transition, rather than clinical transition, enabled reconciliation of body and identity. Evie noted the 'joy' of changes to her body related to hormone replacement therapy, but prioritized social transition, suggesting that physical changes have 'just been more helpful to other people', enabling them to 'latch on to what it is I'm trying to project'. As a result, Evie felt that surgery had become, while potentially helpful, less urgent. For Pat, 'masculinizing traits' as a result of polycystic ovaries led to a feeling of disconnection between embodiment and identity, prior to coming out to herself as non-binary. For Pat, self-understanding, rather than surgical treatment, was key to reconciling body and identity.

The nuances of participants' understandings of the disconnection of body from identity and the ways in which they had sought to overcome this disconnection is striking. While medical ethics is beyond the scope of this project, it seems important to note that, for some participants, non-clinical changes enable reconnection, whereas for others surgery is essential. This diversity should be represented, without judgement, in theological reflections on trans identities. If theological reflections on trans identities focus overly on the body as distinct from the mind, they impose a dualistic narrative. Further, the overemphasis on surgery objectifies trans people, overly simplifies our experiences and impacts people's understandings of trans identity. This pathologizing understanding is prevalent in trans-related healthcare in the UK, with the National Health Service (2020) describing gender dysphoria as the result of 'a mismatch between [a person's] biological sex and their gender identity'. This common assumption ignores the realities of trans people who are intersex, trans people who experience congruence between some parts of their sexed embodiment and their identity, and trans people whose sexed embodiment and/or gender identity change over time. Further, this understanding pathologizes and problematizes trans and non-binary identities. It does not correlate with the ways in which interview participants describe their identities and embodiment.

Wholeness and authenticity, as opposed to fragmentation and hiddenness, was expressed as being important to several participants. River explained, 'If I'm much more open about who I am, I do not have to play this game with myself and with the world about wanting to create coded ways of being in the world.' For River, who experienced life before transition as 'compartmentalized and fragmented', moving towards wholeness and authenticity was essential. They also related having felt 'guilty' regarding their prior lack of authenticity. Similarly, both Evie and Ellen expressed feeling that their inauthenticity prior to transition was problematic. Stacey suggested that authenticity is 'key' to transition and is 'empowered' by God. If transition is a form of revelation, perhaps authenticity is akin to being revealed.

This kind of revelation of God through the authentic human self, however, is linked for participants to a congruence between identity and presentation. For several participants, a lack of societal understanding contributes to a continuing incongruence between their authentic identity and the presentation of that identity which they reveal to those around them. Sam and Evie described their incongruence between identity and presentation, prior to transitioning, as 'repression', each explaining that they had tried, for many years, to hide their gender identities due to external expectations. Similarly, River described previously creating a 'performance of a kind of gender that took me just as far as I needed to go to be slightly more comfortable in my skin', rather than transitioning, and compared this to the freedom experienced in coming out.

However, Jack reflected that 'Spiritually I'm more non-binary' but that he introduces himself as 'a trans guy' because, 'You have to go with people's level of understanding', as many people 'just go, "What?"' This suggests that Jack is unable to reveal his authentic spiritual identity due to a lack of societal awareness and understanding. As someone with a binary identity, Ellen enjoys the congruence between her identity and presentation, and explained, 'I do have passing privilege and, as a result, I can just go shopping and I'm a woman.' This leads me to wonder whether revelation might be more fulsome if other people were able to see Jack similarly intuitively as non-binary. While, for trans people with binary identities, incongruence between identity and the perceptions of others can be overcome, for non-binary people it is sometimes a continuing difficulty.

As well as enabling the reconciliation of body, identity and presentation, transition was also described as a journey from limited life towards life in all its fullness, which Jesus describes as his intention for humanity. Mike echoes Jesus' intention that people 'may have life, and have it abundantly', as opposed to being robbed of abundant life by 'The thief [who] comes only to steal and kill and destroy' (John 10.10). Mike related a journey of moving away from repression and 'a kind of average, OK life', towards a realization that 'actually there's a lot of life and fulness in being authentic to those things'. Stacey described life, pre-transition, as a 'lie'. Jack expressed being in a 'very bad place mentally' prior to transition. In contrast to post-transition energy and purpose, Evie described life, pre-transition, as 'tiring', and also expressed a sense of secrecy and related terror. Ellen suggested that the 'stress' of pre-transition life affected her 'symptoms' of 'Asperger's', meaning that following transition, she is now able to contribute more to society. All participants described ways in which their life has become 'fuller' in coming out and in transition. Perhaps the 'thief' that Jesus describes in John 10.10 can be understood, in this context, as that which limits life, whereas transition enables life in all its fullness.

Considerations of fullness versus limitation do raise the question of dysphoria, a form of suffering that is an integral part of clinical understandings of trans identities and is referred to in several theological reflections on trans personhood. Referring to dysphoria, for example, Chalke (2018, p. 3) suggests that trans people 'feel trapped ... in the body they are in'. This is a problematic trope which I hear frequently as a trans person and relies on the disarticulation of body and mind critiqued above. Additionally, not all trans people feel dysphoric. Some of those I interviewed do experience or have experienced dysphoria, which Mike described as 'gruelling'. Sam explained that dysphoria made her feel unlovable and led to 'breakdowns, emotional breakdowns, mental breakdowns', causing her to realize that she 'had to see a gender specialist'.

However, some participants highlighted limits of the dysphoria model as a framework for understanding trans identities. Despite his experiences of dysphoria, Mike suggested that he has been 'led by the idea of gender euphoria and the idea of what feels right; what feels congruent with who I am internally, externally, psychologically, emotionally', a process that he described as 'following those breadcrumbs of delight'. Stacey explained that 'I have no problem with being transgender' and that she is 'happy in my own skin'. Evie reflected that it is 'tempting' to focus on a model of dysphoria but suggested that it can make trans people 'hard to know how to relate to'. For Evie, a suffering model of understanding trans identities limits the potential for meaningful dialogue, as the assumed suffering is the focus of the conversation partner's attention. Further, Evie highly prizes resilience. Pat noted the personal benefits of a 'euphoria model', expressing that 'I've got a bit of this, and a splash of that', that 'knowing that I'm not a cookie cutter person' deepens her understanding of personhood and that 'God makes us the way we are for a reason, and we can be so much happier if we accept that and get on with it and try to puzzle out what the reason is rather than lamenting.' While experiences of dysphoria are clearly authentic, serious, and deserve attention, it is also clear that experiences of euphoria are an important part of transition. Given the media focus on mental ill health and suffering related to trans identities, it is striking that for participants transition was a move away from suffering towards authenticity and joy. There is a need for theological literature that uses a euphoria framework to consider trans and non-binary personhood. Further, there is a need for pastoral praxis that takes trans euphoria seriously, rather than centring dysphoria.

Mirroring

The understandings and experiences of personhood raised by this group of trans and non-binary Christians suggest that mirroring is an aspect of theological anthropology to which trans and non-binary theologians have much to contribute. 'Mirroring' is my own term referring to the telos, as described by Alistair I. McFadyen (1990) in the seminal theological anthropology, *The Call to Personhood*, of relating to God and to the other in genuine dialogue. In doing so, we hold up a mirror to the other, through which they receive the gift of recognized personhood, and we hold up a mirror to God, through which humans can discern and relate to something of the divine. My MPhil thesis explores the telos of mirroring in relation to trans identities. I argue:

> The ways in which we relate to others should mirror the ways in which we relate to God. It follows that we should allow others freedom and independence while responding to others freely and thankfully. Our relationships with others image God when they are dialogical, as opposed to monological. Dialogical conversations are those in which two or more partners converse with the intention to genuinely hear the voice of the other. (Clare-Young, 2018, pp. 26–7)

The concepts of mirroring and dialogue raised above are inextricably related and co-reliant. In the following sections I explore:

1 Mirroring ourselves – the process of curating identity and embodiment that enables authentic and effective communication.
2 Mirroring each other – processes of dialogue in which we help each other to understand something of what it means to be human.
3 Mirroring God – the ways in which our modes of being, living and communicating demonstrate something of God.

These mirroring concepts are a way of understanding person-hood that is applicable to all. I explore the ways in which trans and non-binary participants' lived experiences and contributions to this research demonstrate these concepts and will point to some broader implications.

Mirroring ourselves

Before we can be a mirror for others some trans people find that we must curate a sense of internal mirroring – a sense of coherence between our identity, embodiment and presentation. Sam compellingly highlighted the importance of mirroring as she described the terror of not recognizing herself in the mirror:

> My first memory is looking in the mirror and not really recognizing the boy that I saw and not being able to make any sense of that experience at all, because in the 50s there was no way of making sense of that experience. It was terrifying, absolutely terrifying. All I could do was try to ignore it and hope it went away, but of course it didn't go away.

River compared the lack of internal mirroring to game play, explaining:

> A lot of what I do around my presentation has been a kind of code for 'Try not to see me as this thing but see me as that thing' but if I'm much more open about who I am I do not have to play this game with myself and with the world about wanting to create coded ways of being in the world.

Mike described 'a rough period' in which he had to work 'to divest from cis-normative concepts of gender and work hard to affirm myself in a society that didn't see me as I was'. This seems to be a process of self-mirroring. Mike was unable to see himself mirrored back by other people in his communities. As a result, he used affirming self-talk to provide that missing mirror. For Mike, the self-mirroring process was not only a process of self-understanding, but also a process of shedding systemically harmful understandings in order to prioritize his own personhood.

When we talk about mirroring dialogue as a key part of our telos, it is important to consider the steps that trans and non-binary people take to enable that mirroring. I would argue, however, that we should also consider these steps as an example of how each person, trans, non-binary or cis, might learn to curate their own authenticity so that each person might attend to their part in dialogue. This has broader implications for how each individual might curate their own identity in order to enable mirroring and dialogue, either intentionally or unintentionally, and how this might inform both theological understandings and ecclesial practice.

Mirroring each other

The way in which others act as mirrors for us, giving us the gift of recognizing our full personhood, can be disruptive or enabling in our attempts to curate a mirroring identity. People act as mirrors through their words and actions in relation to other people. Mirrors reflect an image of ourselves back to us. The mirrored image can be accurate or inaccurate. When people make assumptions about us or misgender us, the mirrored image is inaccurate and problematic. Inaccurate mirroring can be damaging.

We have experienced many examples of inaccurate mirroring, including the male gaze, the problem of assumptions and the use of incorrect pronouns. Evie observed that repeated misgendering often, in her view, leads trans people to focus on surgery, not as related to personal dysphoria but as related to inaccurate mirroring. Sam also found the narrow representation of trans people in the public eye unhelpful. Mike's centring of euphoria led him to feel under-represented, noting that 'My story is not the classic trans narrative.'

Conversely to inaccurate mirroring, when people recognize our identity and respond affirmingly, the mirrored image is accurate and helpful. Accurate mirroring is enabling. Ellen described a powerful moment of accurate mirroring in her interview:

> I remember I was having my one-to-one with my boss and that day I was wearing a dress instead of my usual skirt and T-shirt and I commented to him that I'd gone to check my ID on my belt and realized that I didn't have a belt on that dress, and he just came back with, 'Well, what do the other women do?' I mean, he just said 'other women' without thinking, which was very good – it mattered to me.

For Star, the importance of mirroring goes beyond how other people treat them, to their spiritual practice and scriptural hermeneutics. They explained why it is so important to them to find a mirroring resonance with God and with the characters they read about in the Bible:

> I'm not a-gender – my gender is a very specific and grounded thing that is part of my lived and fleshy experience of the world – so when I think of a gendered God, I need a God whose gender is similarly fleshy. It's the same kind of with like finding characters to relate to in the Bible. I love the whole non-binary angels thing but I need someone with a bit more of a fleshy lived experience. I need it be fleshy – I need it to be about the way they dress, the things that he does with his hair.

Sam and Stacey, similarly, find mirroring in theology. Stacey finds a resonance with St John of the Cross, and asked, 'How can it be that a sixteenth-century Spanish mystic seems to be writing so accurately about me?' Sam remembered discovering the mirroring narrative of Philip baptizing a eunuch (Acts 8), and reflected that 'Wow … salvation really does encompass me.' Pat, Sam and Beth each suggested that the ability to mirror others enhances their ministry. Pat explained that her non-binary identity allows her to be 'the blank canvas on which people can put whatever they need to'. Evie and Beth both described their identities as enabling others to hear their story reflected back, and to share more of themselves.

As explored briefly in reflections on self-mirroring, most of us carefully curate our presentation in order to encourage accurate mirroring and prevent inaccurate mirroring. The responsibility for accurate mirroring is largely placed on trans and non-binary people, not on the others who mirror us. There is a clear need for cis allies to pay attention to accurate mirroring in order to enable trans and non-binary people to flourish. There is also the potential for further research regarding how and why people curate presentation and how this curation weaves itself into hermeneutics.

As we are transformed, we can also act as agents of transformation. We can act as mirrors for others, giving them the gift of recognizing their full personhood, enabling them to curate a mirroring identity. LGBTQ+ communities intentionally practise positive mirroring. All of us spoke of the importance of mutual mirroring within the LGBTQ+ community. Both Ellen and River were enabled to return to church because of mirroring identities. For Ellen, this meant attending a church with a trans friend. For River, this meant attending identity-specific churches.

Trans people often mirror both trans and cis people of the same gender. This can be positive, enabling the formation of an authentic presentation of one's identity and the full participation in society. However, this can also be negative, furthering gender norms and emphasizing toxic forms of extreme binaries. People shared examples of both positive and toxic mirroring, and highlighted the need for diverse visibility, to increase opportunities for authentic and healthy mirroring.

The ways in which we mirror each other point towards potential dialogue between the fields of communication theory and theological anthropology, ecclesiology and missiology. If communicating in ways that mirror the other accurately has positive effects, and vice versa, perhaps learning to mirror well could improve the ways in which humans engage with each other more generally.

Mirroring God

As well as mirroring each other, humans also mirror God. While we will explore understandings of God in more detail in the next chapter, it is helpful to consider here the ways in which participants mirror God in their own lives. The ways in which we mirror God, as individuals and in our relatedness, are central to discipleship. We understand God as gender-full – as a being who contains aspects of all sexes and genders, rather than just some or none. This is foundational to their understandings of God. However, understandings of God's characteristics, beyond gender, were particularly compelling. There are three areas of mirroring God that were important to participants:

1 Creativity, complexity and diversity
2 Suffering, resilience and reconciliation
3 Processes of becoming.

All suggested that God is an active creator who holds within themselves complexity and diversity. Trans and non-binary Christians mirror these aspects of God in creative spiritual practices and in our ability to manage complexity and diversity. Star demonstrated creativity through their playful biblical hermeneutics. Jack described the importance of creation in the spiritual practice that they have developed:

> The third circle is creating, so from the fusion of the talking and the listening from what's come up with what people have shared and then what's coming back from the spirit speaking to people, each person expresses that in their own particular creative way.

Sam highlighted the importance of theatre as a spiritual dis-cipline throughout her interview and exemplified the ability to manage complexity in the matter-of-fact statement, 'I'm a father and a grandmother.' Pat described the complex God that we mirror in a uniquely contemporary way, saying that

God can only be described as 'multifaceted', having 'infinite sides'.

Suffering was a part of the lived experiences of each person. Beth suggested that suffering is central to queer identities. Stacey spoke about how her experiences of suffering were mirrored both in Christ's suffering and in the suffering of mystics, including Joan of Arc and St John of the Cross. She implies that suffering is a necessary component of spiritual growth/ insights. This is problematic, due to the implication that suffering is good. Nevertheless, it is notable that Stacey's suffering draws her to relate most authentically to those theologians who also describe their own suffering. Each participant also demonstrated great resilience. Often this resilience was woven together with suffering, creating a sort of gritty hope that involved a deep desire to contribute to the healing and reconciliation of other marginalized and suffering people.

When I asked Star, who is a priest, if their suffering, caused by the church, has affected their personal sense of calling, they said:

Yeah, it's affected my calling in that it's kind of doubled down on it, I really held on, and the fact that this is the just the right thing for me, and this is what I am called to do, and I will fight every step for it. My entire calling has gotten fiercer. On the darkest days, on the days when I really despair for the church that I'm working for, I remember that there are so many LGBTI people who just need a way out, and if nothing else I'm in a burning building making sure that people get out before the roof collapses but that's the calling if nothing else – that's what I'm left with, when I've not got anything else to do.

Star's vulnerability in the church could cause fear and uncertainty but, instead, Star experiences what I would describe as 'righteous rage', not for themself but for the other. This gritty entanglement of suffering, resilience, hope and reconciliation lead me to consider the cross and resurrection. In his interview, Jack suggested that 'transition is this sort of resurrection experience'. Jesus experienced bodily suffering knowing that it was the key to transformation, not only for himself but also for the reconciliation of others. Trans people experience bodily suffering, knowing that it is the key to our transformation, and finding that it enables us to be reconcilers for others. This lends a new perspective to the hackneyed Christian phrase 'carry your cross'.

Finally, people experience God as in a continual state of transformation, a state that we believe that trans and non-binary people mirror.

Star explained:

> God is becoming – God doesn't sit still – God delights in transformation and its potential is like just the edge of a moment – and so that really feeds into my experience of God through my transition – God doesn't create us to stand still. God creates us to become – God creates us to change – God creates us to grow – because that's what God does.

Beth shared a similar sentiment, and furthered that idea by using dance as an analogy:

> I understand the Trinity, or the church's teaching on the Trinity, this is kind of God's desire for relationship. Also, that movement, that kind of dancing God. I think it is various, for me, there's a very strong sense of love, but also connection, community within that. I think what God wants for us is growing into that love, but also in a way joining into that dance, that trinitarian dance.

In their analogy, Beth showed how by 'joining into the dance', by transforming, being transformed and being in transformative communication with others, we can mirror God. Their analogy links the latter two parts of this section – mirroring each other and mirroring God – together. We mirror God through the ways in which we mirror each other. The ways in which we mirror each other have clear theological implications, if we are understood, as in the doctrine of *imago Dei*, to image

God. If we mirror each other in ways that are inaccurate, we may mirror God in ways that are inaccurate. If we only mirror difficulty and dysphoria, our theological framework is one of suffering. If, conversely, we also mirror joy and euphoria, we can join in with the God who dances.

Personal qualities

Trans theology has often focused on a defence of trans identities in response to critiques. I believe that a shift to theologies that highlight the positives of trans identities is necessary. I notice several striking personal qualities shared by those I spoke with. It is important to note that I am not suggesting that all trans/non-binary people have the same or similar qualities. Rather, I am highlighting the qualities of these ten participants in order to highlight just some of the distinct contributions that they, as individuals, make. This is, in itself, an act of mirroring. By mirroring trans and non-binary Christians' gifts, this book can contribute to affirming literature that counters the negative voices that trans people regularly hear. Further, by learning more about trans and non-binary people's gifts, we more accurately mirror God who looks at creation and says, 'it is good', who looks at humanity and says that 'it is very good' (Genesis 1).

I begin by focusing on some of the personal qualities that participants demonstrated, including authenticity, justice, creativity and resilience. I then move to explore the ways we discussed complexity, in which striking giftedness was demonstrated. I suggest that this is an area where trans and non-binary people can offer guidance to churches and communities.

Authenticity, justice, creativity

Authenticity and truth, combined with openness regarding their personal truths, were held as vital by each of us. Several showed high levels of care for other people. Several participants were extremely humble, sometimes overly so. Most were non-judgemental, even regarding people who had caused them considerable harm.

A clear sense of social justice, intersectionality and caring for others are evidenced by several participants. River chooses to work only in places where inclusion and diversity are embedded and actively considered and is a key player in implementing change. Evie, who consults in the area of human resources, suggested that 'democratizing' and 'inclusion' are central to her practice, in contrast to some others working in the same area. Ellen also showed a passionate interest in social justice, explaining, 'I want to rock the boat, if we are not doing what Jesus told us to do, I want to make a fuss.' Mike expressed frustration at the lack of attention to systemic social injustice in the church. As well as sharing Ellen and Mike's passion for intersectional social justice, Evie expressed an understanding of the intersections between her identity, the business sector and the church. Pat was passionate about ecclesial accessibility at the intersections of gender and disability. Star also described working at the intersections of justice and identity, specializing in theology and neurodiversity. Sam's work as a playwright is influential in improving lives at the intersections of marginalized identities around the world. All participants showed care for others. Poignantly, Jack remembered a spiritual experience when 'the thing that came up for me most strongly was "tell K that she's held and loved"'.

Several participants are creative and open teachers and leaders. Beth demonstrated openness about their own identity in dialogue with others, explaining that 'People ask the questions, and you realize how liberating it can be for people to talk to somebody who is openly out.' Sam described writing plays about being trans when 'nobody wanted to', a practice that has been transformative for many. Star demonstrated creativity in their leadership of a retreat for trans and non-binary people, and Jack described practices of creativity throughout his interview. This sense of openness and creativity often seemed to relate directly to participants' experiences of transition. For example, Evie explained that when it comes to the business sector and intersectional identities, people value her 'ability to connect those two things together'.

Trans and non-binary Christians expressed a high degree of self-sufficiency, self-understanding and humility. When facing isolation, Stacey explained that she continues to 'get on with it', relying on herself and on God. Each participant described processes of identity formation that involved serious examination of their own beliefs and personhood. River explained, 'Who I am in Christ needs to acknowledge that', where 'that' refers to their identity. Each participant apologized at various points in their interviews for talking about their gifts. River exemplified this, explaining, 'Within my field I'm reasonably well known, but I generally do not like drawing attention to myself.' This humility was compelling and is a positive personal quality in itself.

Complexity

Participants displayed striking giftedness in the ways in which they engage with complexity. Complexity and diversity are experienced by some as core elements of being human. Further, privilege and oppression interact in complex ways that, together, can be described as kyriarchy. Several participants were skilled at recognizing complexity, holding seemingly contradictory narratives together and navigating nuance. Some participants had strikingly similar understandings of kyriarchy that recognized the complexities of intersectionality. These understandings of kyriarchy were foundational to their theological understandings and vocational practices. These understandings are especially relevant to churches and communities today.

Mike referred to systemic injustice and kyriarchy throughout his interview and suggested that trans and non-binary identities 'fundamentally disrupt' unjust systems by 'subtly embodying' diversity. Ellen related gender to kyriarchy in theology, suggesting that 'Jesus had to be male because if he had been female nobody would have paid any attention to what he said.' Ellen also showed an ability to recognize and navigate the complexities of gender in theology, stating that 'God the Father is without gender.' Similarly, Sam navigated complexity in her own identity, relating that she is 'a father and a grandmother'. Pat also used nuanced language, referring to herself as a 'non-binary female', and Jack used a variety of terms including 'transmasculine', 'genderflux', 'male', 'demi-guy' and 'non-binary'. The expansive use of gendered language that may be experienced as contradictory by others highlights the nuance with which participants experience, understand and explain the complexities of identity. Participants' treatments of complexity were refreshing, in light of what I have experienced as an increasingly binary, 'either/or' society. It is my experience that society is increasingly divided into 'sides' of debates. Left or right, trans or cis, male or female are just a few of many possible examples. Debates are becoming increasingly hostile. The hateful comments and threats that I, and other trans people in the public eye, experience are becoming a daily reality.

This exploration of each individual's personal qualities points towards the way in which identity-based theological anthropology can celebrate rather than problematize individuals across myriad axes of diversity. Engaging with complexity emerged as a particular skill held by several of us. I am in no way attempting to suggest that all trans and non-binary people hold this skill. I am led to ponder, however, the fact that this skill is not celebrated explicitly in any of the trans-apologetic literature that I have reviewed. In my own vocational process I have not been asked whether I perceived such skills in relation to my vocation. All my participants describe experiences of problematization within churches and denominations, rather than considerations of their particular skills. I wonder whether such organizations are under-utilizing identity-related skills, due to a culture of ignoring diversity at best, and problematizing it at worst, rather than celebrating the resulting diversity of skills and giftings.

Breadcrumbs of delight

The humans who are described in this chapter are humans who mirror. Further, we are humans who seek to mirror delight rather than sorrow. This chapter has shown that research participants have perspectives on theological anthropology that speak both into how trans identities are explored in theology, and what it means to be human more generally. Three key findings are that trans and non-binary Christians:

1 experience continuity in createdness
2 practise mutual mirroring that, in turn, mirrors God
3 use complexity as a lens through which our understandings of what it means to be human are filtered and organized.

These findings suggest the need for further exploration of:

1 continuity versus discontinuity in theological anthropology
2 the way in which binary discussions or hasty marginalization around morality/ethics can limit perceptions of *imago Dei*
3 the potential of applying complexity as a hermeneutical lens in dialogue regarding what it means to be human.

Reflection

Trans and non-binary Christians' understandings of our identities, embodiment and lived experiences are diverse and varied. However, continuity, mirroring and complexity are key arising themes. Here I consider my own responses to experiences of, and insights about, being human. In particular, I explore the ways in which my experiences and understandings of being human have included continuity, mirroring and complexity.

I go on to consider my experiences and insights, and those of participants, in conversation with the theory of identity as performance, as described by Judith Butler (1990, 2004), and the theological anthropology of Alistair I. McFadyen (1990) in *The Call to Personhood*.

As far as I know and remember, I did not meet another trans or non-binary person until I moved to Manchester to attend a music conservatoire at the age of 17. I had come to realize that I did not identify as female some years earlier but had no way to put words to that realization. Instead, I felt that my feelings were errant and possibly pathological. I now realize that I was experiencing considerable dysphoria and that this was one of the root causes of the clinical depression and anxiety with which I had been diagnosed.

During my first year in Manchester, mirroring became possible in two contexts. First, I began to attend a LGBTQ+ affirming church, where members were encouraged and supported to read and interpret scripture for themselves, with reference to helpful supporting literature. This mirrored both God and Christian discipleship in ways that were compelling and helpful, and reignited my faith. Second, I was invited to a LGBTQ+ youth group by a friend who knew that I was struggling. There I met other trans and non-binary people for the first time. It was like looking in a mirror. Reflected back was a sense of who I was, who I could be. In this way, the mirroring of other trans and non-binary people enabled me to understand my own identity and to access transition. In the early days of my transition, mirroring was essential. When I went to youth group, I was referred to by my then new name and pronouns. This enabled me to explore and understand who I was before coming out in less affirming environments, as well as being vital for my sense of self.

Despite this mirroring support, I did initially stumble into some of the trans tropes mentioned above, which meant that it was difficult to mirror myself authentically in early transition. Rather, I bought into the idea that disarticulating my past from my present, and my body from my mind, was the only way to counter the agonizing dysphoria that plagued me every moment of every day. I distanced myself from my past and was unable to see any good in who I had been. Further, I conformed to toxic masculine stereotypes in order to strengthen my rejection of myself as feminine. For me, this disconnection did not feel healthy. I was not living life as fully as I could.

Over time, however, it became important for me to create and sustain a sense of continuity between my past and present, and my body and mind. The hormone replacement therapy that I access has gradually enabled me to understand, live fully within and even enjoy my body. I have also gained a more realistic view of my past, enabling me to both remember and talk about the past, and present more openly and without distress. Further, I now accept and embrace feminine aspects of my personality, identity and embodiment, while still identifying as considerably nearer to male than to female.

In Chapter 4 of this book I raised the importance of forming an authentic frame within which to understand and describe our identities, experiences and insights. As I, personally, developed congruence and continuity between past and present, body and mind, I came to realize that the frame within which I had conceptualized my identity no longer functioned. Dysphoria and maleness were poor representations of the rich tapestry that I have woven of my body, identity, experiences and insights. In the chapter of my previous book entitled 'Transformative', I explain:

> pretending a binary identity was limiting the ways in which I lived and the ways in which I lived out my calling. I think that by identifying solely as male, I tried to hide the more female or feminine aspects of myself in order to fit more easily into church and society. The problem is that doing that hurt me and limited my communication with others (Clare-Young 2019, p. 88).

I go on to describe my non-binary identity as 'living in a state of flux', listening to God's calling, and being 'continually open to be called somewhere else' (p. 89). For me, identifying as non-binary and using the pronouns 'they/them' or just my name enables accurate self-mirroring and is a part of the continuity between various spaces, times and parts of who I am.

Another part of who I am is that I am an autistic adult, which leads me to consider complexity. I have always relished complexity and go out of my way to understand and map complex concepts and apparent contradictions or debates. When someone tells me that something is complicated or impossible, I see a map of stars in my mind, connected by fluorescent strings. I can move the stars around, reconnecting the strings. In this way I can integrate complexity and process what, to others, may seem to be a confused mess. I had always attributed this unusual cognitive process to autism. However, other trans and non-binary Christians' skills in managing complexity and accepting supposed contradictions has led me to give due credit to the ways in which identity formation, transition and related communications have given me valuable skills and insights.

Similar to others, mirroring is key to my anthropological understandings. For me, mirroring has relied on dialogue. I initially noticed this dialogically informed mirroring as I was conducting research on trans-related theological literature during my MPhil degree. The resulting book considered the relevance of McFadyen's (1990) theological anthropology to trans-related theology. As such, I begin this reflection by exploring the theme of 'mirroring personhood' with reference to McFadyen.

Mirroring enabled me to begin to perform masculine identity in a way that was helpful, but not fully authentic. This element of performance in transition, which was also described by several participants, raises the theory of identity as performance, as explored by Judith Butler (1990, 2004). I go on to consider Butler's theory and the ways in which performing gender has been both helpful and problematic for myself and for others.

Although mirroring and performing have been experienced by trans and non-binary Christians, including myself, authenticity is an attribute that we have come to find highly important. I conclude this reflection in dialogue with McFadyen and Butler, by considering the ways in which continuity and complexity are parts of authentic personhood. I argue that these qualities can be life-giving for all people, not only for those who are trans and/or non-binary.

Mirroring personhood

McFadyen's (1990, p. 1) monograph, *The Call to Personhood*, asks and attempts to answer the questions 'What is a person? What is individual identity, and where does it come from?' McFadyen (p. 17) suggests that personhood is dialogical, both in relation to God and in relation to the other. McFadyen further argues that by participating in genuine dialogue, we are able to gift dialogue to the other – that our individual identities are 'a sedimentation of interpersonal relationships' (p. 24). It is this gifting of personhood that I suggest is reminiscent of mirroring. McFadyen also considers the 'distortion' of dialogue that occurs when one dialogue partner makes 'the assumption that one already knows what is right' (pp. 40, 44). It is this practice of making assumptions about others' identities that I describe as inaccurate mirroring.

Mirroring – both accurate and inaccurate – was a key theme throughout my research. Those I spoke with experienced accurate, dialogical mirroring as enabling transition and inaccurate mirroring as disenabling transition. Further, our experiences and insights showed that accurate mirroring among people enabled us to mirror something of God. Mirroring, then, is not only anthropological but also theological.

McFadyen (p. 17) addresses the theological aspect of dialogue, noting that dialogue is both 'horizontal' and 'vertical' – relating respectively to other humans and to God. Further, McFadyen (pp. 17–21) argues that it is in our horizontal dialogues that we form the *imago Dei*, the image of God. It follows that in accurate, dialogical mirroring, trans and non-binary people, and those who engage in dialogue with us, are able to participate in the image of God. Conversely when mirroring between humans is inaccurate, based on assumptions, God is also being inaccurately mirrored.

While accurate mirroring enables us to form authentic identities and to image God, inaccurate mirroring counters this. My participants and I have each experienced both accurate and inaccurate mirroring. This has led to performative presentation, falling short of authentic and open identity.

Performing personhood

The element of performance in trans identities has led me to consider the anthropological theory of Judith Butler. Butler (1990) argues that identity formation develops through both communication and action, which she describes as performance. Butler's theory of gender as performance posits gender as socially constructed rather than biologically implied. For me, it is vital to hold gender as performance in creative tension with the realities of trans bodies and transitions, which go beyond performance to fully incarnate life. Nevertheless, the concept of performed identity correlates with the understanding developed above of identity formed in dialogue by mirroring. For Butler (p. 198), though, individual 'agency' is enacted when one breaks with expected performance in order to act outside those expectations. This enables Butler (pp. 202–3) to show how the normative categories of gender might be destabilized or deconstructed. Mirroring is limiting when it is understood as necessary – the individual must be free to form their identity both in congruence with, and in dissonance with, the mirroring partner.

While identity as performance is congruent with dialogical mirroring, this raises concerns that performance may be shallow or false, particularly where mirroring is assumed, expected or compelled. Further, the suggestion that it is individual performance that destabilizes or deconstructs inaccurate or unjust norms relies on individual confidence, ability and energy. It is unsurprising, then, that those I spoke with and I myself have, at times, found ourselves performing identities that are normative and partial, rather than authentic and holistic, particularly in response to external, relational and/or societal pressures.

The limits of identity as performance relate to audience as well as performer. In *Undoing Gender*, Butler (2004) turns specifically to trans identities. Butler (p. 67) describes trans presentation, particularly in relation to gatekeeping authorities such as Gender Identity Clinics, as a type of performance 'in relation to a certain audience' and in adherence to gendered norms. She goes on to explore the artificial nature of both the norm and the audience's observation, and to suggest that the trans person's self-understanding 'exceeds the norm' (p. 72). Butler (p. 99) argues that diagnostic approaches to trans identities 'assert pressure' to perform gender in particular ways, whereas 'social recognition' is necessary for identity formation and development.

It is this performance that I described as a 'toxic masculinity' that I felt was required to 'pass' as male. I believed that my gender presentation, my clothing, my movements, my attitudes and my actions had to be understood as being masculine in order for my transness to be valid. This binarism risks trapping the trans person in gendered stereotypes and both performing and suffering under toxic masculinity or femininity. It is the part of myself that goes beyond and frankly rejects the norms and/or stereotypes of masculinity that leads me to identify as non-binary. It would be simplistic, though, to suggest that the category 'non-binary' eludes norms and performances. It is all too tempting to perform a non-binary identity in order to justify one's self-identification. The public perception of transition as disjunction is a logical progression of this sequence of partial performances and is a clear problem given the need for social recognition, which McFadyen (1990) describes as dialogue and I describe as mirroring. Perhaps genuine authenticity can provide the necessary communicative bridge of the gap between self and other.

Authenticity is vital to my participants and me. We strive to present our identities honestly and authentically in order to live life fully and mirror God in communications with others. The data described in this chapter suggests that continuity and complexity are key elements of our identities, which must be recognizable if we are to experience accurate mirroring in

dialogue with others and to progress beyond partial performances that are congruent with external norms and pressures.

Butlerian performativity implies an entire disconnection
between body and mind, past and present, sex and gender.
This seems to be overly simplistic, given the complexities of
trans and non-binary people's embodied experiences of gender
identity, or the lack thereof, and the processes of transition –
both social and clinical – that we experience. If sex and gender
were entirely disjoined, trans bodies would essentially be dis-
regarded, irrelevant to our authentic identities. This does not
correlate with the experiences of real trans people.

None of the participants interviewed in this research, nor my
own lived experience, demonstrated the disjunctions between
body and mind and between past and present self that are a part
of Butlerian understandings of trans identities. This suggests
that the image of trans and non-binary identities portrayed in
public discourse differs significantly from the reality of at least
these ten trans and non-binary lives.

Rather, both myself and those I spoke with experience, and/
or work to curate, continuity between all aspects of our beings,
our identities and our lives. This sense of continuity is also evident in our understandings of our createdness and our beliefs
in a God who continues to create and re-create. We do not
experience our identities, actions and embodiment as final and
immoveable. Rather, we experience life as a continuous process, open to change and growth.

The nuanced understandings of complexity described and
demonstrated by participants are essential to our understandings of identity as continuous. Any assumed disjunctions are,
after all, logically straightforward. It is logical to assume a
body/mind disconnection if one sees a straightforward link
between sexed embodiment and gender. Conversely, if one can
accept the complexity of the full variety of human embodiment,
it is possible to understand that bodies and minds can hold
unending possibilities while being continuously connected. It
is logical to assume a past/present disconnection if one sees an
obvious difference between a person's past and current pres-
entations of self. Conversely, if one can accept the complexity

of multi-layered, multi-hued human lives and identities, it is possible to understand that during our time on earth we might hold together multiple truths in an unbroken timeline.

If trans and non-binary people are to participate in the mirroring dialogues that enable relational mirroring of God, public narratives of trans and non-binary identities must embrace the complex authenticity of trans and non-binary people. In doing so, perhaps other problematized and simplified human identities can also be better mirrored. If achieved in the discipline of trans-related theology, this has ambitious far-reaching anthropological and theological potentials that stretch beyond our discipline.

The data explored in this chapter, as well as the reflection above, suggest a need to continue to diversify the way that trans-related theologies explore trans identities. Trans-apologetics have attempted to explain trans identities with reference to norms and narratives that do not correlate with the lived experiences of all trans people. Rather, approaches that take complexity and authenticity seriously, and that take trans theology further than explaining trans lives, have the potential to enable more accurate mirroring of both the people and the God to whom we relate.

Note

1 The Apostles' Creed and the Nicene Creed describe God as 'creator' and 'maker' respectively. Similarly, the United Reformed Church's Basis of Union describes God as 'creator'.

Interlude 5

'Gorgeous Gender Fuckery' – Star

There's been an enormous amount of deconstruction in my faith. Some trans people basically coming from a conservative background decide that one particular thing about their conservative background was wrong – which is the 'trans people are bad' – and so they changed that one bit and that's it. Whereas, for me, once I started to think of a God who loved me for who I was and affirmed me as a trans person, actually everything was different, everything was changed, the whole theological playground was different, and so I've had to rebuild my faith from its very foundations really, so there's been a lot of situations like that and I'm still going with that I think. I think a lot about the exile, and about how like sometimes in transition you're in Babylon and you're far away from where you started and you're trying to work out what serving God means in a whole new land and then some of the time you are sat in the ruins of Jerusalem desperately trying to get together enough stone and mortar to build a wall.

For me, as I have transitioned, things have become a lot less black and white. I'm much more comfortable sitting in grey areas and much more comfortable in not knowing, in not being sure, I think that's really important. So much of my early faith was all about certainty, it was like, 'these are the facts and that is it'. Whereas now it's so much more the case that there are things that I do not know and I'm probably not ever going to know and that's OK and actually my faith is made richer because of that. I think that another thing that is really important is theology being done from a position of compassion. It's really important that actually we use love to read the Bible rather than the Bible to tell us how to love. People cannot just like decide 'This says this, so this is how I'm going to love every single person.' Instead, you have to start with love and empathy and compassion and all that kind of stuff.

Now I focus much more on the things that I know for certain about the character of God before I approach scripture, before I approach the traditions of the church, and anything else really. Where you begin the journey is really important. That changes how I understand God because it changes how I read God's actions and how I read God's church and how I read God's people.

One of the things that's always really important to me is the fleshiness of God. I do not really sit very well with a kind of floaty transcendent idea of God. I need God to be walking in the garden. I need God to be hungry. I need God to be incarnate and not just incarnate in Jesus but in the people around us and in creation. For me that is the key, that God is involved, that God is right in there in all our experiences. The other key thing for me is that God is becoming – God doesn't sit still – God delights in transformation. God is like the potential perching just on the edge of a moment. That really feeds into my experience of God through my transition. God doesn't create us to stand still. God creates us to become. God creates us to change. God creates us to grow. Because each of those things – creating, becoming, changing, growing – that is what God does.

One of the things that I'm kind of struggling with at the moment as a non-binary person is the way that literature and people in general assume that people relate to God as non-binary by relating to God as transcendent. God does transcend gender, God goes beyond the binary, and that's really cool, but for me, needing a fleshy rooted in the earth kind of God, the kind of transcendent floaty idea of God beyond gender just doesn't work for me. My experience in my own gender is that it's not that I'm not outside gender – I'm not agender – my gender is a very specific and grounded thing that is part of my lived and fleshy experience of the world. So when I think of a gendered God, I need a God whose gender is similarly fleshy and so I'm still really struggling with that.

It's the same with finding other characters to relate to in the Bible. I can roll with Joseph being transgender and I can run with people breaking gender roles and stuff but I need ... so, the thing is, I love the whole non-binary angels thing which crops up in quite a lot in trans and non-binary Christian communities, but I need someone with a bit more of a fleshy lived experience to relate to. The closest that I've got is Samson. Like, proper headcanons, Samson is transgender and again I need it to be about the way they dress, the things that he does with his hair. Similarly with God – I need God, the gendered nature of God, to be about how God reveals Godself to the world in creation, and in Jesus, and all that kind of stuff.

I love the medieval period. It seems to be like a wonderful time of crazy relating to God in all kinds of weirdly gendered ways. I mean we start off with Christ as our mother hen and all the gorgeous gender fuckery that comes with that, but then the medieval period they are like, 'No we will go one step further actually and they have a whole thing about Christ breastfeeding on the cross', and all this kind of really weird wacky stuff.

I really want to be able to play around with Jesus like that and I think the Gospels really invite us to do that. We're invited to look at Jesus and see ourselves – whatever gender we are – and so that's really important to me. I think just being playful with that really helps me and being playful with Jesus does. I do not want to say, 'Oh, Jesus was definitely trans' or 'Jesus was definitely autistic' or 'Jesus was definitely intersex' or anything like that. I want it to be playful every time. I want to read Jesus as transfeminine one day and transmasculine the next day.

At the moment, at this stage, I'm deconstructing and reconstructing my faith. Sin is not a thing that I can get too close to without bringing up all the loaded baggage from my past, but I do really like playing around with the fall because all my trans stuff comes from earlier in Genesis so I had to early on play around with the fall and I really like the idea of binary understandings of sex and gender being the result of the fall and the curse that Eve and Adam experience in Genesis 3 being gendered lives. God curses them and basically says, 'Adam you're a man and this is your job, and that's what men do and Eve you're a woman this is what women do, and this is your job.' For me the idea that that's the result of whatever the hell is happening in the fall ... I really like that idea. You hear a lot from some people that being trans is the result of the fall and I want to flip it the other way round and actually say that binary understandings of gender and gender roles and all that kind of stuff; that's the result of the fall.

My understanding of redemption sits more with my understanding of the incarnation than with the crucifixion. It's Christ's life as well as Christ's death that redeems the world and it's the fact that Christ experienced what it's like to be a human being and all the shit that we have to deal with that comes with that, that's the redemptive power. And the crucifixion is the result of that enormous act of empathy, it's just one of a series of sufferings that God experiences through Christ.

To be honest I'm fucking terrified of the cross right now like I really cannot like go near it, it's got so much baggage from my former life and theology that to think about the cross, it's just really a struggle. I've got on my desk this Indian Jesus who has got gorgeous hips and three nipples for some reason. He hangs up my desk while I'm working and that is as close as I get to understanding any theology of the cross really. It's stuff I'm still working on I guess.

6

Dancing with God:
Theology

Narratology informs theology. Themes of suffering, resilience and joy were apparent in participants' experiences and understandings of God. In the following theological explorations I highlight the ways in which themes of suffering, resilience and joy shaped participants' understandings of God.

I introduce our experiences of, and insights about, God. I begin by exploring conversation partners' contributions regarding how well we can understand God, before moving on to consider our understandings of God as Creator, Spirit and Christ.

Can we understand God?

Throughout our conversations we reflected on the limited nature and scope of our human understandings of God. Every person I spoke with questioned how much we can really know about God, considered how limited language affects the way that we talk about God, and explored how understandings of God's gender are sometimes overly impacted by these limitations.

Knowing God

The idea that God cannot be fully known was sometimes informed by experiences of suffering as a result of theological certainty – their own or that of others. We have experienced

the suffering caused by theological understandings and feel
that theology that confines or over-defines God is limiting and
can be harmful. Mike noticed the difficulty of limited understandings of God in his own lived experience, arguing that
'Some bad Evangelical theology is behind the anxiety that I
experience.' Mike's comments specifically referred to the problems of a judgemental understanding of God. Before speaking
about personal harm, Mike also highlighted the wider harm
done by these understandings and questioned 'whether there
is anything still good, whether there is still something valuable
here, or whether it all needs to go'. Mike cited 'the idea that the
Old Testament God is big and scary' as evidence of harmful
understandings of God.

Similarly, Stacey pointed to the harm that limited understandings of God can cause, reflecting on the anger that she has
perceived God as holding 'because of my experiences of human
nature, basically, that's robbed me of everything'. Stacey's lived
experiences of human injustice, combined with her understanding that humans reflect the image of God, led her to feel that,
perhaps, God is also unjust. This focus on harm and injustice
seemed to be related to Mike and Stacey's regular questioning
of their sense of belonging and faith. In Chapter 4, I suggested
that Mike's narrative was framed by joy whereas Stacey's was
framed by suffering. The similarity between the theological
understandings that they critique, however, is striking, though
the conclusions they come to are different. Whereas Stacey
seemed to accept that there is a judgemental aspect to God,
Mike focused on filtering out harmful understandings in order
to further social justice and limit harm.

Sam also recognized the danger of narrow understandings of
God and cited the Bible as cause and even perpetrator. Referring to a play that she wrote, Sam said:

> I tell the story of God getting unhappy and grumpy. This is
> recorded in the Bible. I held the Bible responsible, the Bible
> as corrupted. The Bible as a work of pornography. In that
> sense, the Bible was put on trial and found to be guilty.

This reflection was Sam's response to the treatment of God's gender in the Bible, which is explored in more depth later in this chapter. Sam explained that she believes that the Bible confines God through over-defining God as male. Further, she related the harm of confining God to the confining of the humans who image God. In this exploration, Sam pointed towards the theological harm, as well as the personal harm, of narrow understandings of God. Narrowness or definitiveness limit our theology as well as our lives.

Similarly, Evie and Ellen both questioned treatments of God that are overused or, in Ellen's words, 'well-worn'. Ellen described her pre-transition picture of God as 'a man with a long white beard sitting on a cloud', an image from her childhood which she 'never unthought'. River analysed similar treatments succinctly, reflecting that 'it feels like you are making God smaller'.

For some participants, understandings of God were described as being inextricably linked to understandings, processes and experiences of trans identities and transitions. Mike's transition relied on a broadening of his theology, a process through which he said that his understandings became 'less dogmatic and authoritarian'. Sam experienced a similar process of theological expansion preceding and enabling transition, seeing something of herself in the gender-full God described above. It seems that theological resources and skills were, therefore, essential to their transitions.

For Ellen and Evie, transition preceded, and enabled, their theological transformations. Ellen explained that 'Transition was what prodded me into asking the questions.' Similarly, Evie noted, 'It was literally at the point where I transitioned that my intellectual and emotional grasp of the salvation message made me say, "I am a Christian and before I wasn't."' Despite many years of church membership prior to transition, it was transition that ultimately informed Evie's theological understanding and Christian identity. Similarly, Beth credited their non-binary identity as a key element in their theological understandings, noting that their identity is 'very enriching' in relationship to their theological studies. It seems that, for Ellen,

Evie and Beth, their identities and/or transitions are essential to their theological understandings. This suggests a practice of theological resilience, whereby participants are able to rethink understandings that have previously limited their perceptions of God.

Rather than being certain, fixed and comprehensible, participants generally expressed an understanding of God as beyond the realm of human understanding, suggesting resilient responses to more rigid understandings of God. Sam pointed out that God is 'a short word to say, but the essence of God is completely beyond our understanding'. Mike explained, 'I cannot pin God down.' Ellen expanded on similar understandings:

> God has no physical form. There's a problem there. God is spirit. I can meditate, which I'm not very good at, I can pray, which I'm a bit better at but not that good, and I can have a relationship with God in that way ... But who is God?

For Ellen, God's form as spirit logically dictates an element of mystery, liminality or slipperiness. Ellen suggested that we can reach towards relatedness with God but can never fully explain who God is.

Participants also framed lack of knowledge regarding God positively, as mysterious, as liminal. Pat highlighted the importance of an understanding of God as 'multifaceted'. Beth described an intentional practice of 'praying more with the Trinity' and 'inhabiting the different places within it', which they said is 'a growing thing for me, just trying to shift between the aspects of it', and also described as 'joining into a dance' with God. When Pat and Beth describe the Trinity, there is a distinctive hermeneutical style, which is exploratory and playful rather than definitive. Pat refers to 'viewing' or 'trying on' different characteristics of God by using the images of rolling a dice or playing dress-up. No side of the dice, or set of clothing, is preferrable to any other. Rather, it is the process of play itself in which one meets God, not in finding a supposedly correct answer. Beth's shifting between different aspects of God is similarly playful given its intentional motion, rather than any attempt to reach a view from any one specific location. They describe this motion as 'dancing'. In these practices of exploration and play, participants strived to connect with God, developing their understandings through intentional, joyful, creative practice.

Talking about God

As with the limitations of knowledge, we explored the limitations of using human language to refer to God. Perceived limitations related to attempts to concretize or unify understandings of God in absolute language. Ellen pointed succinctly to the problem of describing God, stating that 'our language doesn't cope'. Evie noted the problematic lure of 'well-worn language'. Similarly, when asked to describe God, Beth noted that it is 'hard to put words to it', and Pat suggested that 'God is all things to all people'. All four seemed to hint at limited or fractured language. River suggested a rationale for this difficulty, explaining that it's 'quite difficult to articulate in some ways, because my experience of God is quite intangible'.

Relying on limited language can cause harm. When reflecting on how to describe God in worship, Jack explained that limited 'language will put people off right from the start'. Mike reflected that 'It is scary when you've been used to living within a very small box to then expand into a new understanding', highlighting the potential harm that language can do to an individual's faith journey when used in a limited way.

However, several participants suggested that expanding and multiplying descriptors can move us closer to helpful language about God. Reflecting on changes in their use of religious language over time, Star also questioned concrete descriptions, sharing that 'Things are a lot less black and white – I'm much more comfortable sitting in grey areas and much more comfortable in not knowing, in not being sure – I think that's really important.' Similarly, Ellen listed multiple roles as descriptive of God, including military roles and parenting roles, noting that each of them is 'true' but that they are also 'just fragments'.

Star expanded further, highlighting the creative imagery of Christ as 'mother hen' and 'Christa'. Evie highlighted the ways in which expansive understandings of God enter lived experiences, expressing that 'God is a whole range of things and God is interwoven into so much of my life in so many ways.' This interweaving strikes me as an image of God in motion. Rather than Evie dancing with God, like Beth, God dances into Evie's life at particular moments, in varying ways. God is not a person or object that Evie can view from an objective distance, rather a dancer who reaches in and invites Evie to notice their presence. Similarly, Star said, 'God is becoming – God doesn't sit still.' These descriptions of a living, moving, weaving God highlight the difficulties of describing God in static or concrete language. Beth noted the personal growth that comes from expanding language and images, suggesting that 'It's good to use images that stretch our understanding.'

Some people went further than expansion to explain how exploring and complexifying descriptors can help us to find new ways to speak about God creatively and joyfully. Jack described God as 'God, Goddess and Deep Mystery'. For Jack, 'God' refers to the 'God who speaks', 'Goddess' refers to the one 'who listens', and the 'Deep Mystery' part of God is liminal and playful and is present when we engage in dialogue and communal creativity. The contemporary imagery Pat used to describe God as multifaceted is particularly compelling. Pat asked me to 'Imagine a 100-sided dice that gamers use but more and more and more and more sides than that, infinite sides – if I could picture God that way then there's nothing God cannot be or do.' Many-sided dice are used in gaming and, like a conventional dice, the number on top, facing upwards, is read. However, due to their shape, the more sides the dice has, the more visible other sides and numbers are. When you focus on one side of a many-sided dice, you can glimpse some of the other sides but cannot see the whole picture. Similarly, when focusing on any one aspect of God, we might glimpse some other aspects but will not be able to see every aspect. Each side is intrinsically related to, and reliant on, each other side, and yet each side is distinct. By rolling the dice, we are enabled to explore diverse aspects of God.

For example, if God is number 16 on a 20-sided gaming dice, you can see the number 16 front and centre, you can also see numbers 3, 6 and 8 – representing the parts of God that you see most intuitively, around the side – and you can glimpse the numbers 20, 14, 9 and 19 at the very edges – those aspects of God that you see but do not prioritize. The dice has 14 sides that you cannot see at all without moving the dice. That does not mean that those sides of the dice – of God – do not exist. Rather, you have to roll the dice – experiment afresh with your understanding of God – to understand something more. Alternatively, Sam found joy simply in the fact that God cannot be defined, expressing that 'Of course at the end of the day we cannot, and is not that wonderful?' For Sam, embracing the limits of human language and knowledge is key to creative linguistic freedom.

I have observed that some trans and non-binary folks, like Pat and myself, work creatively to discern and explain aspects of God's identity and attributes in part due to their experiences of discerning and explaining their own identities. I also feel that some trans and non-binary folks, like Sam, are better able to embrace God's being beyond definition because of our own experiences of living lives that cannot be trapped in small boxes and insufficient words.

God's gender

The limits of knowledge and language also affect understandings of God's gender. Many participants highlighted that God is not exclusively male. For some, this is integrated into their understandings of, and relationships with, God. For River, God is simply not gendered and, therefore, not male. For Jack, God is male, female and non-binary; described as 'God, Goddess and Deep Mystery'. Pat noted that 'God is not just one gender.' Stacey simply stated that 'God is not male.'

For some, decentring God's masculinity is more complex and/or challenging. Ellen introduced complexity with the idea that 'God the Father is without gender.' Ellen went on to explain that 'If God created mankind, humankind, male and female in their image, then they are male and female. And I would say that includes non-binary of various sorts.' Mike and Evie both reflected that they are on a journey in relation to their understandings of God's gender. Mike noted that this is:

> something that I need to work on and reflect on because I've always felt very comfortable with the idea of God being male. There's always been a very rich appeal to me in being fathered by God. I know how patriarchal and exclusionary that is. Theoretically, I do not think that God has one gender. In terms of how I will instantly picture God, it feels masculine, and I do not think that's what I want to always feel.

Similarly, Evie recognized:

> I always use 'he' pronouns for God and I think that is just literally the way I've been socialized into my relationship with God. I have tried of late, actually. I've read your little booklet that you've published recently online, and I noticed that you're using 'they' pronouns for God. There's a lot to be said for that. It just feels weird not to call God he, but I guess I'm probably on a journey with that one.

Both Evie and Mike referred here to the understandings of God that have been part of their psycho-social-spiritual development. Both suggested a dissonance between their spiritual and intellectual understandings, and both expressed a desire for expansion. This highlights the power of linguistic norms and the importance of expansive language and understandings.

Ecclesial understandings of expansive language regarding God's gender can, however, be problematic. Beth shared their thoughts on the limitations of gendered language:

> It's actually something I've been thinking about in the last couple of weeks because my boss here insists on calling God Mother wherever possible. Using that kind of very gendered language, I'm realizing that I never found it helpful. I notice

a lot of people do and I'm willing to do it, but it's just, I do not know ... I like the idea of using more provocative images, provocative gender imagery around that. Feeling very progressive by calling God Mother is already so obvious that it almost doesn't ... it doesn't add much for me. God is beyond gender almost. Just traditional gendered language for God ... I do not find that particularly helpful in the context of theological literature.

It seems as if supposedly expansive descriptions of God in Beth's context are limited to the addition of – or perhaps even an entire shift to – female descriptions, rather than a broader expansion. While expansive language does include masculine and feminine language, it is important to consider whether reliance on gendered language furthers binary normativity and alienates those who do not relate to gender and/or binary gender roles/norms.

Beth's concerns also raise the question of whether God is gender-less or gender-full. Beth's concept of God as almost 'beyond gender' implies gender-less-ness. River expressed a definite understanding of God as gender-less, explaining, 'I do not think God has a gender; I know that people talk about God having a ... but it's just meaningless to me to suggest that God would have a gender ... Just ... No!' This description of God as gender-less seems to be a resilient countervoice to the pain caused by male-only or binary understandings, and to River's struggles with embodied dysphoria.

Several of those I spoke with, however, challenged this understanding, relating more intuitively to a God who is gender-full; whose gender is actual, specific and enfleshed. Mike explained that he doesn't 'think that God has *one* gender', implying that God has multiple genders. For Ellen, God's specific gender is related to the gender of human beings, as noted above. Ellen suggested that 'God created humans in his – or their – image, male *and* female.' Evie described God as 'genderfluid' and Pat suggested that God is 'so many genders'. Star spoke more specifically about their preference for an enfleshed, gendered God, explaining:

God goes beyond the binary of gender – and that's really cool – but for me, I need a fleshy rooted-in-the-earth kind of God. That gender-less God doesn't quite work for me. My experience in my own gender is that I'm not outside gender – I'm not a-gender – my gender is a very specific and grounded thing that is part of my lived and fleshy experience of the world. So when I think of a gendered God – I need a God whose gender is similarly fleshy.

Like Ellen, Star said that they relate to God as that which is reflected in human identity, including their own identity as non-binary. For Star, understandings of God as gender-less correlate directly with assumptions that God is flesh-less, and that non-binary people are both gender-less and disconnected from their bodies. Rather, Star advocates for a playful, enfleshed God who mirrors – or even shares – and enjoys trans and non-binary people's complex, nuanced, changeable, fleshy nature.

Pat explored the possibility of God's gender as gender-full and yet also gender-less by suggesting that 'God is without gender and is with so many genders.' This suggestion seems, in its simplicity and in its complexity, to reflect many of the nuances and tensions above. Much like understandings of God more generally, understandings of God's gender are both constrained and enabled by the limits of language. This is one of many topics explored in this work for which a sense of holding seemingly contrasting understandings in tension is evident. This suggests an ability to hold creative tensions in a way that embraces and celebrates liminality and contrast, rather than becoming mired in binary over-definition or debate. For trans and non-binary people, it is entirely possible for God to be both entirely gender-less and entirely gender-full. This holding of tension allows for a nuanced and diverse set of understandings and descriptions of God.

Christ, Spirit, Creator

The focus in this chapter now changes from how we define and speak about God and God's gender to understandings of God's character more broadly. Participants related to God in some senses as the traditional trinitarian persons of Christ, Spirit and/or Creator. These categories are loosely used to organize the material in this section. It is important to note, however, that the three are interrelated and overlapping. In particular, both God as Spirit and God as Creator were frequently used by participants to refer to God more generally/holistically.

Christ

Participants' understandings of God as Christ/Jesus are diverse and complex. Some participants suggested that Christ provides God with incarnate lived experience, gaining lived experience through injustice and empathy. Stacey noted Christ's suffering and its relation to her own lived experience, recognizing that 'Christ went through the ultimate and so must we.' Pat, however, referred to the absence of ecclesial attention to Jesus' suffering and, similarly, to expansive understandings of masculinities as a barrier to a fulsome understanding of Jesus, explaining:

> We need to get rid of the white-bearded buddy Christ, the kind of cheesy Jesus, holding a lamb and being so very white. We do not see, ever see Jesus really looking weak – unless we're talking about the passion – men are men, strong men – we need to think about the imagery we have.

Star explained that for them:

> It's Christ's life as well as Christ's death that redeems the world and it's the fact that Christ experienced what it's like to be a human being and with all the shit that we have to deal with that comes with that, that's the redemptive power, and

the crucifixion is kind of the result of that enormous act of empathy, and the crucifixion is just one of a series of sufferings that God experiences through Christ.

For Star, understandings of redemption that rely wholly on the crucifixion and resurrection are problematic. Rather, Star believes that all Christ's lived experiences, not only those of suffering, are redemptive. Star's reference to empathy is both key and interesting. If God cannot change, a conventional theological understanding, the idea of God gaining empathy might seem problematic.[1] And yet God's empathy as related to Jesus' experience, if understood as extratemporal, is compelling, involving both suffering and joy. The joy of eating and drinking, of making friends around many diverse tables, is intermingled with the sorrow of Lazarus' death, and Jesus' own torture and crucifixion. For Star, Christ is a complex character whose lived experiences include experiences of tangible humanity and emotion that counter strength-based masculine gender norms.

Rather than focusing on redemption theory, Pat explained that she relates to Jesus as:

> a moral exemplar – I do not believe he won a victory over death, I do not believe he is the lamb that was slain for my misdemeanours, I do not believe he wrestled with the devil so that I might have eternal life, but I do see Jesus as a moral exemplar.

While no other participant rejected traditional atonement theories this clearly,[2] no other participant referred to them at all. It is clear, therefore, that traditional atonement theories were not vital to the participants of this research. Rather, several participants described Jesus as a moral exemplar. Evie explained:

> Jesus is actually more of a role model about how I want to live my life. I mean obviously I respect and understand him as God intellectually but actually it's more like a brotherly relationship with someone who is helping me to see the kind of person I want be.

Evie feels that she is supposed to understand Jesus as God, in theory, but in her own experience, Jesus is clearly human and, further, Jesus is a human whose example she feels compelled to follow.

Participants' understandings of the example that Jesus provides are particularly compelling to me. For Pat, love and non-judgement are key aspects of Jesus' example. Pat noted that 'You do not see Jesus judging anyone – all of the individuals he meets he treats as valuable.' Similarly, Sam highlighted Jesus' command that people 'love your enemies, bless those who persecute you'. Conversely, despite arguing that God loves evildoers, River also argued that 'their day of judgement will come'. They were clear, however, that 'we cannot say that God doesn't approve of' any particular 'point of view'. River's understanding of judgement here, however, seems to be eschatological, rather than related to Jesus' lived example. River points to spiritualized judgement after death rather than of temporal justice here and now. At other points in our interview, however, River points to social justice as a moral norm.

Rather than judging and problematizing, Star believes that Jesus humanizes people and gives them agency. Reflecting on both their own experiences and on scripture, Star explained:

> It's the classic thing of seeing me as a problem and not as a person. You see over and again in the accounts of people who Jesus encounters, they have spent their lives being treated as problems and not people and the first thing that he does is that he humanizes them. My favourite passage of all time is the woman caught in adultery, because she's just this object, and Jesus personalizes her, and humanizes her and puts agency into her hands, and all that kind of stuff, it's really powerful.

It strikes me that Star's example, here, refers to someone who would be seen by those with power as problematic, as someone to be judged. This suggests that Jesus' practices of humanizing people and giving them agency applies to those who are often judged and problematized. Similarly, Mike sees Jesus' example as having a particular focus on social justice. Mike noticed a 'lack of integrity and hypocrisy' when 'people are preaching about love and being Christlike' and yet they do not 'ask questions' about injustice or 'treat queer people with gentleness and with dignity and empathy'. For Mike, the Jesus who Christians are called to image does question injustice and treat people well. Beth described a process, throughout their faith journey, of 'moving away from a mainstream hermeneutic to hermeneutics of social justice'. Similarly, River described their secular career as 'very much aligned with my faith – focused on human rights, social justice, dignity, equality'. Pat connected social justice with eco justice suggesting that 'We are supposed to live caring for the earth, caring for fellow humans.'

There is a sense of both resilience and joy in participants' reflections on a non-judgemental Jesus. The freedom and social justice that participants both long to experience and work to enable for others is apparent in their descriptions of Jesus. Rather than focus on the cross, most participants focus on the positive ways in which Jesus treats others. In their desire to be understood as fully human, participants also humanize Jesus by refusing to objectify him based solely on his suffering.

Christ was understood in a subtly different way from Jesus by some participants. These participants understand themselves as playing a part in Christ. For Star, this is a mirroring relationship whereby 'We look at Christ and see ourselves.' Similarly, Pat understands everyone as 'being made in the image of Christ and that everyone is different and seeing that being non-binary is part of the amazing difference; knowing that I'm not a cookie cutter person deepens my understanding of that'. For Pat, then, non-binary identity is an explicit and valued part of the image of Christ. For Jack, Christ is internal, whereby a person finds 'the Christ within yourself'. Ellen referred to Christians as 'members of the Body of Christ' and went on to note that in Christ 'there's no slave nor free, Jew nor Greek, male nor female, so we're all non-binary'. For Ellen, the non-binary nature of Christ frees her to understand herself as eschatologically non-binary, as stretched beyond her human identity as a woman. While, for now, Ellen's identity and lived experiences are definitively female, she holds a theological understanding that gendered identity and experiences are temporal and, as such, finite. Ellen presents this as an academic rather than personal reality. In this understanding, Ellen highlights both the challenge and the potential, for everyone, of life in Christ. The potential to be freed from the gender binary is also a challenge, if that binary is an important part of one's identity; a part that one has struggled and fought for.

Further, Ellen highlighted the scientific impossibility versus what she understands as the miraculous reality of Jesus' maleness:

> Jesus was male. He had to be one or the other or ... I mean he might have been intersex. You know, nobody did a chromosome test did they? ... And parthenogenic births do happen. They're very rare but they do happen. The offspring is always female, so Jesus was a trans man ... Alternatively, Mary was XY and totally androgen insensitive, so she was a trans woman ... Now, I do not actually believe that, what I believe is that God did a miracle because God does miracles. But it's an interesting argument.

When I challenged Ellen as to whether science and miracle could be one and the same, rather than either/or, she clarified 'Why not? I think with any miracle you ask how God did it and the answer is that it doesn't matter. The point is that he did.' In considering Jesus' scientifically impossible sex and gender as miraculous, Ellen elevates trans, non-binary and intersex bodies/the bodies of people who live with intersex traits to the realm of the miraculous. This is in stark contrast to the pathologization that many trans people experience.

Spirit

Several participants related predominantly to God as Spirit. Pat described God as 'heart', 'centre' and 'spirit', highlighting 'spiritual' practice as key to relatedness with God. Pat explained:

I think the Holy Spirit and God are largely interchangeable for the main ... The Holy Spirit is exactly that multifaceted thing that is all around us all the time in everything we do, say, feel. I think that the Holy Spirit is much more useful as an idea than God the Father.

For Pat, God as 'Father' and as 'Spirit' were described as, in essence, inextricably related, perhaps even identical. Pedagogically and personally, however, Pat's preference for understanding and relating to God as Spirit was clear. Mike, similarly, described God as Spirit, suggesting that God is 'nonhuman, hard to grasp, transcendent'.

For Ellen, God's spiritual nature, and transcendence, are related to understandings regarding God's gender. Ellen expressed that 'It's difficult because God has no physical form, so ... I'm not one of these who, as some of our friends are, would say that God is exclusively male. Yeah, there's a problem there. God is Spirit.' The connections Ellen made hint at the Spirit as a way of describing God that transcends sex, gender and norms.

Other participants also relate to Spirit as between and beyond genders. Jack referred regularly to God as 'Deep Mystery'. For Jack, Deep Mystery is the 'Spirit' aspect of God, in which genders and other characteristics overlap and combine. Pat expanded on this concept of the genderqueer Spirit, explaining that 'I know it is often portrayed as female, but somehow it is a lot easier for us to allow the Holy Spirit to float between genders and ages and classes and forms than it is to allow God to.'

Ellen also connected Spirit to genderqueering, reflecting somewhat inaccurately but, nevertheless, tellingly that 'The gender of the Holy Spirit is an interesting one. In the Greek and the Hebrew, it is a neutral word that is gendered variously in translation. I liked that one when I found that out.'[3] Here Ellen pointed to the ways in which the translation of the Bible from biblical Hebrew, Aramaic and Greek, through Latin, to English, and our understandings of biblical translation, affects our understandings of God. The queer potential of Spirit enables creative exploration of God, of the self, and of the other, as well as resilience in light of masculine treatments of the other two trinitarian aspects of God. The Spirit's popular feminization is a barrier and an issue with regards to both accuracy and expansiveness for some.

Creator

Several participants described how God the 'Creator' is understood through actions that lead to an understanding of the Creator's essence. Star related to God as incarnate, stating that 'I do not really sit very well with a kind of floaty, transcendent God. I need God to be walking in the garden, I need God to be hungry, I need God to be incarnate.' Evie explained that she experiences talking to God as like 'talking to another human being' while also recognizing a sense of 'intimacy' in relation to 'a spiritual entity'. Mike described 'the times when I felt like I've heard from God', recalling:

> the first time that I had sex and wasn't married, and it was like, oh, I think this is OK, actually. I think God is OK with this. I had had this image of God in the sky, just waiting to pounce on me for any mistake that I made. That is shifting.

This suggests that Mike's perceptions of God's actions have shifted from a feeling of judgement, drawing on experiences of being judged by humans, to a feeling of affirmation, drawing on positive experiences of gender euphoria during transition. Continuing the theme of affirmation, Pat explained that her understanding of God includes the idea that 'Like any good creator-slash-parent, God chooses to see those good times rather than those bad times – I certainly do not think God judges me for anything that I am because I think he made me to be me, and to be free, and to be ...'

For Ellen, describing God started with noting that God 'is the creator' and that 'God is the ultimate cause and the ultimate reason.' Ellen also referred to God as the doer of miracles and as nurturer. Again, these descriptions reference action rather than essence. Sam described God's protective action when 'I almost died, but God was inside my body. I kind of knew about this theoretically, but it was amazing that intelligence was trying to keep me alive.' In this case, Sam's experience of God's action in her life correlates with her theoretical understandings of God. Star's understandings of God are intertwined with a different part of their life – transition. Star explained:

God is becoming. God doesn't sit still. God delights in transformation and like, it's all potential ... just the edge of a moment. And that really feeds into my experience of God through my transition. God doesn't create us to stand still. God creates us to become. God creates us to change. God creates us to grow. Because that's what God does.

For Star, God's constant action is reflected in the actions of human transition, change and growth. Similarly, Beth described the Trinity as God's 'desire for relationship. Also, that movement, that dancing God. There's a very strong sense of love, connection, community within that.' There is a sense in Star and Beth's descriptions that it is difficult to define that which is in constant motion and that that difficulty releases creative potential and connections.

Three key aspects of God's actions are loving care, creation and recreation/transformation. River said that 'God is love' and explains that 'God loves even Donald Trump. I do think that it is our job as Christians to proclaim that.' For River, God's universal love is central. Mike credited that love with his continued faith, reflecting that 'The thing that keeps me in the game is the moments when I feel like I have felt God's presence and God's love, and that knowing what that feels like it feels almost impossible to walk away from.'

For Ellen, God's central action is creation, which impels theology to be theocentric. Ellen explained that God:

is the creator, it's ... One thing I do see as fundamental to my theology is that this is God's world, he made the world for his purpose and put us in it. Any theology which starts with mankind and then says 'that's God' has got it wrong. Even Christians do that. They say they're not, but their world view is human centred. God is the ultimate cause and the ultimate reason.

Further, Ellen added that 'God created humans.' For Ellen, God's identity as Creator is linked to our identity as created. The latter, Ellen suggested, is entirely dependent on the former. Similarly, Pat reflected on God's creative action, suggesting, 'I've got a bit of this and a splash of that – you know a dollop of this and that … a kind of cartoonesque recipe idea when God is making a person.' Further, Pat said, 'God is what's behind it all.' Pat's understanding of God is artistic rather than ordered, focusing on creativity rather than power. She retains, however, a strong understanding of God as the foundational source.

For Sam and Star, God's continued role in our lives, in sustaining, transforming and re-creating us is central. Sam explained above the feeling of God being inside her body, keeping her alive in a time of ill health. She went on to relate this to God re-creating her through her transition. Similarly, Star linked God's creativity with transition, highlighting 'becoming' as a key divine characteristic. Whereas Ellen and Pat's reflections largely defined God in the initial act of creation, Star and Sam's understandings relied more specifically on present and continuing creativity and care.

In participants' understandings, then, the Creator creates and loves humanity and continues to act through processes of transformation, which may be described as loving recreation. These are understandings of a God who fully loves the human beings whom they create and transform.

Dancing with God

The God who is described in this chapter is a God who dances. Further, they are a God who dances with their created and creative people. Any sense of certainty or univocality in knowing or talking about God is challenged. God is considered to be gender-full and gender-less rather than merely male. Finally, God, experienced as Creator, Spirit and Christ, is continually in positive action, communication and transition, working over and against forces of normativity, judgement and injustice.

Reflection

It is clear that participants' understandings of theological knowledge, language and of God themselves are affected by their experiences and narratives of suffering, resilience and joy. In research involving gay and lesbian participants, Kirk A. Foster, Sharon E. Bowland and Anne Nancy Vosler (2015, p. 195) found that 'transforming theological meaning' was foundational to forming resilience after experiences of homophobia. This process of transforming meaning may include deconstructing a prior understanding of faith, often formed in childhood, and discerning an alternative system of meaning. Similarly, for the trans and non-binary participants interviewed in my research, theological transformation via deconstruction and transformed/transformative rebuilding is foundational to forming resilience after experiences of transphobia. Further, they engage in joyful participation in the theological narrative.

As a child, God was my friend. My dad was a Church of Scotland minister and a hospital chaplain and faith was an important part of my childhood. I spent much of my time in the faith space in the Edinburgh Royal Infirmary and, with our church congregation, on the Isle of Iona, and both of these entirely different spaces, one very urban, the other very rural, felt like 'thin' places to me, places where the tissue between this world and another world, the world of God – of spirituality, of justice and of peace – was incredibly thin (see Burgoyne,

2007). These were places where God and I could enter into dialogue with one another. Dialogue with God felt like freedom; conversations in which I could really express anything, and where responses were loving and creative.

When I was 13 and my dad moved to full-time chaplaincy, I began to attend a city-centre church alone. During my time at that church, the experiences of God that I had centred around control and obedience. My accessory choices exemplified that control, and my efforts at obedience. I wore a cross around my neck representing not Jesus, the person, but crucifixion, the punishment for my wrongdoing. I never removed a What Would Jesus Do? (WWJD) wristband, reminding me of the commitment to sinlessness that I believed Jesus held me to. I also wore a purity ring, given to me by an emotionally abusive boyfriend, symbolizing my commitment to abstaining from sex until after marriage that was enforced by both a controlling boy and a judgemental Father God.

That church was unable to welcome me fully as someone who was starting to explore my LGBTQ+ identity and, after a very difficult time of debate and prayer that was intended to change me, I was asked to leave. This led to my being out of church for two years, during which time I struggled with severe anxiety and depression as I attempted to reconcile my experiences of church and God with my understandings of who I was.

At university I was able to reconnect with the church. I began to attend a church related to the university. Food and hospitality were core to their ministry, and this has influenced my own understanding of ministry. Genuine, all-encompassing welcome was a given, and it was made very clear to me that I was welcome as an LGBTQ+ person from the moment I stepped through the door. At that church I was encouraged, for the first time, to read the Bible for myself, without relying on devotional booklets or a minister or youth worker's interpretation. This was transformational for my own spiritual and theological journey.

I feel that my transition, vocation and understanding of God are deeply intertwined. In transition, I was not only able to not re-enter into dialogue with God, but also to participate in the

Body of Christ. In *Transgender. Christian. Human.* I refer to 'God's creativity, grace and love' (Clare-Young, 2019, p. 16). In the chapter 'Transforming Discipleship', I paraphrase Isaiah 43.1, suggesting that 'God created me, formed me, shaped me and calls out to me' (p. 55). Throughout that chapter, I highlight the way in which I believe God transforms or recreates (pp. 55–60). In exploring the image of God in humanity, I suggest that God is reflected in our 'flexibility; our ability to transform and to be transformed in communication with God and with other people' (p. 87).

Much of the above refers more to God's actions, perceived by human beings, rather than God's essence. I describe God, throughout, more in action than in essence. My personal understandings of God's essence, I now realize, are largely informed by the experiences that I and others have of God's actions. As such, I am generally reluctant to attempt to describe God's essence, knowing that such attempts will always fall short. Rather, I attempt to participate in God's actions, to dance with God in my own small ways by working for social justice, freedom and peace, and by resisting over-definition, instead playing with new ideas and experiences.

I have been struck by Pat's image of God as being like a many-sided dice. Further, it was notable that participants had varied understandings of God, particularly around God's gender-less-ness and gender-full-ness. As Sam quips, 'is not it wonderful' that we rely on each other to glimpse ever more sides of God, and still cannot claim to see the whole picture or comprehend the whole of God? My own understandings of God, described above, suggest that at various times in my life I have been looking at various sides of the God-dice.

As a child, I saw God as friend or dialogue partner. As a teenager, I saw God as a Father and ruler and Jesus as both moral exemplar and victor over my supposed sins. As a dechurched young adult, I saw God as a mystery, a puzzle to be solved. At university, I saw God as teacher, carer and kin, and began to understand Jesus as a radical rebel. In transition, I saw God as creator and re-creator. Now I see God as many of those things and many more things still. I focus less on what side of the dice I see and more on the ways in which I can participate in God's action.

Participants' understandings, and my own, incorporate many more characters of God, or sides of the dice. One trans-related theological text that explores theology in a broadly similar way is Barnsley's (2013) 'Grounding Theology'. I am struck by the ways in which the understandings of research participants, and my own understandings, are similar to, and diverge from, Barnsley's theology.

Barnsley's dice, differing from Pat's, might be described as three-sided, inasmuch as it mirrors the identities of three research participants, who Barnsley views as *imago Dei*. Rather than hearing participants' own theological insights, Barnsley analyses their lived experiences and theologizes from them. Barnsley suggests three arising divine metaphors: 'Thinness', 'Proteanism' and 'Opacity' (p. 322). Barnsley capitalizes these characteristics when referring to God and uses lower case when referring to human research participants. I have retained this pattern. The Thinness of God that Barnsley (pp. 322–3) describes is correlated with the thinness of their participant Leigh's gender. Thinness refers to a sort of transparency whereby the viewer can see something extraordinary in and/ or through the ordinary. Thinness relies on and celebrates embodiment while also suggesting that the image of God can be seen both in and through/beyond it. Thinness, for Barnsley, challenges rigid definitions of gender and of God. Proteanism is witnessed by Barnsley (pp. 323–5) through the experiences of their participant Robin and highlights the mutability and complexity of both human embodiment and of God. Barnsley uses this concept to challenge ideas of orthodoxy and idolatry and suggests that God's identity and embodiment mirror the internal inconsistencies of human identities and bodies. It roots God firmly in flesh while also freeing them from any particular enfleshed body. Barnsley draws the idea of opacity from their participant Sol's story. This refers to the aspects of ourselves, of each other and of God that we cannot see. Similar to Pat's many-sided dice above, opacity recognizes that no one can see every side of God and that the very opacity, or mystery, is an important part of how we understand God. To deny it, Barnsley (pp. 325–6) argues, is unethical; this quality is related to God's presence in, around and outside every aspect of the material, rather than any artificial separations.

Thinness posits the body as a site of potential connection – primarily between God and the human person – rather than as an essential facet of who a person is. This is similar to the concept of 'thin places', wherein the physical place is the site of potential connection between the spiritual and the material, rather than being defined by its physicality. Similarly, God's Thinness is a liminal characteristic that enables connection between the human person and God.

This Thinness is congruent with some of the theological insights of participants, in particular the sense that God 'dances', 'plays' or otherwise enters into human, material space. The sense of Thinness is especially relatable to Evie's relating to God primarily as Spirit, and Jack's sense that God, both as Christ and Spirit, can be located within a human being through spiritual practice and attention. Beth's intentional praxis of engagement with each person of the Trinity suggests the human quality of thinness, whereby Beth decentres themselves in order to meet the divine. Conversely, Star and Ellen express a relationship with a fleshier God, who is concretely accessible to human beings as the person of Christ. Nevertheless, their God is still a God who enters into human realities, albeit as a human being Godself.

As noted above, Barnsley suggests that Leigh's thinness, the indefinability of their gender, mirrors God's Thinness. The idea of personal thinness, particularly as relates to gender, is compelling to me. I certainly do not define myself in a static or material manner. Rather, my identity is liminal, fluid and often incoherent. It makes sense, to me, that this thinness mirrors both thin places and the Thinness of God. This is not, however, mirrored in the God to whom I most intuitively relate. Rather, like Star, the God with whom I relate is inherently fleshy. I hold in tension a belief in the Thinness and/or liminality of God, particularly as Spirit, while personally struggling to relate thereto. Rather, I relate to Christ, both in the flesh of

Jesus and, latterly, in the flesh of the human beings who strive to be the Body of Christ, the Church, on earth. This is not to deny God's Thinness, but rather to suggest that the ways in which my non-binary identity mirror it do not mean that it is a central tenet of my own beliefs.

The concept of Proteanism is, therefore, more relatable to me, given that it highlights God as material, as well as liminal. Proteanism is also described as the capacity to change in substance as well as character. In other words, it is explanatory of a God who has the capacity to be both Spirit and Flesh, or only Spirit, or only Flesh, at any given time.

While Proteanism is congruent with the varying understandings of, and relationships with, God that participants of this research hold, it is not an understanding that many participants explicitly shared. Rather, most participants related more to God as Spirit *or* as flesh, rather than relating to God as changeable. Conversely, both Beth and Jack engage in practices that intentionally recognize God's changeability and are intended to enable relationship thereto. It is notable, though, that this recognition is not innate but, rather, takes practice.

This is similar to my own personal experience of logically understanding God as Spirit and Flesh, as Creator, Redeemer and Sustainer, while also recognizing that I relate most intuitively to one aspect of that Trinity, an aspect that is definitively and expansively enfleshed. Nevertheless, I do wonder if my understanding of Christ as moving from the Body of Jesus to the Body of Many Believers is, in itself, reliant on Proteanism, on changeability.

Barnsley's final characteristic of God, Opacity, is entirely congruent with the insights shared by participants of this research. Each participant is keen to point to the mysterious nature of God, to the aspects of God that could not, as yet, be known. Concern and/or suspicion in relation to theological understandings that rely on or assume certainty repeatedly arise.

In our current, temporal reality, I share this concern or suspicion about certainty, which I view as an idol, and believe that the capacity to accept mystery is important in relating authentically to God. Nevertheless, I do not believe that this mystery is without end. Rather, congruent with strong objectivity, I believe that the truth(s) of God will be discernible in the eschaton, by which time the understandings of all people will be contributed to our theological knowledge. In other words, I believe that we currently see God as in a mirror dimly (1 Corinthians 13.12), whereas we will ultimately see God clearly. This relies on the gathering of multiple truths, or multiple mirrors. The image of God is clarified as each new voice is heard.

This reflection leads me to consider how the image of God functions. The theological concepts that Barnsley explores are clearly congruent with my own understandings and the understandings of my research participants. Nevertheless, I find myself yearning to know what Barnsley's interview participants experience of God in their lives and where they see the image of God in other people. Further, I wonder how the way in which they form this mirror has changed throughout their experiences of identity formation, coming out and transition.

Throughout this chapter it has been clear that participants' understandings of God are intertwined with, and mirrored in, their experiences of humanity. It is the way in which they recognize and express that mirroring as reciprocal, though, that is compelling, rather than the phenomenon itself. Barnsley observes God through the mirror of the participant. My interview participants meet God through the mirror of their dialogue partners in each of their lived experiences. They can only see the God-likeness that is reflected in them because it is reflected back and forth in relationship and community with others. That communal, participative aspect of discerning the image of God is a key finding of this research: the God who is known and yet unknowable, gender-less and yet gender-full, enfleshed and yet transcendent, fully, often reciprocally, involved in our lives and yet just beyond our grasp.

Speaking with other trans and non-binary Christians about our understandings of God has helped me to gain confidence in my own understandings, particularly where they differ from commonly held or denominational understandings. As expressed in the Introduction, one of the reasons that I undertook this research was the need for increased theological output from trans and non-binary people, which relies on increased confidence in expressing and amplifying our experiences and theological understanding. I have come to realize that my previous experiences and their harmful effects have undermined my theological confidence. This process of research, analysis and writing has helped me begin to reclaim it. As such, I feel that there is a clear need for spaces where trans and non-binary people can, as members of the Body of Christ, engage in mutual theological discernment, writing, curation and amplification.

In considering Barnsley's research further, though, I also realize that it is my relationship with each participant, as a trans non-binary researcher, that has made me feel enlivened by the process of research. I have come to a more authentic and nuanced understanding of God through the dialogue that I have personally experienced with each research participant. This has been similar to my growth in dialogue with fellow ordinands when training for ministry, and yet has been so much more meaningful to me. I believe that these relationships of 'similar difference', wherein a core identity characteristic is shared by dialogue partners, have been vital for me. I am also strongly aware that very few trans and/non-binary ordinands, or even Christians, can hope to find such a community. In the future, I would love to bring together a community of trans and non-binary participants to discern how we form, transform and reform the image of God together in a dialogical, practical process of theological formation.

Notes

1 See R. T. Mullins, *The End of the Timeless God* (Oxford: Oxford University Press, 2016) for an exploration, and rebuttal, of divine immutability in Christian theology.

2 See Ben Pugh, *Atonement Theories: A Way Through the Maze* (Cambridge: James Clarke and Co., 2014) for an exploration of traditional atonement theories.

3 Ellen's recollections regarding the Holy Spirit's gender are inaccurate. Rather, *ruach* in Hebrew is grammatically female, whereas Hebrew does not have a neuter. Regardless, her recollections regarding the gender of the Holy Spirit, though inaccurate, are relevant to her theological understandings. For an exploration of the Holy Spirit's gender in early Christianity, see Johannes van Oort, 'The Holy Spirit as Feminine: Early Christian Testimonies and their Interpretation', *Hervormde Teologiese Studies*, 72, 1 (2016), pp. 1–6, https://www.pro quest.com/scholarly-journals/holy-spirit-as-feminine-early-christian/docview/1817997487/se-2 (accessed 1 December 2021).

Interlude 6

Is Not That Wonderful? – Sam

Well, this is how we understand who we are. We understand who we are as human beings through stories. We need stories to make sense of our lives. When I grew up, women, their stories, those little stories around me or something reinforced the sense that I wasn't really a human being, but I am and I have a right to exist and there should be stories about people like me. I saw it from a documentary called *Disclosure*, which you've probably seen. One of the things about it was the trans men and women who were in it were gorgeous. Oh my gosh. They were so glamorous. They worked so hard to conform to conventional cisgendered heteronormative norms of beauty. As they have to. I mean, if they're going to make any kind of career in the media in America, that's what you have to do, but it doesn't necessarily help.

Most of us are not so gorgeous and not so beautiful. We're not about to actually go into all that work of transforming ourselves to conform to that. It's an impression. I do not want to buy into that. I think it's especially important for people, trans people and cis people, to see a performer like myself who is old, who is not glamorous, but is very confident in themselves, likes themselves basically, playing a trans woman, playing a very positive, trans role model. I think that is actually very important for everybody.

It's like saying, well, OK, you do not have to be impossibly handsome just to be accepted in this world. You can just be an old person, you can go to the supermarket, it's all right. You do not look like a film star. It's OK. You're all right. You are a good person. You're not necessarily going to be judged by your appearance. I'm assuming that you know all about how that feels, that judgement ...

And God ... It's funny, is not it? 'God' ... that's a short word to say, but the essence of God is completely beyond our understanding. After my wife died, one of the valves in my heart stopped working properly, so I almost died, but God was inside my body. I kind of knew about this theoretically, but it was amazing that that intelligence was trying to keep me alive. You can just see how there is this amazing, incredible intelligence inside all our bodies that preserves our health as best it can, but there is also something that seems to be looking at getting us through this world. I think you must be aware of it as well because we could all have gone so completely wrong. We are so lucky to be ourselves. Somehow, we have been guided to meet the right group at the right time so that we are able to be OK.

So that's one understanding of what God is. It's that intelligence. But, of course, it's much greater than that because if you look at the world religions there's this wonderful concept in India that there is some enormous, incredible intelligence that is doing its best to look after us despite a war, despite crap humans. I would call that another dimension of God.

Beyond that, there is something that keeps us on the tracks ... but there's also so much room, so much space. We know it intellectually, but somehow gravity functions. Somehow $e = mc^2$. Somehow this universal will seems to operate. And we do not understand all of God because that's beyond our understanding. That is maybe the biggest cosmic dimension of God.

If you try and put all these amazing intelligences together and add something – goodness knows what it is – then maybe you'll get close to describing it. Maybe then we'd be getting close to being able to define God. But, of course, at the end of the day we cannot, and is not that wonderful?

Is not it wonderful when we meditate some, when we pray, we are turning our attention to something, and we are entering that beautiful cloud of unknowing? That, of course, is also where creativity comes from because we create something that wasn't there before. And it's just incredible that we try to use a one syllable word to define that.

I would say for most of my life my experiences of church

have been very negative. Negative in the sense that just to get into a church I had to lie. I have a strong memory of being in the chapel of my public school as a very small boy, 14 years old, and everybody was singing. I couldn't join in. I was ashamed of my voice. My voice was still high. I was wearing suits like everybody else, there was a sense of crushing uniformity ... It felt like a very unsafe place. It was a place full of hypocrisy that preached love, but didn't put love into practice. It was horrible.

Then when we moved we lived really near a chapel. God, what a beautiful chapel, and the vicar was such a lovely, very nice man. The chapel was beautiful. I got a sense of the beauty of that church. But when I was on the vestry committee it was like a fucking snake den of vipers. That put me off church for a long time. The Metropolitan Community Church was very wonderful until I got terribly involved in that church. Again, the way people being on the management committee behaved I just thought, 'God, this is awful.' People are just horrible. Why are they treating us with such a lack of respect? It's very difficult to experience.

Now I'm in an inclusive church and I stay as far away as I can from the management side of things. I end up standing at the door, greeting people. I love reading the lesson. I love being seen as a trans person without any questions in that church. It liberates me hugely and helps undo a lot of the hurt that I suffered in churches when I was young. It's very important to be seen as myself and see other people like me there. That's very important. And it's important to be accepted and be part of this community of folks – straight, cis, hetero, queer – just a very wide community that embraces us. The worship is important and the prayers, who is preaching and what we preach, so many people have a lot of really interesting things to say. I think that what that community is doing is limited. It's not revolutionary, more could be done, but everybody's doing their best. That's a good thing to be part of.

7

Concluding

In this book I have tried to do justice to ten incredible and unique individuals who have gifted something of their identities, experiences and insights to me so that I can curate material that makes clear steps towards grounding theologies and anthropologies in the authentic identities, lived experiences and insights of trans and non-binary Christians.

This is an essential step in the inclusion of trans and non-binary voices in Christian theology, which begins to work, create and play in the knowledge gaps created throughout theology by the current marginalization and under-representation of trans and non-binary theologians. This theology is not complete in itself, forming a crucial part of a sorely needed watershed of support and platforming of trans and non-binary theologians and our resulting theologies, both in the academy and in the church.

In researching theology and anthropology with ten other Christian trans and non-binary research people, I discovered that we share valuable, nuanced and hard-won experiences and insights about aspects of theological and anthropological method that are unhelpful and must be addressed in trans-related theological literature.

Gender norms

The assumption of gender norms is both prevalent and limiting. While treatment of these norms in theological literature is varied they are often centralized. Some writers critique gendered norms and posit the defence thereof as the reason for transphobia. For them, gender norms play a foundational role in the suffering of trans people. Other writers suggest that trans people should embrace, and Christians should witness to, gender and sex norms. For them, such norms are foundational to the construction of gender – by both trans people and our critics. Sadly, this norm-based approach is still prevalent in ecclesial conversations about trans identities, such as the 'Living in Love and Faith' report and in legislative documents such as the 'Gender Recognition Act'. Gender norms are reinforced by trans-related theological literature that relies on binary accounts of gender. This is not good enough. Theological literature and ecclesial praxis must thoroughly deconstruct binary gender and associated norms.

The deconstruction of gender norms is central to my research and writing paradigm, which is both grounded and queer. Grounded research is rooted in the lived experiences of participants, rather than in norms, theories or assumptions about their identities. Queer theory, further, seeks to que(e)ry and deconstruct norms. Further, queer theory is definitively non-conforming. As such, queer theorists must question and deconstruct norms without inadvertently imposing new ones. Trans-apologetic literature, conversely, risks reinforcing normative modes of trans identification in order to defend the existence of trans people. This problematic impulse is common to all 'teaching transgender' disciplines, a fact that highlights the need for a move from literature about being trans towards literature by trans people about a wide range of topics. Far too much trans-related theological literature is trans-apologetic and, therefore, focuses much of its content on 'teaching trans'. This reinforces the gender norms that harm us. As such, it is beyond time to move on from 'teaching trans' to actually hearing trans voices.

I find that my conversation partners, even those who hold binary identities, que(e)ry and deconstruct gender norms, rather than reinforcing norms or suggesting new ones. Stacey, whose narrative is informed and shaped by a theme of suffering, posits societal norms as foundational to her life pre-transition. Jack, whose narrative is shot through with gritty resilience, experiences considerable difficulty in mirroring or enacting gender norms. Similarly, River posits norms around motherhood as foundational to their 'gender struggle'. Those whose narratives are framed by joy actively deconstruct norms. Pat proclaims that 'Blessed are those of us who defy sex and gender norms because Jesus said so.' Similarly, Star plays with norms, deconstructing them in describing a 'breastfeeding Christ' and a 'transgender Samson', as they explain their process of 'genderfluid hermeneutics'. Mike moves beyond the importance of deconstructing gender norms to argue that the ways in which trans and non-binary people do so are a key to the deconstruction of societal norms and injustice more generally. In doing this, we pose a clear challenge to theologians who rely on gender norms to defend trans identities. We show the limitations of these norms and highlight creative alternatives.

When it comes to God, participants further dismantle gender norms, with no participants experiencing God as entirely male. River suggests that the idea of God having a gender is 'meaningless', Beth describes God as 'a dancer' and Mike suggests that God has many genders. Ellen and Evie posit God as 'genderfluid', male, female and non-binary, and Pat compares describing God to describing a multi-sided gaming dice. Star describes a God whose gender is 'fleshy' but nevertheless queer. Pat sums up an understanding of God that is both entirely outside of, and yet entirely embraces, gender, stating simply that 'God is without gender and is with so many genders.' Even the idea that 'gender-full-ness' and 'gender-less-ness' can co-exist deconstructs binary norms of sex and gender.

It is clear that trans-related theology must not rely on gendered norms. Gendered norms are experienced as problematic and are not central to the theological understandings of participants. Rather, participants actively deconstruct and re-imagine ideas of gender both in relation to being human and to God. Further, some participants suggest that this deconstruction and re-imagining stretches beyond trans identities to a dismantling of all kyriarchal structures.

Non-binary voices, however, are still in the minority in this book. The strong challenge posed to gender norms herein could, as such, be further strengthened by the inclusion of additional non-binary perspectives. There is scope for further deconstruction of gendered norms in theology, and for new queer theologies grounded in non-binary identities, experiences and insights. This has the potential to impact all normative assumptions, not only those concerning gender. The deconstruction of norms cannot, however, start from a place of defence against those who reify them. If it does, it will only ever be partial and reactive rather than fulsome and authentic.

Understanding gender

Prevalent models of exploring gender do not encapsulate the diversity of trans and non-binary people's lived experiences. Nevertheless, trans-apologetic accounts are reliant on them. Given the toxic and binary debates about gender in public discourse, it is clear that new ways of talking about gender are desperately needed. Trans-related theological literature that relies on prevalent models of gender marginalizes trans and non-binary people's lived experience. It is vital that new ways to explore and understand gender are found and considered.

I found that trans and non-binary Christians are exploring emerging models of gender and creating new ones. None of us 'teaches transgender' in a typical way. Rather, each of us explicates our own unique identities and understandings. This shows the value of a trans researcher, with whom participants can be in authentic dialogue rather than in a teacher–student relationship, as is logically the case when trans participants are interviewed by cis researchers. Our explanations of gender include concepts as diverse as eschatology, euphoria, complexity, gift, pilgrimage and empathy. None of us talk about sex and gender being entirely different or separated, a common misconception. Most of us continue the process of gender-exploration even as we tell our stories, suggesting that these explanations of gender identity are not definitive but, rather, provisional. We enjoy playing with new understandings of gender and exploring the gaps in old ones. This sense of provisionality touches on the way in which normative theological understandings of 'truth' can be dismantled through deep engagement with lived experiences. The truth of gender is rarely static but, rather, is a perpetual process of discovery.

For Mike, being trans is much more about euphoria than dysphoria. For Evie, her gender as perceived by the other is of primary importance, more so than her embodiment, and is primarily relational rather than internal. For Ellen, gender identity has an eschatological element – with all people ultimately being gender-less children of God. Sam embraces the apparent contradictions of her non-binary identity as both father and grandmother without over-defining what being non-binary means to her. Star plays with gender. Jack experiences gender as a pilgrimage, with a non-binary destination. For Pat, gender, particularly non-binary gender, is that which enables empathy with the other – whatever their gender. For River, gender is a process of autonomy enabling authenticity – a series of autonomous choices that allow one to present authentically to the world.

These ways of understanding gender are individual and personal, not generalizable or academic. They are lived and embodied, not written or abstract. They are complex and contradictory, not straightforward or coherent. It is vital to recognize that participants' experiences and understandings of gender do not align neatly with gender theory or trans-related theological anthropology. Rather, trans and non-binary Christians' experiences and understandings of gender que(e)ry theories highlight the provisionality of anthropological knowledge.

Trans-related theology must engage with emerging models of gender and suggest new ones. It must also, however, avoid creating new normative models. There is still a sense in which emerging and new models of gender fail to capture the variety and complexity of trans and non-binary lived experiences. There is a risk of suggesting that there are correct and incorrect ways to understand, and live out, trans and non-binary identities. As such, there is scope for further theological writing that deals in detail with the lived experiences of trans people without attempting to codify those experiences into a coherent, apologetic narrative.

Churches must stop engaging in processes that rely on

'teaching trans', as if there is one fixed way to understand trans identities. This does not lead towards trans inclusion, affirmation or liberation. Rather, it codifies new norms and reinforces new hierarchies, suggesting that there are correct and incorrect ways to be trans and/or non-binary. Churches must actually lift up and listen to the voices of a diverse range of trans people in the same way that they lift up and listen to the voices of a diverse range of cis people. On a personal note, I am sick and tired of being asked to 'represent' trans people in meetings of tens, or even hundreds, of cis people who are not asked to represent anyone other than themselves. We are not representatives, we are individuals with unique identities, experiences and insights. This thesis proves that.

Diversity and lived experience

The lived experiences of a diverse selection of trans and non-binary people are largely absent from theological discourse. Trans-related theology often draws on a limited sample and homogenizes trans narratives. Non-binary identities are largely excluded, and biblical interpretation focuses on texts that have been used to critique trans identities, and those used to defend them. Trans-apologetic literature focuses on points that are disputed by trans-critical writers. Literature that moves towards a broader theology still focuses on topics that are associated with being trans. Hartke (2018, p. 5), whose writing is a step towards trans-authored theology, writes:

> Christians these days have questions about what the Bible has to say regarding clothing, changing bodies, new names, and the way God created human beings to exist in this world. I am thankful that trans Christians, who have been living and studying these questions for years, have come up with some pretty fascinating answers.

This is clearly true and yet limits trans and non-binary Christians to answering the questions posed to us by others, questions that assume that clothing, embodiment, names and creation are the only topics on which we have something to contribute. It is appalling that trans and non-binary Christians are rarely if ever asked about our relationships with God, our thoughts about what it means to be church, our Christological and eschatological understandings, our perspectives on theological hermeneutics or ecclesial praxis.

The identities of the ten interview participants whose identities, experiences and insights are explored alongside my own in this book are diverse in every sense, and particularly in terms of gender or gender-less-ness. The participants whose identities, lived experiences and understandings are explored here are variously agender, androgynous, genderflux, genderqueer non-binary, genderqueer, living full time as female, male, man, mtf, non-binary transmasculine, non-binary, simply female, trans guy, trans, transgender female, transgender, transmasculine, woman. This breadth of gender identities is not found anywhere else in the literature.

This is not simply a methodological or inclusion-related observation. Rather, the methodology impacts the arising insights. By including a wide range of trans and non-binary peoples' voices in this work, I have moved beyond trans-apologetic topics to highlight the diversity of trans identities, lived experiences and insights. Folks raised topics as broad as suffering, resilience, euphoria, the continuation of createdness, the problem of the Cartesian split, vertical and horizontal mirroring, kyriarchy, complexity, the limits and risks of theological hermeneutics, God as gender-full and gender-less, God as participative, and God's fleshiness. These topics go far beyond the specifically trans-related, contributing insights that speak into theology and anthropology more widely.

Further, this diverse sample of people highlights the problem of trans-related theology's attempts to homogenize trans and non-binary identities, experiences and insights. Rather, this thesis highlights several points of diversity and divergence. This diversity begins in the realm of narratology, where I show that participants variously frame their narratives with themes of suffering, resilience and joy. These varying frames contribute to the diversity of participants' anthropological and theological understandings.

We differ, for example, in our understandings of the connections and disarticulations between body and identity, which is also variously referred to as mind and/or spirit. While most participants suggest a progressive congruence between body and identity, River and Ellen variously highlight the disconnections between body and identity. River cites this fracturing as a pre-transition reality whereas Ellen believes it is part of our earthly existence, with the full spiritual connection of body and identity only possible in the eschaton, where both body and identity are non-binary. Further, Ellen highlights the importance of surgery, and Evie and River reference surgery as a site of hope, whereas other participants focus on social transition as the primary locus of hope.

However, our divergent anthropological understandings reach beyond our own gender identities. In describing queer identity, for example, Beth focuses on suffering, Mike focuses on euphoria and Pat focuses on the empathy with others that queerness facilitates; three distinctive understandings of being both human and queer. Further, whereas trans and non-binary people are generally assumed to have demonstrated abilities in specific areas, such as change and diversity, the trans and/or non-binary people I spoke with demonstrated a wide range of personal characteristics and qualities, including authenticity, a strong sense of justice, creativity, resilience, empathy, entrepreneurship, honesty and complexity. Further, they each had interesting and perceptive theological ideas despite the fact that most of them were not willing to claim the label 'theologian'. It is also notable that not all participants had the same characteristics or gifts. Again, trans and/or people are not a monolith but are individuals. If you have met one trans and/or non-binary person you have met one trans and/or non-binary person.

In theology, the understandings of my conversation partners differ even more. It is striking that the one point of agreement is that God cannot be fully known or described. Beyond that hermeneutical consideration, participants have diverse understandings of God. In terms of God's gender, some of us understand God as gender-less whereas others understand God as gender-full. Some use male language for God, albeit with some discomfort, whereas others use any language but male language; still others only use language that is explicitly non-gendered. Divergent opinions stretch beyond God's gender to God's materiality, Christ's characteristics and God's perspective. For Ellen, theology should be theocentric and for Mike, social justice is a key priority of God and, therefore, central to theology. Their perspectives are subtly different, though compatible. For Ellen, her primary attention is on God. For Mike, his primary attention is on what he discerns God's primary attention to be on, namely justice. Some people feel that God is distant, whereas others experience God as intimately involved in human life. Some of us experience Christ as spiritual, whereas others perceive Jesus as a human exemplar. Some participants experience God as fully human, others as fully spirit, others as both. For some, spiritual understandings are deeply important whereas, for others, anthropomorphic understandings are key.

The aforementioned indefinability of God leads Pat to describe understandings of God as a many-sided gaming dice, whereby we can only describe the sides we can see at any given time. This highlights the need for attention to diverse perspectives. Trans theologians might be able to glimpse sides of the dice that cis theologians are not looking at. Non-binary theologians might be able to see sides that trans theologians have turned face-down. Further, various trans and non-binary theologians will be looking at different sides of the dice at any given time. In other words, each of us can only glimpse part of humanity and part of God. Each of our perspectives are vital if anthropology and theology are to be further expanded.

Trans-related theology must highlight the experiences and voices of diverse trans and non-binary people. However, attention to the identities, lived experiences, and insights of global majority trans and non-binary Christians and disabled trans and non-binary Christians are still missing. Further, more attention is needed to the identities, experiences and insights of those who hold a number of marginalized identities. While this research and book attempts to prioritize subaltern identities, there are still gaps. In particular, only one Black voice is heard, and treatment of disability is largely limited to neurodiversity. This has also made it impossible to examine the impact of multiple marginalization on identities, experiences and insights. As pointed to in the Introduction, I believe there are particular points of similar interest between disability studies and trans studies.

There is scope for theological research that intentionally explores particular identity combinations. For example, it would be helpful to explore the theological understandings of Black trans people in more depth. Further, this book hints at links between trans theologies and disability theologies. These links deserve further exploration. There is practically unlimited scope for research with trans and non-binary theologians – both researchers and participants – on every anthropological and theological topic that we have no trans and/or non-binary perspectives regarding. There is a lot of catching up to do! This work will not be complete until many, many more books on the shelves of theological libraries are written by trans and non-binary people.

First-person authority

First-person authority means, in practice, trans people being able to form and express our own narrative identity and to be believed and accepted. Each of my conversation partners described times at which they were not able to express their identity and times at which they expressed their identity and were subject to questioning and/or criticism. They spoke openly about the harm caused. They also spoke to the ways in which this harm inhibited their contributions to theological discourse, to churches and to society more widely. I believe that first-person authority should also be central to ministerial praxis and theological research. It is not adequately demonstrated in trans-critical or trans-apologetic literature. Trans and non-binary people are simply asking to be accurately heard and fully believed when we describe ourselves. All too often we are not, and that has consequences not only for us but also for church and society.

Trans-related theology has sought to defend trans identities, rather than fully embrace them. Trans-related theology is often, therefore, rooted in the problematization of trans identities. Rather than continue this legacy of problematization, this book is rooted in the assumption that it is not only acceptable but also positive to be trans; that trans people exist and that God says that we too are good. This intentional embrace of trans identities, experiences and insights draws a route map from theological literature about trans people to theological literature by trans people, about being human and about God. That does not mean that there should not be any further theological research or writing *about* trans and/or non-binary people and not necessarily by us. Rather, this absolutely necessary and valid research should be complemented by wider theological research and writing by trans and non-binary people who can benefit the theological discipline more widely, on an infinite range of topics, rather than only having relevance to trans people and those who wish to discuss the ethical ramifications of our existence.

I note that further theological research and writing about trans and non-binary people, whoever it is written by, is necessary, because literature that fully embraces our identities, from a theological perspective, is still marginal and is entirely lacking in certain disciplines. For example, there is no clear ecclesial embrace of trans and non-binary identities. The church either ignores or problematizes us; more often and more worryingly the latter. A loving embrace by churches is contingent on full, frank and genuine theological explorations of trans and non-binary identities, founded on first-person authority. In other words, churches need to start speaking with us, rather than only speaking about us. I believe that any denomination currently debating trans identities from trans-critical versus trans-apologetic standpoints is failing to respect first-person authority in relation to trans and non-binary people and, as such, is failing us both pastorally and theologically. More broadly, this is a failure to recognize reflections of the *imago Dei*, members of the body of Christ. Surely it should not be controversial to say that this must be challenged and change.

Churches should respect our first-person authority in dialogue with – not about – us. Only once churches stop debating and start fully embracing trans and non-binary people exactly as we are will it be possible for churches to draw on our identities, experiences and insights to contribute to anthropological and theological knowledge.

This book is personal. And as it is personal – deeply involved in ten real lives – it is also provisional. As I have been writing, our lives have moved on. Our identities, relationships and experiences have changed. We may struggle to recognize our living selves in some of what is written here. And yet I have been regularly – and rightly – encouraged to remove from my doctoral book, and then from this book, the tentative language that comes naturally to me. I have done so gladly, as I am confident in what the data are asking me to write. However, I feel strongly that theology – particularly where related closely to the personal – must relearn humility.

The curation of this book has, undoubtedly, been personal as well as academic, humble as well as confident, provisional as well as actual. It would be disingenuous to ignore my role as participant-researcher. However, far from overwriting participants' identities, experiences and understandings with my own, my own identity, experiences and understandings have been enriched and transformed by participants. The level of challenge and encouragement that I have experienced has been far beyond my expectations.

I have historically framed my own identity, experience and understandings with the theme of suffering. I now realize that this framing was an apologetic response to the trans-critical understandings against which I attempt to offer a differing perspective. Further, I had not found trans, non-binary, Christian kin who could demonstrate a framing of joy. This narrative shift, as well as participants' understandings of humanity and of God, has affected my own understandings and altered the ways in which I describe them. I now describe God as being gender-full and relate this to the continuity of my own identity, enabling a self-understanding that is celebratory, rather than apologetic. This has led to a change in practice too. I no longer participate in debates about, or offer explanations of, trans and non-binary identities. Rather, I participate in events that celebrate or affirm trans identities, and in academic work that describes our identities, experiences and understandings, rather than seeking to explain them.

It is my fervent hope that trans-related theology, more widely, may be on a similar journey. It is a journey from suffering to joy, from defence to affirmation. It is a journey from merely persuading others to accept trans and non-binary people, to wholeheartedly celebrating our identities, experiences and understandings. It is a journey from inclusion for its own sake towards a recognition that our anthropological and theological understandings, and our churches, will be incomplete for as long as the voices of trans and non-binary people are not being heard.

In October 2022, I was pleased to be able to speak about trans theology for ten minutes, as part of the final of SCM Press's 'Theology Slam', a competition for young theologians. I would like to share my reflections and talk here, as they indicate the way in which my own, personal theological understandings have been reframed and have flourished as a result of doing the research on which this book relies. They were originally published on my blog, with the title 'Christ's Queer Body'.

* * *

Theology can inspire either hope or fear in the body. The linking of personal guilt and shame to the cross is an oppressive practice that embeds fear deep in our consciousness. The cross is misused as an instrument of oppression based on simplistic, supposedly either/or truths. Divine or human, good or bad, innocent or guilty. This misuse means orientating our gaze towards binary division, towards the piercing and splitting of the body and – ultimately – towards death.

My name is Alex and my pronouns are they/them. My journey started with the obscuring, fear-inducing divisiveness of guilt and shame. When I was a child I felt like an alien, completely unable to comprehend where I fit in a binary – male or female – world. That alienation led to terror in my teens as I began to understand the complexity of my identity but had no words to express it.

When I began to describe my complicated relationship with my body, I was diagnosed with gender dysphoria – extreme discomfort with my body and the way that society perceived my gender. The word 'dysphoria' is heavy with the assumption that my mind cannot embrace and love my body. This supposed division of body from mind mirrors the divisive binary of man = XY/phallus versus woman = vulva and XX chromosomes – a false binary that both school and church had tried to teach me as a child.

Theologians who start at guilt and shame often ask if I think God made a mistake with my body. I wonder why they assume that I hate this wonderful, resilient body, which I love. In asking this, they imply that body and mind can be separated, and that bodies should be revered. The cross alone doesn't allow for this supposed reverence for the human body, though. Instead, on the cross the body is obliterated by hatred born of systemic oppression. The cross – with attendant guilt and shame – is a part of the Christian narrative that I have heard and experienced over and over since birth.

The incarnation, less so. Perhaps the inherent queerness of incarnation is why churches seem to talk about it less. Incarnation is all about changing things. God stretching flesh by bursting into time ruptures our normative understandings. In kenotic incarnation, God tumbles out of power into fleshy vulnerability. In prophetic creativity, Mary's autogynephilic – or virgin – birthing of God stretches flesh, science, credulity and respectability politics to their very limits by producing a son who should, if genetics are to be believed, have been female. Jesus' masculinity shatters the idea that you need X and Y chromosomes to be male.

The Queen in Lewis Carroll's *Through the Looking-Glass*

exclaims: 'Sometimes I've believed as many as six impossible things before breakfast.' To believe in Jesus, I had to believe in complex bodies. I had to believe that the human body can be stretched to birth, to cradle, to contain and, yes, to touch divinity. I even came to believe that the body can be stretched beyond death to new, transformed life.

After going on that theological learning journey, I began to experience my own trans, genderqueer body through the lens of transformative incarnation. I came to realize that my body is not a static fact but, rather, a queer, living, fluid collection of cells into which God breathes almost infinite potential. My queerness mirrors the seahorse, which both fertilizes the eggs that their mate creates and carries them in their brood pouch, bursting forth in a display of androgynous birth. And my queerness mirrors the incarnate God, who chooses to embody fleshy transformation. My queerness is *imago Dei*. My queerness is part of the Body of Christ.

So why is the body ecclesia – the church – still stuck at crucifixion, at division, at an orientation towards death? My complex body is both part of the church and reflective of the body of Christ. Or to put it another way, the body of Christ is both trans and genderqueer. The church includes members who are male, who are female and who are not defined by binary gender. And that has to impact how we do things. We cannot go on pretending that the church is only one thing or one way. We – the body of Christ – cannot, must not be limited to normative binaries or polemical debates.

St Paul refuses to separate mind from body from community. Paul's vision of Christ is an image of unity in diversity, of a body that contains millions of human hands and feet and eyes and ears and – yes – genitalia in a complex creative being that is all the better for its internal contradictions and constant recreation. Elizabeth Stuart (2007, pp. 65–76) suggests that the body of Christ is stretched by each new believer that joins it. Christ's body is inevitably trans, inherently queer, beautifully beyond binaries.

The church must urgently learn to mirror incarnation, relying on the capacity to stretch, to grow, to change. We need to practise queerness, to pay attention to those voices who challenge normativity, ready to be transformed rather than to debate. We need to speak about the fleshy hope that we embody more loudly than we squabble over the norms we should be reaching far beyond.

And so I choose the lens of incarnation over the blindfold of crucifixion. I choose hope over fear. I choose to dance towards new life, rather than to trudge towards inevitable death. You can choose to be a part of the sorely needed transition from a terrified church that clings on by its fingertips, to a euphoric church that allows for the stretching of its skin to embrace its many unique parts, so that every person may encounter Christ's queer body.

Interlude 7

'Those Mirroring Things Matter' – Pat

I certainly see open and out trans people within the church setting and my church setting is in a small town but there are people who openly identify as trans. I also see people who, although they may not openly use the words non-binary in a church setting, are people who are non-binary – who are masculine women or effeminate men or androgynous people somewhere in the middle, so yeah you do see us in church settings – it will depend I think very much from church to church how open people are about it. I think it's harder in ministry – I think people are more likely to assume that you subscribe to and fit into the gender binary. I do not think it even crosses their minds. So in some ways it's harder to express myself, but in some ways as a minister I also have more freedom to express myself. I certainly have a public platform to express myself on and I do not have a traditional workplace that I need to fit into. I can certainly wear trousers every single day of the year and no one thinks any different of it – so in some ways I do have freedom.

I feel able to speak out explicitly about being non-binary but I do not choose to. I think part of ministry is allowing yourself to be to some extent nondescript, the blank canvas on which people can put whatever they need to, so I do not feel the need to declare my sexuality at the start of every conversation but if there is a conversation about sexuality then it is important that I at least mention that mine is not perhaps the norm. Again, if there's likely to be conversations about gender then I would probably mention that my gender is not exactly typical. But I do not necessarily feel the need to be out and proud about it.

Being non-binary is a positive in ministry. I think if I was particularly stereotypically right at the end of femininity, whatever your definition of the end of femininity is, that makes it harder in some ways for men, particularly men of a certain age, to relate. I think the fact that I am, in old-fashioned parlance, a tomboy makes it easier for men of a particular generation or men of a particular mindset to talk to me without having all that baggage of femininity. I think to some extent that is an advantage that it allows me to cross the gender divides. It's certainly an advantage with younger people particularly if they are non-binary or otherwise not normative. It makes it easier for them to talk to me because I do not fit in the boxes.

I think we all want to see someone who looks like us – and the more ambiguous we are as a person the easier it is to focus on the bits that do look like us. I think there are specific situations where you're looking for someone where you can see a mirror, where you can see someone who is going to understand you, someone who's going to be sympathetic to you, someone who you immediately have some points of reference with. I do not need to look for that kind of person when I'm buying shoes or when I'm seeing my GP about athletes foot but if I'm seeing a counsellor or talking to a minister or looking for a friend then those mirroring things matter.

I think my gender and my theology are definitely intertwined. For a start, the painful parts of not having a standard gender have an outlet in lament, in the screaming at God, the 'Why won't you fix this?' the 'Why didn't you make me one or the other?' In the other direction, I hold the understanding that everyone is made in the image of Christ and that everyone is different and that being non-binary is part of the amazing difference. I'm neither male nor female, I'm more one than the other and I've got a bit of this and a splash of that. Knowing that I'm not a cookie cutter person deepens my understanding of God's creativity. I think we are who we are. God makes us the way we are for a reason and we can be so much better and so much happier if we can accept that and get on with it and try and perhaps puzzle out what that reason is rather than lamenting.

God is ... God is what's behind it all – but I do not claim to understand it – I still find comfort in using the traditional words I grew up with – Father, He, Lord – I understand all of their complexities or their difficulties and I understand that actually they're not that helpful but that's what I grew up with. I absolutely one hundred per cent accept that God is without gender or is in fact with so much and so many genders but I just find it really hard to stop using the words.

My relationship with God is as a Father – I appreciate that I have all these other strands and relationships to God and I think I need to explore them more. I think God is just the heart and centre of everything and I think that all the things that we define God as – whether it's people talking about Mother Nature, people talking about being spiritual but not religious, people finding peace in the seaside, all of those are aspects of God because God is not just one thing, not just one gender, not just one anything – it's so multifaceted.

I do not think it's even that important to me to use those traditional words anymore, it's just habit, but the more I use those words the more I reinforce to myself that image of God. I think that's when I doubt my faith – when I've gone back into that 'he lord father' whereas all the best I can come to visualizing God is this multifaceted ... I know! Imagine a 100-sided dice that gamers used to use but more and more and more and more sides than that ... You know, infinite sides obviously. If I could picture God that way then there's nothing God cannot do so I think actually using those gender words and those gender roles limits God and I think that seeing God as also being trans and non-binary makes our understandings of God all the more powerful.

To me sin is a very unhelpful word. I try to avoid using it except in a very sarcastic – 'you dirty sinner' – kind of way. The word sin is an unhelpful word because we are all sinners, we are all people who do not do exactly as God might wish us to do – or rather exactly as our fellow humans might wish us to do, exactly as the rule of love would have us do – we all act contrary to the commandment to love one another, to love our neighbour, we are all acting contrary to the commandment to love our God at which point it becomes unhelpful because there's no 'sin' bigger than another. The whole concept is completely unhelpful.

I do not think transness being sinful would even have crossed Jesus' mind because it's not hurting someone else. I mean, he talks about eunuchs being blessed. You can easily rewrite the Beatitudes to read, 'Blessed are the non-binary, blessed are the trans people, blessed are the other people who just refuse to fit in a box, blessed are the women in jeans and the men in skirts.' The church should be the first place where anyone who does not fit into society's little boxes could feel at home so, therefore, there is a role for the church in first accepting people who are different, and then second in pushing that acceptance outwards from itself. There is a role for the church in saying to people, 'You are OK exactly as you are.' And standing up for those people when anyone outside the church says, 'No you should be male, you should be female!'

But the first thing the church has to do is an audit of itself. We need to audit all attitudes to gender. That's not just about the physical building that we call church. We do need that, we need things like having toilets that are accepting or accessible to different genders. But it's also about looking at our language. It's eliminating that constant microaggressive bloody painful repetition of brothers and sisters, men and women, boys and girls, Christian men and women. I'm not saying that we take a sharpie and cross out Genesis 2 and Proverbs whatever it is but we certainly treat them the same way as we now treat teachings on divorce and things like that. We certainly take the sting out of them and say, 'OK that was then this is now.' We just need to think about all our language, all our attitudes, not having men and women's groups, not calling it mums and tots. We need to do a really serious audit at all levels from the simplest things outwards.

8

Erring

It's not usual to write a chapter after the conclusion, is it? This is the chapter that shouldn't be here. You might choose not to read it – please do! If you do read it, you might choose to then go back and read the conclusion again – please do! I have wrestled with the order of these chapters more than is reasonable. There were lots of things that I said I wouldn't do in my doctoral research. I said I wouldn't try to explain what it meant to be trans. I said I wouldn't dignify anti-trans theological writing with a citation or a response. I said I wouldn't broach the contentious and politicized topic of so-called 'detransitioning'. And yet, finding myself with the opportunity to publish words that people might actually read, I realize that I cannot leave these topics alone. They represent the questions, concerns, hate mail and threats that I have to cope with every single day.

So this is my response, today. I hope it might give me the courage to stop using my limited spoons[1] to respond every day, an exhausting practice of over a decade that frankly affects my capacity to live life to the full. This chapter is different from the other chapters because it is not grounded in my doctoral research. These are my opinions and understandings, formed over time and rooted in a lot of reading, conversation and discernment. Do with them what you will.

Defining

The first part of this chapter serves to define words that I am often asked about. Rather than a concise dictionary definition, though, what I am offering is my own understanding and experience of each word, and some of the ways in which I have experienced them being problematized in conversation.

Trans

Trans simply means across. Transform, transmit, transatlantic, translation ... To transform something is to change it across from one state to another. To transmit something is to communicate it across from one person to another. To go on a transatlantic voyage is to travel across the Atlantic. To translate is to move a message from one language across to another. To be transgender is something like translation – trans folks move the language of gender from a language that is used to describe our sex observed – and correlated gender assigned – at birth to a language that more accurately and authentically communicates ourselves to the world.

Trans is what is often referred to as an umbrella term. That means that it is a term that includes a whole lot of other terms. Words like transmasculine, transman and ftm – all terms describing a transition towards male, each with its own particular nuances and debates. Words like transfeminine, transwoman and mtf – all terms describing a transition towards female, each with its own particular nuances and debates. Trans is a word that describes me and also describes people who are nothing like me. If you have met one trans person you have met one trans person. We are not a monolith, hive mind, movement or agenda ... We are simply people who are trans, who move across.

There is no one way to be trans. Some trans people experience gender dysphoria – some do not. Some trans people experience gender euphoria – some do not. Many trans people transition socially, perhaps taking steps like changing our names, pronouns, appearance, documents and so on. Some do not. Some take some of those steps but not all. Some transition socially in some contexts and not in others. There is no one way to transition socially. Some trans people transition clinically, perhaps taking steps such as hormone replacement therapies and surgeries. Many do not. The gender-affirmative care that trans people often seek is not unusual or unique to us – each treatment is also available to cis people for different reasons. Some treatments that are no longer available to trans young people – for example so-called hormone blockers – are still available to cis young people. Discrimination? Certainly looks like it. But not all trans people have any clinical care at all, and that too is of course valid. There is no one way to transition. There is no one type of body that can be labelled 'male', 'female', 'cis' or 'trans'.

So to summarize, trans means across. Transgender people are human beings who transform other people's perceptions of us, sometimes transitioning socially, sometimes clinically, to transmit an authentic self and to translate that self for accurate communication with other people and with God. Transform, transmit, transatlantic, translation, transgender.

Non-binary

As well as being trans, as having travelled and translated across a gulf of gender, I am also non-binary. Non-binary is another umbrella term. Some people would also say that non-binary fits under the trans umbrella. I think it is kind of staggered, as some non-binary people also think of themselves as trans and others do not. For example, in this book, River is both trans and non-binary whereas Pat is only non-binary and not trans.

Non-binary refers to people who identify and live in varying ways outside the binary identities of male and female. It includes people who are genderqueer – who play with gender – people who are genderfluid – whose gender identities change – and people who are agender – people who do not identify with gender. Like any definition, these are partial. Similarly to trans people, if you have met one non-binary person then you have met one non-binary person. Because of that, I would like to tell you a bit about what being non-binary means to me, but I would also beg you not to simply apply these experiences, traits and opinions uncritically to any other non-binary person;

we are each distinct. For me, being non-binary is mainly about five things: history, embodiment, politics and theology, play, and sense of self.

History I was raised female and now move around the world as pretty much male. I am certainly read as male. Many trans people have been raised in a gendered way that does not correlate with their gender identity. That doesn't necessarily mean that they are non-binary. But for me, it has been important to understand my history, present and future in a congruent way, and to not try overly hard to change every stereotypically feminine aspect of myself. Further, I believe that cross-gendered formation teaches us all sorts of things. I have seen the world through the eyes, body and experiences of someone who was raised and assumed to be female and I have seen the world through the eyes, body and experiences of someone who has transitioned and is assumed to be male. I do not believe that it is possible or even desirable for me, personally, to erase those experiences and understandings. They are part of what makes me who I am and a part of what it means to me to be non-binary.

Embodiment I am one of countless trans people who has had some gender-affirming care and who has not had all of the gender-affirming care that is available to me. Again I must stress that I do not believe that there is any such thing as a male body or a female body. Having said that, in terms of sex, my body is now definitively beyond the male/female binary and, rather than experiencing dysphoria about that, I experience comfort and correlation, euphoria, the feeling that this is the way that my body is meant to be. My whole body is a part of what makes me who I am, a part of what it means to me to be non-binary.

Politics and theology I do not believe in the gender binary as a positive. If anything, my feelings about gender would not be too different from Star's belief that it is 'fallen'. Any system that divides people by one aspect of who they are is, quite frankly, seriously messed up. I hold the binary gender system responsible for patriarchy, gendered violence, toxic masculinity, stereotypes, inequality ... The list could go on. But I also genuinely do not believe that binary gender is core to who we are created to be as human beings who image God. The Genesis creation narratives point to communication across similarities and differences, eunuchs are held in high esteem throughout scripture, and both Paul's writings and philosophical/theological reasoning more generally strongly suggest that the body of Christ is non-binary along with our eschatological realities. I believe that, fundamentally, human being is simply not binary.

Play I like playing with my presentation, embodiment and so on. It's as simple as that. I love creativity and queerness. I do not always 'look non-binary', whatever that means, but I reserve the right to play with gender in a way that stretches reality beyond binaries simply because I enjoy doing so. And, finally, sense of self. I am non-binary simply because I am. I spent years trying to be 'certain' that I was male, only to realize that I have no idea what that even means. The whole concept of gender is not something I completely understand and it certainly is not something I feel I fit into. There is simply a true-ness about me being non-binary. I cannot explain it and I shouldn't have to defend it. I am.

Pronouns

Pronouns are the words that we use to identify people and things, often standing in for their name. In terms of people, when the pronouns we use accurately mirror the self-understanding of the person we are defining, that is a correct, respectful use of pronouns. When the pronouns we use do not accurately mirror the self-understanding of the person we are defining, that is an incorrect, disrespectful use of pronouns. Everyone makes mistakes, but it is vital to practise using people's pronouns so that we can refer to each other in ever more correct and respectful ways.

My pronouns are they/them, or just my name. You will hear people I am very close to using other pronouns for me, but these are the pronouns that I would like most people to use. It's really, really important to me that people use these, but I feel I have yet to explain why in a way that really helps people to understand. They/them is a gender-neutral pronoun. We use it all the time when we wonder if whoever was sitting at this table before us realizes that *they* left *their* umbrella behind.

Often when I talk about being non-binary, or using the pronouns they/them or just my name, people point out my masculine presentation. Although I do occasionally wear nail varnish, usually wear a fair amount of bracelets, rings and necklaces, and almost always wear clothes from the 'women's' section of the store (who doesn't?!), I accept that a person with a beard, fairly bland clothing and a flat cap, is often assumed to be male.

And that's where the problem lies: assumptions. My natural home or affinity is certainly slightly nearer to the location 'male' than the location 'female'. My body seems to work significantly better when it is regularly given testosterone, I really like my little beard, and I am acutely uncomfortable, to the extent of nausea and physical pain, when people use my old name or female pronouns to describe me. And yet to assume that that means I am a man is inaccurate, and means that you only glimpse the very surface of who I am.

For me – and please note that this is something I only say for myself, not for others who rightly form and describe their own identities in an infinite diversity of ways – my lived experience, embodiment and characteristics lead me to feel that I am non-binary, not male. I believe that gendered stereotypes are just that, stereotypes, and yet they function.

So having been socialized as female, finding that I am always talked over by men in boardrooms, being the type of autistic who masks impeccably while knowing I shouldn't have to, being naturally polite and quiet and conflict-avoidant and having to wrestle with myself to speak up and out and not panic about what others think ... Having lived through periods and sexual assault and teenage battles with makeup and being patronized and ignored ... Loving sewing and playing the harp and whispering through images instead of shouting through words ... Having experienced all of that, I am absolutely sure that those things do not necessarily make a person a woman. But I am also absolutely sure that they do not necessarily make a person a man. Rather, they make me me.

Some people have asked why I insist on continuing to use the pronouns they/them, when I am so clearly not terribly upset by he/him. For me, it's a matter of truth. I genuinely believe that I am non-binary, that I am they/them. Those pronouns provide an accurate mirror of the fullest possible version of myself. Maleness is an insufficient mirage that does not expose the fullness of who I am. Authenticity matters to me. You matter to me. And so I want to give you the gift of my true self. It is up to you whether you honour it or whether it is easier to refer to me in part. If you call me he/him, I won't mind, but I will know that at that moment you are only seeing, only addressing, the part of me that you can see. So if you would like to know me better, as I really am, my name is Alex, and my pronouns are they/them or just my name.

Dysphoria/euphoria/realism

Some trans people experience gender dysphoria. Dysphoria is often described as extreme discomfort. I would also describe it as a sense of unreality. It is that moment when you look in the mirror and your breath catches in your throat, heart thudding, because you do not quite recognize the image staring back at you. It is the dithering in a clothes shop between what you can afford, what fits, what you love and what you know is seen as 'normal'. It is the itching under your skin when parts of your body feel like they do not belong. It is the sudden onset of nausea when a stranger refers to you as 'ma'am' or you hear the name that you have struggled to forget was once used to describe you.

Dysphoria can be related to the body and/or related to societal perceptions. For some people, dysphoria is intensely and particularly physical. For other people, dysphoria is intensely and particularly social. For many it is a bit of both. Dysphoria is not limited to particular body parts or words, it is distinctive to every person and may be surprising. For example, I used to have the most dysphoria about my arms and hands. That is no longer the case. Some trans and non-binary people do not experience dysphoria at all. However, dysphoria is often the experience that a trans person is trying to travel away from.

Euphoria is ostensibly the opposite of dysphoria. Made famous by Elliot Page and his topless selfies, euphoria is often described as extreme joy. I would also describe it as a sense of reality. It is that moment when you look in the mirror and recognize the person staring back at you and feel more whole than you ever have before. It is finding the perfect jumper in TK Maxx (other stores are available) and knowing that it will fit perfectly before you even try it on. It is ceasing to care about what is seen as 'normal' because you love yourself just enough to let go of other people's perceptions. It is the comfort in your skin when your body is finally your body. It is the sense of warmth when you are gendered correctly, and hear your name with love in the speaker's voice.

Euphoria can be related to the body and/or related to societal perceptions. For some people, euphoria is intensely and particularly physical. For other people, euphoria is intensely and particularly social. For many, it is a bit of both. Euphoria is not limited to particular body parts or words, it is distinctive to every person and may be surprising. For example, I experience euphoria when someone asks me about or compliments my embroidery, because I know that they are starting to see the whole of me, not just stereotypically gendered parts. Some trans and non-binary people do not experience euphoria at all. However, euphoria is often the experience that a trans person is trying to travel towards.

Realism, however, requires the reader to understand that euphoria and dysphoria are not straightforward constants. The reality is that many trans people experience a mixture of both in all sorts of ways at all sorts of times. The trick is to not limit us to one experience or another but to understand that, just like anyone else, we are complex human beings with myriad emotions and experiences. We do not fit in any one narrative, frame or box. Life simply ain't like that.

Cis

Cis should be a relatively easy word to define, given that it is simply the opposite of trans. If trans means across, cis means on the same side as. In other words, a cisgender person is someone who remains with a similar gender identity to their sex observed and correlated gender assigned at birth. Cis is not a slur or a derogatory term, it is simply a functional word that describes a common state of being. The problem with avoiding the word cis is that you end up saying 'not trans' a lot or, worse, 'normal'. If someone argues that there is no need for the word cis, they are implicitly stating that to be cis is to be normal and that, therefore, to be trans is to be abnormal. That is not an implication that I can accept.

The most reasonable objection to the term cis that I have heard is the argument that a person does not identify wholly with the assumptions and stereotypes that are correlated with their sex or gender identity. And that makes sense. Just as every trans person is an individual, and every non-binary person is an individual, so too is each cis person an individual with their own diverse identities, experiences and insights that will be distinct from any other cis person. If you have met one cis person, you have met one cis person. And so, not identifying with the term cis does not eradicate its usefulness or prove it to be a problem. Rather, if a person genuinely does not identify with their sex, they have the free choice to describe themselves as trans or non-binary. If they do not, it is a simple fact that they are cisgender.

Responding

In the second part of this chapter I grapple with some of the topics that are often brought to me as the subject of debates. My responses to them come from a mix of lived experiences, spiritual discernment, academic research and personal opinions. It is also my experience, however, that people are often not willing to listen to or be swayed by anyone's experiences, discernment, research or opinions in the context of debates where they have already made up their mind. That is why I no longer participate in debates. I do not believe that other people's unwillingness to accept what many of us hold to be true makes those beliefs any less true or valid. When I disagree with other people's views I wholeheartedly defend their right to hold them. I wish that others would do me and other trans and non-binary people the same courtesy.

Genesis

The Genesis creation narratives are often a divisive topic among trans and non-binary Christians. I've yet to meet someone who feels lukewarm about them. Generally folks either find them immensely helpful or affirming on the one hand, or intensely unhelpful and wounding on the other. Many of us have been on quite a journey between those two experiences. I used to detest the Genesis creation narratives. The words, 'You're either a man or a woman' and similar sentiments have been central to every incident of abuse – psychological, spiritual, verbal, sexual or physical – that I have suffered since the beginning of my transition, and there have been several. Worse, when I read through the reports about trans folks murdered in advance of Trans Day of Remembrance each year, I can surmise undertones of these sentiments in the words and actions of the perpetrators of those tragic, violent and transphobic crimes. The reality is that people use the sort of logic underlying a binary reading of the Genesis creation narratives to build a foundation for the claim that people like me – trans and non-binary people – do not and should not exist.

The problem, though, is that the words do not warrant such a reading. Often trans-apologetic texts cite this as a 'literal' reading of the Genesis creation narratives, but it is not even that. At best it is a 'reading in' to the English translations and interpretations of the Genesis creation narratives. At worst, it is a facet of puritanical morality imposed on scripture from culture as a part of colonialist attempts to flatten diversity and impose English normativity around the world. If you have no idea what I am on about, google the so-called 'Breeches Bible'.

My relationship with the Genesis creation narratives changed drastically when I was training for ministry and was encouraged to study Hebrew. In fact, I would not have completed my doctoral research nor written this book had Hebrew not been a part of my early ministerial studies. Before that, I pretty much detested Genesis. It had been used to hurt me and, subsequently, I had been advised by a spiritual director to avoid it altogether. Learning Hebrew, an accident of timing more than anything else, enabled me to explore underneath the blunt English polemic and to begin not only to understand but also deeply feel and embrace the fact that trans and non-binary people too are created in God's image.

The problem is one of translation. As the Italian saying goes, translators are traitors. It is not possible to translate, you see, without making decisions, and plenty of decisions were made, and continue to be made, in the translation of biblical Hebrew. Why? Because every language is different and the gap between modern and ancient languages is significant. Biblical Hebrew has many fewer words than modern English and the nuance and creativity possible within those words is vast. To interpret biblical Hebrew 'literally' in English, a person would need to provide countless options for each word or phrase. There is no such thing, therefore, as a literal reading of the Genesis creation narratives. These are not literal texts.

That doesn't mean they are not important. Discussion of these texts often regresses to a binary 'conservative' versus 'liberal' debate as to whether they are 'true' or 'myth'. That debate makes no sense. Mythic writing contains truths that are different from, and as vital as, scientific writing. The question is, what are those truths? What is the text trying to communicate? In my view, the primary purpose of the Genesis creation narratives is not to point out sexual dimorphism and construct an ethic around sex and gender. Rather, they are getting at something far more significant about what it means to be human.

In Genesis 1.26 the word אָדָם (pronounced something like *ha'adam*) has been variously translated as 'man', 'mankind', 'humankind', 'the man', and 'Adam'. *Ha'adam* is a singular or collective, referring variously to the human as an individual and humankind as a group. Its masculinity is likely an accident of the fact that every neutral object, person or group in Hebrew is masculine in form. There is no neutral. It would be equally accurate to translate *ha'adam* as the whole of humanity, containing both masculinity and femininity, or as one human being containing both masculinity and femininity.

We read that God created human beings or the human being in their own image, and here is where gender is officially brought into the equation. In Genesis 1.27 we read that humankind are created 'male and female', but this form can be adjective or noun, not needing to refer to an objective fixed state, and the joining word – the 'and' – could be any joining word. It would, I believe, be just as accurate to suggest that 'God created the human in their own image. Masculine to feminine God created them.' I wonder how much that changes the narrative from one of binary thinking to one of fluidity and diversity. I wonder if the concept of a range of masculinity and femininity queerly expressed within one creature is closer to androgyny than more traditional translators and interpreters dare to suggest.

In Genesis 2, the narrative becomes more creative still. After some sort of divine–human animal naming game, *ha'adam* is still looking for 'a help to mirror him'. It is not until that mirror is created – pulled out of *ha'adam*'s androgynous self – that *ha'adam* recognizes himself as 'ish' – man – and his mirror image as 'ishah' – woman. This mirroring wordplay suggests similarity and diversity, but not binary distinction. If anything, this moment reads, to me, as a coming out narrative, wherein *ha'adam* – the androgynous human – is enabled to recognize their diversity and transition variously into their masculine and feminine forms.

These aren't the only readings of the Genesis creation narratives, but they are also not unfaithful to the text. If more traditional readings can be described as 'literal', then so can these. I feel that neither can. Rather, we are given this wonderful world or myth from which to discern something about what it might mean to be human, in dialogue with communities of mirroring and diversity, created to communicate with other people and with God. There is no literal reading, but there are plenty of readings that hold truths vital to what it might be to be human. That vitality has little or nothing to do with what is in our pants. It's way past time to decry the Breeches Bible once and for all.

Mistakes

'But God doesn't make mistakes …' If I had a pound, or even a penny, for every time I heard that argument, I could probably fund hostels around the world to support the many gender-creative children and young people who are thrown out of their homes every day. Sadly, anti-trans sentiments do not usually come with charitable donations, so that is not an option. I'd better counter the thing here, instead.

First, God does change their mind. I get that that is an unpopular opinion, but it also comes pretty directly from scripture. 'And the LORD changed his mind about the disaster that he planned to bring on his people' (Exodus 32.14). 'The LORD relented concerning this; "It shall not be," said the LORD' (Amos 7.3). And it happens again in verse 6. I could give many more examples from scripture of moments where God has been about to do something and has had to step back and think again. God does change their mind. And that doesn't make God any less – well – God.

Second, and I believe more importantly, how come I'm

figured as a mistake all of a sudden? If it were not for the evidence above, I wouldn't be too worried about accepting that God doesn't make mistakes because I do not think that I am one! If trans people's very existence is evidence of a 'mistake' on the part of God, what does that reveal about people's attitude towards us? Honestly, the more I think about it the more angry I get. We are not mistakes. We are beautiful, wonderful, complex, ordinary, extraordinary, cracked, perfect, imperfect, transforming human beings. We are God's beloved creations, children, vessels and mirrors. We are certainly not errors.

If your triple bypass did not suggest that God made a mistake, then neither did my chest surgery. If the cream you use to change the pH of your skin does not suggest that God made a mistake, than neither does my testosterone. If the changes you made to your name, style, appearance and so on as you grew from childhood to adulthood does not suggest that God made a mistake, then neither did my social transition. Every single human being's body changed over time. And most human beings also change their own communicated identities and bodies over time in some way or another. That does not remove my belief that God 'knit me together' in the womb (where, by the way, my transness may stem from) or that my body is a temple. Rather, it means that I'm a pretty wonderful piece of handicraft, and it's only good and proper to renovate any living home of the divine's breath. We aren't mistakes. Stop, please.

Nature

An argument against trans people is often made from the perspective of what is 'natural'. This is another one that confuses and frustrates me. The binary of 'natural' and 'unnatural' is one of many false binaries that have become contemporary idols. There is no such clear distinction that can be made. Intersex people – people with chromosomes, sex characteristics or secondary sex characteristics that differ from the binary norm – exist. Trans people exist. Non-binary people exist.

And, more so, we see intersex, trans and non-binary existence across the spectrum of human and non-human animals and even plants. It is simply not possible to claim that it is 'unnatural' to be trans or non-binary.

Two arguments are vaguely possible. First, to discuss nature pre and then post something that is described by some as a 'fall' and, second, to discuss medical ethics. These questions go beyond 'natural' versus 'unnatural' to broader questions of what it means to be human, to be loved by God and to make decisions about our bodies and about how we function in the world. It is important to consider these questions, but not allow them to function as weapons against intersex, trans and non-binary people. We exist, we are the same muddled tangle of nature and synthesis as any other human or non-human animal.

The concept of 'fall' is one that is problematic in myriad ways that multiple theologians with significantly more knowledge and experience than me have expressed over the decades. Nevertheless, it is an idea that persists. So if the fall did exist, what would it mean for trans and non-binary people? To me, similarly to Star, it seems that the first human beings were non-binary or androgynous and that sexual distinction – such as it is – came later. It is even clearer that the human beings did not have a full understanding of sexual distinction until they realized that they were naked, existing without a sense of gender difference until that fateful apple. The supposed consequences of the so-called 'fall' are highly gendered. As such, the fall, if we must, would not rule out transness and non-binaryness but would, rather, point to the broken reality of a binary, hierarchical gender system.

The topic of medical ethics is a complicated one that stretches far beyond trans and non-binary folks. Any medical treatment can be argued to be 'unnatural' and, indeed, is by some. But again, I feel that this overly simplifies the meaning of 'natural'. Medical procedures utilize organic and synthetic materials, human intelligence, skill, touch and movement, and the body's own capacity to change and to heal. They are both natural and unnatural, both mundane and miraculous. Do careful decisions have to be made? Of course, for all of us, not only for trans and non-binary people.

The reality is that countless people have medical interventions every single day. Very few people will get through their lives without some form of intervention. For the majority of adults and young people above the age of Gillick competency,[2] clinical treatment is offered and carried out with the main case-by-case 'gatekeeping' being mostly in the form of informed consent, whereby the person is given all the available information about the procedure or medication and its risks and benefits and is then free to choose whether to accept the intervention or to say no. Conversely, trans and non-binary people are subject to years of invasive psychological testing and decision-making in order to access any form of gender-affirming care. Further, Gillick competency is not accepted in the case of trans and non-binary young people. To me, this clear discrimination, whereby trans and non-binary people are treated differently from everyone else, is a key question in medical ethics that ought to receive more attention than it does.

So am I natural? Yes. Am I also unnatural? Yes. And so are you, whoever you are.

Harm

Some of the most recent arguments against trans people are founded on the premise that we have an agenda and cause harm. The facets of this that I encounter most often are accusations of grooming, and of the erosion of safe public spaces. These accusations are never supported by anything more than anecdotal accounts and are often accompanied by a great deal of hyperbole. And yet they persist. I am often told by people who are otherwise very reasonable and caring that they are completely fine with trans and non-binary people, and support me, but that they are appalled by what 'we' are doing – insert violent misrepresentation here. While I accept that these people are genuinely concerned and are coming from a good place, I find it so hurtful that they believe what they read to such an extent that it erases all that they know about trans people through our conversations and shared lives.

Grooming

Trans and non-binary people are often accused of having a political agenda in relation to gender and of grooming young people to be trans and/or non-binary. That is not my experience of working with young people in a trans-affirming role, nor do I believe it to be possible. To address this, I think it important to consider three issues: education, identity and clinical care.

I have been involved in advocating for gendercreative children and young people in the education sector. Usually this has involved sessional work in schools with mixed groups of teachers and pupils. Once this also involved working on a one-to-one basis with a young person over the period of a school term. I have never advocated that young people 'should become' trans and/or non-binary. Nor have I seen any evidence that any other individual or organization has done so. To me, that would be both harmful and counterintuitive.

Being trans is not a fad, phase or choice. It is not cool. When people suggest that it is 'popular' among young people to be trans, I wonder if they have ever been in a school or other group setting with young people. Being different in any way is not cool, it's bloody hard work. Many children and young people who I have spoken to about being trans do not want to be trans. More often, it is a prospect that is somewhat frightening. Rather, children and young people want to understand what it is to be trans and/or non-binary so that they can support their trans and non-binary peers.

The individual I met with was a good example of the value of experimentation and the lack of grooming involved in good pastoral care work with gender-exploring young people. They thought they might be trans, so their school consulted me. I met with them over a period of six weeks and used whatever name and pronoun they asked me to and we simply talked about all sorts of things. At the end of our time together, they told me that they did not think that they were trans, and went back to using their birth name and pronouns. Was I disappointed? Not one bit. It was clear that some time to experiment and discuss had enabled that young person to gain confidence in their identity and live authentically. That is my hope for all young people, gendercreative, trans, non-binary and cis.

Safe public spaces

Safe public spaces are often cited as a central concern around trans rights, particularly in relation to debates around gender recognition – more specifically around whether trans people should have the right to self-determination in relation to their gender marker on official documents. These concerns often centre on spaces such as public bathrooms, changing rooms and prisons. They are about physical spaces rather than space in a more metaphorical sense.

Those who are keen to ban trans people from spaces that are correlated with our gender identity found their arguments on the implicit premise that gender-divided spaces are safe spaces. I disagree strongly with that premise. My experience of both attending and working in schools and youth spaces has suggested that gender-divided toilets and changing rooms are the nexus of bullying for trans and cis people alike. These spaces become normative and that normativity is policed socially. Gender-divided spaces – and indeed any space where people are segregated due to an aspect of biology or identity, because of who they are – are spaces that call out difference, rather than protecting those who are seen as different. In particular, I have spoken to many women who self-identify as 'butch' or have masculine physical traits who have experienced bullying, exclusion and even physical assault in gender-divided toilets and changing rooms.

My own experience, growing up assumed to be female, was that gender-divided spaces were not safe spaces. I experienced bullying verging on abuse and assault in gendered toilets and changing rooms throughout my childhood and young adulthood. I should stress that these experiences were not related to being trans – I was bullied precisely because I was using the gendered spaces supposedly appropriate to my sex and because other people of that sex did not want me there. I still experience anxiety using public toilets and changing rooms as a result, and use single stall spaces wherever possible.

Which points to the solution, does it not? Debates about trans and non-binary people in gendered spaces assume that gendered spaces, when 'correctly' policed, are safe and private. The problem is that they are not. Even if you ignore the experiences and concerns I have outlined above, having to pee and change in spaces where other people can see and hear private aspects of your body is not something that I feel we should accept. If people feel unsafe in multi-stall and/or no-stall public toilets and changing rooms, I do not blame them. They aren't safe spaces.

And so the solution must be to provide single-stall, lockable, completely private toilet and changing facilities wherever possible, each of which should include a bin, toilet and sink. That does not rely on gender-segregation but protects all people from harm. And do not even get me started on urinals … A terrible idea.

Transitioning (Again)

The final subject I address is that of so-called 'detransitioning'. 'Detransitioning' is a word that I find utterly inaccurate. It implies that something is being undone, whereas it is more accurate to suggest that, for some people, a further transition is desired or required. Some people use the term 'retransitioning' to describe this process. This, however, still implies a return to the pre-transition state and is therefore inaccurate. I wonder if a simple change to speaking about 'transitioning again' may be the most accurate and non-judgemental choice of language.

The reality that some people do transition again is often raised in debates about trans people, and it is a tricky one. However, the rhetoric shared often differs from the reality –

not least because the number of those who transition again is vanishingly small. I also believe, though, that the way in which transitioning again is spoken about exposes a broader problem in the ways we conceive of and discuss trans identities in church and in society more widely.

The obsession with detransition has, in my opinion, much to do with responses to trans bodies and, more particularly, the objectification of trans people; a belief in the importance of the body as a static item rather than a malleable aspect of human personhood. The belief in the body as absolute immutable fact leads to the reification of body parts. This is often correlated with sexism and/or internalized sexism. For example, there are countless social media accounts that exist solely to share stolen photos of transmasculine people's chests post-top surgery and to cite this practice as a mutilation of 'healthy breasts', which are, therefore, reified and sexualized.

People who have 'transitioned again' are subject to this objectification in the form of the belief that having one's body altered and then altered again, but not returned to its initial state, is a particularly horrific situation to be in. They are objectified doubly by being instrumentalized as a tool of anti-trans rhetoric, sometimes for financial or political gain. If, instead of objectifying trans and non-binary people by attaching their worth to embodiment, we saw the entire person, then it would be easier to accept that people do change, in mind, identity and body, repeatedly over the course of life.

Objectification often includes the control of the object by the active player in any given situation. As explored earlier in this chapter, trans and non-binary people are objectified in the way that our informed consent is not respected in relation to gender-affirming care. In any clinical treatment, informed consent does not rule out the person subsequently regretting the treatment and wishing they had not given their consent. This is not considered as invalidating the treatment or suggesting that it should not have been offered. Rather, the individual concerned has exercised their own bodily autonomy and experiences the consequences of the decisions that they, both rightly and alone, have the authority to make.

Further, regret is not experienced by all the people who transition more than once. I know three people who have 'transitioned again'. In one case, the person cannot take gender-affirming hormone replacement therapy due to clinical incompatibility, and ultimately found it too hard to identify and live in a gender identity that others repeatedly failed to recognize. In another case, the person was removed from their home and ostracized from their family, faith community and friendship circle due to transitioning. Sadly for them, due to transphobic hatred, transitioning again felt like the only way to live a liveable life. Finally, I know a person who transitioned and lived happily in their gender for decades before transitioning again for the latter part of their life. None of those three people regrets transition or uses the word 'detransition'. Instead, they recognize the complexities of the world in which they live and have followed paths that enable each of them, as individuals with particular circumstances, to live as fully as they may.

I feel strongly about narratives of 'detransition' in part because I have experienced being labelled as a 'detransitioner' and having my identity and choices questioned as a result. I originally transitioned to male and transitioned again to non-binary. This change in self-understanding did not lead to me regretting any of the clinical procedures that I have undergone, nor have I stopped taking testosterone. It did, however, alter my ongoing clinical plan and the way I describe and present myself. People often meet this reality with 'What if?' questions. The answer is that at each moment I discern decisions that will enable me to live life to the fullest extent possible at that time, with the full knowledge that a different decision might be necessary in order to do that again at a different time. I believe that all people should be free to autonomously make choices, even those choices that may seem to be in internal contradiction to another person who is assessing our lived experiences from outside us.

None of the above denies the fact that some people do transition again, some of them do identify with the term 'detransition', and some of them have regrets and share those regrets publicly. Nevertheless, I fully support their right to bodily autonomy both in transition and in subsequent transitions and detransitions. They deserve appropriate respect and care. They do not deserve to be used as a reason to remove care based on informed consent from every other trans and non-binary person. We are all human beings, all individuals, and each of us has the right to make our own choices about our bodies and our lives.

A conclusion after the conclusion: being the body

How to conclude after I've already concluded is a tricky one. Is there still more to say? It feels like it really matters where our journey together as writer and reader ends. Throughout this process of research and writing, several key principles have remained important. Many of them were described at the beginning of this book. Four things in particular have become increasingly important throughout this four-year process. These were not considerations that I was previously unaware of, but realities I hadn't really focused on as key considerations in my prior life or, indeed, in previous writing:

1 Bodies matter
2 Authenticity matters
3 Peer groups matter
4 No one should have to debate their identity with others.

Bodies matter

And that includes trans and non-binary bodies. Being trans and/or non-binary doesn't suddenly disembody us. Nor does it separate our body from our mind in some form of Cartesian split. Church and society ought to explore the realities of being fleshy a whole lot more. I wonder how you relate to your body?

Authenticity matters

And that includes trans and non-binary authenticity. Being trans and/or non-binary should not remove our freedom to express our authentic selves to our peers, communities and the world. Nor should we be treated poorly, abused or marginalized for doing so. Church and society ought to support people to express themselves more authentically. I wonder what your authentic truths are?

Peer groups matter

Including for trans and non-binary Christians. Prior to this research and writing, I lacked a peer group. Now, together, we have challenged, affirmed, queried and mirrored each other. I have not been left unchanged. Rather, I am transformed and transforming. Church and society ought to recognize the importance of peer support. I wonder who your unknown peers are?

No one should have to debate their identity with others

And I am done with it. God loves me, exactly as I am. God loves you, exactly as you are. God's grace is never limited or withheld. Church, this shouldn't be a complicated truth to accept, celebrate and share. I wonder how you experience God's love? I wonder how you might share it?

This book is entitled *Trans Formations* not only because trans and non-binary people are, indeed, transformed, transforming and transformational. Additionally, my formation for not only ministry but also life has been massively grown by the amazing trans and non-binary people who I have conducted this research with, and continues to grow and to flower with the support and companionship of the countless trans and non-binary people who are now a part of my huge, extended chosen family. I honour each one of you, and I honour our transformational web of connections and dialogue. I am close to done with speaking about my own transness and non-binaryness, and yet I will continue to do everything I can, as an individual member of Christ's interconnected body who happens to be trans and non-binary, to centre your voices and protect your rights in church and society for as long as such efforts are needed. Not in my own power but by the grace of God. May it be so. Amen.

Notes

1 Spoons refer to units of energy in spoon theory, which was coined by Christine Miserandino to describe experiences of fatigue correlated with chronic illness and/or disability.

2 Gillick competency refers to the point in medical law at which a child has reached the maturity required to make decisions about their own healthcare. It is used to determine when a child can make their own informed consent without the consent of a parent or guardian.

Postlude

Euphoria – Mike

In terms of my personal journey, I can only say that I've been led by the idea of gender euphoria and the idea of what feels right; what feels congruent with who I am internally, externally, psychologically, emotionally. I guess my story is not the classic trans narrative, where people assume that all trans people have always known that they were trans from a young age and things like that. I think for me that sense was there, but it wasn't so prominent or intense. It didn't feel like something I had to act on or pursue. I mean, I remember asking my mum if I could be a boy, but I asked it in a really theoretical, hypothetical way, as kids do. From her response, I understood that that was something that society would frown on. That was the end of the conversation for me at that point.

It was like, 'OK, well, I guess I'll just be a girl.' Honestly, I probably could have lived a kind of average OK life that way. But then, when I realized I was bisexual, it meant that I stopped living for the male gaze for the first time and started dressing and presenting more authentically and inhabiting masculinity more. I guess I felt like I was able to do that. And the more I did that, the more the gender feelings became quite pertinent, and I sensed there was something else at work there.

For me the journey, at least at the start, wasn't led by dysphoria. It was about finding things that made me feel good. It was about the fact that the first time I tried on a binder, I felt like I could breathe. It was about being in a space where people weren't assuming my gender for the first time. It felt very freeing, and it was following those breadcrumbs of delight that led me to my final realization and the point where I am now.

More recently, with transition and things like that, the first steps out of the closet were particularly hard. Being visibly trans, or in any way not conforming to people's notions of gender in public, was very hard. It was a gruelling experience for me, it was a really hard time to navigate and to get through. That was a rough period. I really had to dig deep into self-affirmation to get through that time and into trying to divest from cis-normative concepts of gender and working hard to affirm myself in a society that didn't see me as I was.

My relationship with faith feels quite ambiguous at the moment because it's certainly shifted over the last four years since I first came out as a queer person. I think it is partly because there is not really room for queer or LGBT Christians in the church. I mean, there are spaces, and there are corners, and there are shadows, and there are fringe groups, which I have been part of, which I'm still part of and which I do think are really important. I do not say that to be dismissive of them, but I think that really the experience of realizing the hypocrisy of most churches and most Christians, and the ways that the church enshrines a lot of injustice structurally, has been a real reflection point for me.

Because I think it takes me to a place of thinking, 'What is this all about? What's the point of all of this? Like, what is the purpose?' If you talk about love, but you are structurally harming people, I think it takes me to those kinds of big questions like, 'What's the substance here?' Simultaneously, I think I've started to have broader theological questions, partly through queerness, but I think also partly through being Black as well. Questions around the Bible or interpretations of it and questions around the personhood of like Jesus and God. I guess that it's a hodgepodge right now, lots of reflections on where things have been abused or misused or in harmful ways. I guess I am trying to decide whether there is anything still good, whether there is still something valuable here, or whether it all needs to go. I currently feel like there is something good. I currently feel like I do not want to throw the baby out with the bathwater. I still have a lot of questions.

I think the other thing as well was that growing up, my spirituality was very built on spiritual experiences and feeling God's presence and things like that. And I haven't had that for years. I have it occasionally every now and again, but I haven't had that feeling really for years. I think, again, that's another part of feeling so disconnected from faith or certainly engaging with it in a different way. I think maybe we're getting to the hard part of the heart of the issue, which is that it feels a bit like ... this sounds dramatic, but it feels a bit like God abandoned me.

It feels a bit like, well, 'What happened?' I went from feeling very close to God to, for quite a long time now, not feeling that. What is that about? And particularly when there's been some very painful and difficult things to navigate in that time and feeling like God is not close. I think that's another aspect of my spirituality at the moment, and my faith. I'm just a bit like 'What's going on?'

I think that my concerns are probably less about specific passages and perhaps more about certain themes, or motifs. For example, what are the consequences of the idea that the Old Testament God is big, scary, and then the New Testament God is loving and kind again? And passages that talk about like sexual morality, I do not really know how you could or would redeem those because, first of all, I do not think there's a coherent sex ethic in the Bible anyway, but secondly, from the bits that are there, I do not really agree with them and I do not think that they are healthy, which feels like a very scary thing to say as someone who grew up evangelical and it's God's word and there's not really room to question those things.

I guess I mentioned the sexual and morality passages in particular because I think that has been significant to me, and my journey of coming out has been moving away from that sense of regret, like repressing things and desires, that part of me, and realizing that actually there's a lot of life and fullness in being authentic to those things, obviously within respectful and consensual boundaries.

But I think that it probably does go even wider than that to the concept of sin and salvation and what that means, which again feels like the crux of some forms of Christianity. I do not agree with the way most churches handle sin. I do not agree with sin being seen as this thing on a personal level. I think that's where the idea of repression and like being guilt-ridden and things like that comes in. So much of the way that people have spoken about sin and salvation is very individual. I think the lenses through which I view the world now are very structural and thinking about structural patterns of injustice and oppression.

I think that we can hold people accountable for the ways in which they partake in systemic oppression. I just think, from what I read and understood about sin in the Bible, I do not think that Christianity speaks enough to structures of power. While I think how we treat people on a personal and individual level and our interpersonal politics are important, for sure, I think I struggle with how it's not hugely apparent in terms of looking at structural systems or certainly not in the way that the church talks about things. Otherwise it wouldn't partake in some of those structural injustices. That makes no sense to me. The Bible has been used a lot to kind of prop up structural injustice.

At the moment I would find myself inclined to agree that church is the opiate of the masses in the form that it currently takes where it's a bit of Sunday comfort for people and it gives people some meaning. And those things aren't wrong at all. I support them and I actually strangely enough do feel called to be a minister someday. I do feel like an important part of ministry is pastoral care and looking after people. But I also think that the Church is so insular at the moment in terms of the conversations it's having, in terms of the vision it has. It's always about making more people Christian or it's about doing good on a very individual level. It feels like it's not really connecting the dots in terms of, OK, so the church helps run a food bank, but why is there a need for a food bank? It feels like the church doesn't ask those questions.

I think partly that's because of some of the class interests of some of the people who are in the church. I think that's one of my issues with it at the moment. I think the other thing is a lack of integrity, and hypocrisy, which is such an obvious thing to say, but I think from a queer perspective, having seen it so close up where, the church that I grew up in people there were very

... there for me and very kind of present. As soon as I came out as queer that vanished, and similarly, even among some of the more progressive parts of the church, I know ministers who are LGBT-affirming, but do not want to say anything because it's going to cost them something. I just see so many layers of like people preaching saying 'Speak the truth in love' on a Sunday morning, but they cannot say it themselves, or people preaching about love, but then being very callous and unbothered by the harm done to LGBT people.

Honestly, in the end there's so much that the church could learn from trans perspectives and a trans lens on theology. It's really frustrating that it gets stuck in apologetics because there's a real liberty that comes when you start to unpick gender, because gender can be so informative of how we live our lives. I think it's probably part of the reason why the church has just ignored trans people. I think that anything that seems to challenge binaries is something that the church doesn't know what to do with.

Appendix 1:
The Theology in Theory

When concluding my PhD thesis, I shared two summaries of the theological material that had arisen from our views. The first version was theoretical, explaining the views in recognized academic language. I share this version below.

God is participative. God is fully gendered and fully without gender. God is flesh and spirit.

God cannot be fully defined or explained. Nevertheless, we desire to understand God. This causes us to separate ourselves from God and examine them, creating theological theory. This, however, limits our understandings and descriptions of God.

Theological certainty leads to a 'them and us' dynamic, wherein those whose views are considered unorthodox are subject to attack. It becomes difficult to question or challenge inherited theological understandings. Questions feel threatening.

We mirror each other. That mirroring enables us to begin to question our understandings of anthropology and theology and to be open to transformation. We need the other – the one who is both similar and differentiated – to enable accurate mirroring. However, the assumption of both a Cartesian split of mind from body, and a temporal split wherein we disown our past selves, creates barriers to authenticity.

When we hear the stories of trans and non-binary people in their own words, moving beyond assumption, we learn that trans bodies and minds, pasts and presents, are not split but congruent. This congruence indicates a process of continual becoming. It defies the logic of binary categorization.

Being open to continual becoming allows us to fully participate in God's dance of creation. Mirroring enables us to enter into dialogue with others and to form communities of likeness and distinction. The instinct to categorize can hamper these processes.

The recognition of the authentic self by the other is essential to congruent personhood. We receive our personhood from the other who recognizes us even as we recognize them. This is how we mirror each other – it is a reciprocal process. This mutual recognition helps us to begin to glimpse the problematic orthodoxies and missing elements in our partial theological constructions.

We cannot become our full selves in isolation; we rely on dialogue partners who see us as we truly are and show us the beauty and potential in the parts of ourselves that we have tried to hide away.

Only once we can see the other as they truly are and accept both ourselves and the other can we begin to see that our theological understandings are never complete in and of themselves and, therefore, deconstruct problematic theological constructions.

Together, we can approach deconstruction. That does not mean throwing out inherited traditional and theological understandings or devaluing them. Rather, it means recognizing their use as components that must be reconsidered in the light of new contexts and knowledge.

Deconstruction allows us to fully recognize the participative nature of God and to participate in turn. God is creative, inspirational and wounded. We must recognize God in the wounded other, allow God to inspire change, and co-create with God.

Appendix 2:
An Open Table Communion Liturgy

Many readers will be a part of a church or other community of faith. At the time of writing, I am co-chair of the Open Table Network, a network of local Christian communities facilitating safer, braver spaces for LGBTQ+ folks around a communion table. I have written this liturgy to honour them, to acknowledge some of the teachings in my conversations with trans kin, and to enable churches to repent of transphobia and honour the trans people in their midst.

Welcome *(written or spoken)*

Welcome to this time where we will share in God's meal together. We are taking some time and space today to focus on trans and non-binary people. Some of us who join together are trans and non-binary. Many of us love and support people who are trans and non-binary. Some of us come with a history of ignorance and transphobia. All of us live in a world where trans and non-binary people are not given much time and space where they – we – are not debated, not rejected, not merely tolerated but, instead, celebrated exactly as we are. And so during this meal each of us is welcomed, celebrated and honoured as God's guest, created as a reflection of, and continually being shaped more and more into, God's holy image.

Gathering

Out the dirt and the dust and the mud of a nascent world, God created *ha'adam* – humanity – in their image. From masculine to feminine, from androgynous to genderqueer, from diversity to diversity God created us. *(Words inspired by Genesis 1.27)*

God we come to you with dirt under our fingernails and a thirst in our throat.
You shaped us from mud and, touching your lips to our own, breathed your life into us.
God of dust and dirt, thirst and breath, we gather.

God, we come to you with dysphoria in our skin and euphoria in our blood,
with bodies stretching and growing and changing by hormones and hand.
We come with wonder and admiration, with love and with care, with respect and with nurture.
God of all folks, trans, non-binary and cis, we gather.

God, we gather at a meal, hungry or full, in faith or in doubt, in trust or in terror.
We want to believe your welcome,
and yet humans have often made us feel unwelcome.
We want to love each other, and yet we have often experienced hatred.
God of grace, whether we are ready or not, we gather.

Thanksgiving

Let no one suggest that we are like dead, withering wood and should be cut off, excluded. Because God will give us their home, its walls a memorial to us and a name better than binaries. God will give us a name of freedom that will last for ever. *(Isaiah 56.5)*

God, we are alive, green, new, here …
We thank you for new names, reshaped bodies, reclaimed narratives.

Creator, we are clay, malleable, real, messy …
We thank you for imperfection, scars, journeys.

Christ, we are your kindred, siblings, body, broken …
We thank you for being with us in an authentic way.

Spirit, we are inspired, attempting, creating, uncertain …
We thank you for stirring up all sorts of emotions.

Letting go

Of one thing I am certain: each of us regrets something. Some of us have been unkind, confused, unknowing or intentional. Some of us have been stalling, afraid, hurt, beaten down or angry. Let's spend a moment letting go.

I invite you to sit comfortably, to consider closing your eyes if you feel safe and willing to do so, and to breathe with me.

(Facilitator, say slowly, one word per second):
In-two-three-four-out-two-three-four-five-pause.
In-two-three-four-out-two-three-four-five-pause.
In-two-three-four-out-two-three-four-five-pause.
In-two-three-four-out-two-three-four-five-pause.
In-two-three-four-out-two-three-four-five-pause.
We bring to mind those things we would like to let go of,
to let God take care of. *(Pause)*
We imagine them floating up from our hands like clouds.
(Pause)
They gather above our heads as a storm cloud. *(Pause)*
As we let go, rain begins to fall. *(Pause)*
It is refreshing, it feels cool, it tastes sweet. *(Pause)*
Above us, the cloud grows lighter and lighter, fading to reveal the bright blue sky. *(Pause)*

God's rainbow shines brightly. We are loved. We are
witnesses to grace. We are free.
Let's gradually come back into the room. Wiggle if you need
to, stretch if you need to. Open your eyes when you are
ready.

Invitation

We cannot invite God into this space because God is already
here and God is waiting for us, ready to invite us to a feast.
There is not much food. There is not even a whole lot to drink.
What there is is love, grace, acceptance and celebration for
everyone who wants to remember Jesus' lived-out justice, and
live in Christ's new, just, euphoric, better world.
We are kindred of God, beloved simply because we are human,
celebrated because God drenches us in grace. This meal doesn't
fit into the binary logic of the world. It doesn't quite belong
in heaven or on earth. This meal is part of God's queer logic,
which breathes beyond binaries and loves beyond judgement.
Jesus invites all who are a part of Christ's body to put Jesus'
justice back together again by eating and drinking in the way
that Jesus did, instead of buying and selling in the way that we
so often do. And so God invites us to their meal, where binaries
are broken, where tables are turned, where all are beloved.

Peace

And although the invitation comes without exceptions or
limits, it's always more fun to eat with those who we love,
so it is good to make peace with each other.
The peace of God be always with you.
And also with you.
We share the peace of God in ways that respect and honour
each other, asking each other if we would prefer a handshake,
a hug or a namaste; respecting those who prefer to simply close
their eyes and breathe in God's peace.

The big story

> In the just, euphoric, better world of God there is diversity
> and unity: of faith, of culture and, yes, of gender, because the
> body of Christ contains all of us. *(Words inspired by Gal-*
> *atians 3.28)*

The body of Christ was there in the beginning, both clay and
potter, both human and divine, both dawn and dusk.
The body of Christ was there in the prophets, both truth
and courage, both anger and righteousness, both holiness
and doubt.
The body of Christ was there in Jesus, both justice and peace,
both creator and created, both broken and free.
The body of Christ was there on the cross, both wounded and
healer, both scarred and beautiful, both forgiven and forgiver.
And so we remember together:
Christ is born, Christ is stilled. Christ rises up.

The body of Christ was there in resurrection, both present
and transcendent, both the same and changed, both known
and unknowable.
The body of Christ is here in us, both trans and cis, both
non-binary and binary, both flesh and spirit.
And so we raise our voices together:
Holy, holy, holy God, from the very beginning until the very
end. Heaven and earth are full of your stories. Hosannah!

The table story *(Words inspired by Mark 14)*

On a day of festival and sacrifice, of remembrance, storytelling
and protest, Jesus' kin – the chosen family he travelled around
with – asked him: 'Where do you want us to go and make the
preparations for you to eat the Passover?' So he sent two of his
disciples, saying to them, 'Go into the city, and a man carrying
a jar of water – transgressing gender in doing so – will meet

you; follow them, and wherever they enter, say to the owner of the house, "The Teacher asks: 'Where is my guest room where I may eat the Passover with my kindred?'" The owner will show you a large room upstairs, furnished and ready. Make preparations for us there.' So the disciples set out and went to the city and found everything as he had told them, and they prepared the Passover meal.

When it was evening, Jesus joined them. And when each person had taken their places and were eating, Jesus said, 'Truly I tell you, one of you will betray me, one who is eating with me.' They began to be distressed and to say to Jesus one after another, 'Surely, not I?' Jesus said to them, 'It is one of the twelve, my kin, one who is dipping bread into the bowl with me. For humans betray each other, do they not?'

While they were eating, he took the bread, and after blessing it he broke it, gave it to them, and said, 'Take; this is my body.' Then he took a cup, and after giving thanks he gave it to them, and all of them drank from it. He said to them, 'This is my blood of the covenant, the new promise, which is poured out for many. Truly I tell you, I will never again drink of the fruit of the vine until that day when I drink it new in God's new, just, euphoric, better world.' Even as Jesus did this, Christ knew that not one, but two of their chosen kin would betray them. Judas, who sold Jesus out, and Peter, who denied Jesus' lived reality.

The sharing

And so let's eat, building up our memory of what it means to be part of the body of Christ.
And so let's drink, mourning the ways we have betrayed and been betrayed, and swallowing the liquid truth of God's promised grace.

Our stories and their stories

There are people who live beyond the binary boundaries of
sex and gender because of the facts of their birth, because of
the experiences of their lives, because of the calling of God,
because of God's new, just, euphoric, better world. You
should accept this. *(Words inspired by Matthew 19.12)*

Thanks be to God for these gifts beyond words.
Let's pray, lifting up our own stories and the stories of people
around the world.
In the vast potential of your mercy and grace,
Inspire us, transform us, reconcile us.

Where there is conflict ... *(Silence)*
Where there is binary debate ... *(Silence)*
Where there is oppression ...*(Silence)*
Where there is protest ... *(Silence)*
Where there is pain ... *(Silence)*
Where there is too much silence ... *(Silence)*
Where there is too much noise ... *(Silence)*

We say together:
Creator and Kin, as near as breath,
And yet far beyond our understanding,
holy is your name, your new reality come,
your justice be done, here and now.
May we feed each other, as you feed us.
You hold us in grace when we do not 'get it'.
May we hold others in grace too.
May we resist complacency,
and strive for justice and peace,
For all people, and all times. Amen.

Dispersing

What is to stop us from being blessed, so that we might go on our way rejoicing? *(Words inspired by Acts 8.26–39)*

We go with the blessing of Abba, Imma,* Creator,
To live creatively, for a just world.

We go with the blessing of Christ, Kindred,
To live honestly, for a peace-filled world.

We go with the blessing of the Spirit, Breath,
To love each other, and all of God's children.
Amen

---

*abba – father; imma – mother

Bibliography

Abraham, Amelia, 'Exploring the cult appeal of Maggie Nelson with the writer herself', in *Daze Digital* (2019), https://www.dazeddigital.com/life-culture/article/45446/1/cult-writer-maggie-nelson-interview-the-argonauts-jane-a-murder (accessed 25 February 2022).

Ahmed, Sarah, *Living a Feminist Life* (Durham, NC: Duke University Press, 2017).

Althaus, Paul, tr. Schultz, Robert C., *The Theology of Martin Luther* (Philadelphia, PA: Fortress Press, 1966).

Althaus-Reid, Marcella (ed.), *Liberation Theology and Sexuality* (London: Taylor & Francis, 2009).

Althaus-Reid, Marcella and Isherwood, Lisa, *Trans/Formations* (London: SCM Press, 2009).

Althaus-Reid, Marcella, *Indecent Theology* (London: Routledge, 2001).

Althaus-Reid, Marcella and Isherwood, Lisa, *Controversies in Feminist Theology* (London: SCM Press, 2007).

Anderson, Leon, 'Analytic Autoethnography', *Journal of Contemporary Ethnography*, 35, 4 (2006), pp. 373–95, https://doi.org/10.1177/0891241605280449 (accessed 25 February 2022).

Anselm, St, *Basic Writings: Proslogium; Monologium; Gaunilo's In Behalf of the Fool; Cur Deus Homo* (La Salle, IL: Open Court, 1962).

Armour, Ellen T., 'Transing the Study of Religion: A (Christian) Theological Response', *Journal of Feminist Studies in Religion*, 34, 1 (2018), pp. 58–63, https://doi.org/10.2979/jfemistudreli.34.1.07 (accessed 25 February 2022).

Austin, Ashley, Craig, Shelly L., D'Souza, Sandra and McInroy, Lauren B., 'Suicidality Among Transgender Youth: Elucidating the Role of Interpersonal Risk Factors', *Journal of Interpersonal Violence*, 37, 5–6, pp. 1–23, https://doi.org/10.1177/0886260520915554 (accessed 10 March 2022).

Badenhorst, Cecile, Arif, Abu and Quintyne, Kelvin, 'Doctoral writing and the politics of citation Use', *Discourse and Writing/Rédactologie*, 32, 1 (2022).

Barnsley, Jennie, 'Grounded Theology: Adopting and Adapting Qualitative Research Methods for Feminist Theological Enquiry', *Feminist Theology*, 24, 2 (2016), pp. 109–24, https://doi.org/10.1177/0966735015612175 (accessed 30 May 2022).

Barnsley, Jennie, 'Grounding Theology in quotidian experiences of complex gender: a feminist approach: PhD' (Birmingham: University of Birmingham, 2013), https://etheses.bham.ac.uk/id/eprint/4188/ (accessed 25 February 2022).

BBC, 'Germaine Greer: Transgender Women are not Women', BBC News Online (2015), https://www.bbc.co.uk/news/av/uk-34625512/germaine-greer-transgender-women-are-not-women (accessed 25 February 2022).

Beagan, Brenda L. and Hattie, Brenda, 'Religion, Spirituality, and LGBTQ Identity Integration', *Journal of LGBT Issues in Counselling*, 9, 2 (2015) pp. 92–117, https://doi.org/10.1080/15538605.2015.1029204 (accessed 25 February 2022).

Beardsley, Christina and O'Brien, Michelle, *This is My Body: Hearing the Theology of Transgender Christians* (London: Darton, Longman & Todd, 2016).

Beischel, Will J., Gauvin, Stéphanie E. M. and Anders, Sari M. van, 'A little shiny gender breakthrough: Community understandings of gender euphoria', *International Journal of Transgender Health*, 23, 3 (2021), http://dx.doi.org/10.1080/26895269.2021.1915223 (accessed 11 March 2022).

Belkhir, Meriam, Brouard, Myriam, Brunk, Katja H., Dalmoro, Marlon, Ferreira, Marcia Christina, Figueiredo, Bernardo, Huff, Aimee Dinnin, Scaraboto, Daiane, Sibai, Olivier and Smith, Andrew N., 'Isolation in Globalizing Academic Fields: A Collaborative Autoethnography of Early Career Researchers', *Academy of Management Learning and Education*, 18, 2 (2019), https://journals.aom.org/doi/full/10.5465/amle.2017.0329 (accessed 23 September 2022).

Bell-Metereau, Rebecca, *Transgender Cinema* (New Brunswick, NJ: Rutgers University Press, 2019).

Benson, Kristen, Westerfield, Eli and van Eeden-Moorefield, Brad, 'Transgender people's reflections on identity, faith, and Christian faith communities in the U.S.', *Sexual and Relationship Therapy*, 33, 4 (2018) pp. 395–420, https://doi.org/10.1080/14681994.2018.1472375 (accessed 25 February 2022).

Berk, Ronald A., 'Microaggressions Trilogy: Part 1. Why do microaggressions matter?', *The Journal of Faculty Development*, 31, 1 (2017), pp. 63–73, https://www.proquest.com/docview/1907273559?sourcetype=Scholarly%20Journals (accessed 25 February 2022).

Bettcher, Talia Mae, 'Trans Identities and First-Person Authority', in Shrage, Laurie (ed.) *You've Changed: Sex Reassignment and Personal Identity* (Oxford: Oxford University Press, 2009), pp. 98–120.

Bindel, Julie, 'Gender Benders Beware', *The Guardian* (1 January 2004), https://www.theguardian.com/world/2004/jan/31/gender.weekend7 (accessed 25 February 2022).

TRANS *FORMATIONS*

Birks, Melanie and Mills, Jane, *Grounded Theory: A Practical Guide* (Thousand Oaks, CA: Sage Publications, 2011).

Blumer, Herbert, *Symbolic Interactionism: Perspective and Method* (Englewood Cliffs, NJ: Prentice Hall, 1969).

Bockting, Walter O., 'Transforming the paradigm of transgender health: a field in transition', *Sexual and Relationship Therapy*, 24, 2 (2009), pp. 103–7, https://doi.org/10.1080/14681990903037660 (accessed 25 February 2022).

Boersma, Hans, 'Calvin and the extent of the Atonement', *Evangelical Quarterly*, 64, 4 (1992), pp. 333–55, https://mail.biblicalstudies.org.uk/pdf/eq/1992-4_333.pdf (accessed 25 February 2022).

Bolz-Weber, Nadia, *Pastrix: The Cranky, Beautiful Faith of a Sinner and Saint* (New York: Worthy Publishing, 2014).

Bolz-Weber, Nadia, *Shameless* (Norwich: Canterbury Press, 2019).

Bornstein, Kate and Bergman, S. Bear, *Gender Outlaws* (Berkeley, CA: Seal Press, 2010).

Bornstein, Kate, *My New Gender Workbook* (Abingdon: Routledge, 2013).

Boylan, Jennifer Finney, 'Throwing our Voices', in Erickson-Schroth, Laura (ed.), *Trans Bodies, Trans Selves: A Resource for the Transgender Community* (Oxford: Oxford University Press, 2014), pp. xv–xviii.

Brennan, Samantha, '*The Argonauts*: Review', *Kennedy Institute of Ethics Journal*, 26, 3 (2016), pp. 19–22, https://doi.org/10.1353/ken.2016.0029 (accessed 25 February 2022).

British Association for Counselling and Psychotherapy, 'Memorandum of Understanding on Conversion Therapy in the UK, Version 2', *BACP* (2021), https://www.bacp.co.uk/media/13265/memorandum-of-understanding-on-conversion-therapy-in-the-uk-september-2021.pdf (accessed 25 February 2022).

Brosnan, Mark and Mills, Elizabeth, 'The effect of diagnostic labels on the affective responses of college students towards peers with "Asperger's Syndrome" and "Autism Spectrum Disorder"', *Autism*, 20, 4 (2016), pp. 388–94, https://doi-org.ezproxyd.bham.ac.uk/10.1177%2F1362361315586721 (accessed 9 March 2022).

Brown, Jonathan, 'Transgender teacher sought protection from intrusive press coverage', *The Independent* (23 March 2013), https://www.proquest.com/newspapers/transgender-teacher-sought-protection-intrusive/docview/1318868442/ (accessed 3 April 2022).

Brueggemann, Walter, 'Testimony that Breaks the Silence of Totalism', *Interpretation: A Journey of Bible and Theology*, 70, 3 (2016), pp. 275–87, http://dx.doi.org/10.1177/0020964316640506 (accessed 2 December 2021).

Bryan, Audrey and Mayock, Paula, 'Supporting LGBT Lives? Complicating the suicide consensus in LGBT mental health research',

Sexualities, 20, 1–2 (2017), pp. 65–85, https://doi.org/10.1177/1363
460716648099 (accessed 9 March 2022).

Bulmer, Martin, *The Chicago School of Sociology: Institutionalization, Diversity and the Rise of Sociological Research* (Chicago, IL: University of Chicago Press, 1984).

Burgoyne, Mindie, 'What is a thin place?' (2007), www.thinplaces.net/openingarticle.htm (accessed 24 September 2022).

Burnier, DeLysa, 'Encounters With the Self in Social Science Research: A Political Scientist Looks at Autoethnography', *Journal of Contemporary Ethnography*, 35, 4 (2006), pp. 410–18, https://doi.org/10.1177/0891241606286982 (accessed 9 March 2022).

Buser, Juleen K., Goodrich, Kristopher M., Luke, Melissa and Buser, Trevor J., 'A Narratology of Lesbian, Gay, Bisexual, and Transgender Clients' Experiences Addressing Religious and Spiritual Issues in Counseling', *Journal of LGBT Issues in Counseling*, 5, 3–4 (2011), pp. 282–303, https://doi.org/10.1080/15538605.2011.632395 (accessed 9 March 2022).

Butler, Judith, *Gender Trouble* (London: Routledge, 1990/2007).

Butler, Judith, *Undoing Gender* (Abingdon: Routledge, 2004).

Butler, Judith, *Bodies That Matter: On the Discursive Limits of 'Sex'* (London: Taylor & Francis, 2014).

Calvin, John, tr. Beveridge, Henry, *Institutes of the Christian Religion* (London: James Clarke, 1962).

Campbell, Mitchell R., 'The substantial effect of microaggressions', *Talent Development*, 74, 11 (2020) 58–63, https://www.proquest.com/trade-journals/substantial-effect-microaggressions/docview/2457731498/ (accessed 10 March 2022).

Caprioglio, Teresa, 'Does "Queer Narrative" Mean "Trauma Narrative" on TV? Exploring Television's Traumatized Queer Identity', *Journal of Trauma & Dissociation*, 22, 4 (2021), pp. 452–64, https://doi.org/10.1080/15299732.2021.1925865 (accessed 11 March 2022).

Chalke, Steve, *The Gender Agenda: Towards a Biblical Theology on Gender Identity, Reassignment and Confirmation* (London: Oasis Books, 2018).

Charmaz, Kathleen M., *Constructing Grounded Theory: A Practical Guide through Qualitative Analysis* (Thousand Oaks, CA: Sage Publications, 2006).

Charmaz, Kathleen M., 'Grounded Theory Methods in Social Justice Research', in Denzin, Norman K. and Lincoln, Yvonne S. (eds), *The Sage Handbook of Qualitative Research* (Thousand Oaks, CA: Sage Publications, 2011), pp. 359–80.

Carroll, Lewis, *Through the Looking-Glass, and What Alice Found There* (Minneapolis, MN: Lerner Publishing Group, 2016), p. 51.

Church of England, 'What we Believe', https://www.churchofengland.

org/our-faith/what-we-believe/apostles-creed#na (accessed 10 March 2022).

Claassens, Juliana M. Mourner, *Mother, Midwife: Reimagining God's Delivering Presence in the Old Testament* (Louisville, KY: Westminster John Knox, 2012).

Clare-Young, Alex, 'Towards a Theology of Trans Personhood': MPhil Dissertation (Cambridge: University of Cambridge, 2018).

Clare-Young, Alex, *Transgender. Christian. Human* (Glasgow: Wild Goose, 2019).

Clare-Young, Alex, 'Book Review: Owen Strachan, Mark A. Yarhouse, Julia Sadusky, Megan K. DeFranza and Justin Sabia-Tanis, *Understanding Transgender Identities: Four Views*', *Anglican Theological Journal*, 103, 3 (2021), https://doi.org/10.1177/00033286211017127 (accessed 28 May 2022).

Clark-King, Ellen, 'The Divine Call to Be Myself: Anglican Transgender Women and Prayer', *Anglican Theological Review*, 98, 2 (2016), pp. 331–9, https://doi.org/10.1177/000332861609800208 (accessed 10 March 2022).

Comstock, Gary David and Henking, Susan E., *Que(e)rying Religion* (New York: Continuum, 1997).

Cone, James, *A Black Theology of Liberation* (New York: Orbis, 1970).

Conroy, Melissa, 'Treating Transgendered Children: Clinical Methods and Religious Mythology', *Zygon*, 45, 2 (2010), pp. 301–16, https://doi.org/10.1111/j.1467-9744.2010.01082.x (accessed 10 March 2022).

Cornick, David, *Under God's Good Hand* (London: The United Reformed Church, 1998).

Cornwall, Susannah, *Controversies in Queer Theology* (London: SCM Press, 2011).

Cornwall, Susannah, 'Recognizing the Full Spectrum of Gender? Transgender, Intersex and the Futures of Feminist Theology', *Feminist Theology*, 20, 3 (2012), pp. 236–41, https://doi.org/10.1177%2F0966735012436895 (accessed 10 March 2022).

Cornwall, Susannah, 'Healthcare Chaplaincy and Spiritual Care for Trans People: Envisaging the Future', *Health and Social Care Chaplaincy*, 7, 1 (2019), pp. 8–27, http://dx.doi.org/10.1558/hscc.37227 (accessed 25 February 2022).

Cornwall, Susannah (2022), *Constructive Theology and Gender Variance: Transformative Creatures* (Cambridge: Cambridge University Press).

Creamer, Deborah Beth, *Disability and Christian Theology: Embodied Limits and Constructive Possibilities* (Oxford: Oxford University Press, 2009).

Creswell, John W. and Poth, Cheryl N., *Qualitative Inquiry and Research Design: Choosing among Five Approaches* (2nd edn) (Thousand Oaks, CA: Sage Publications, 2007).

Davy, Zowie, 'Transsexual Agents: Negotiating Authenticity and Embodiment within the UK's Medicolegal System', in Hines, Sally and Sanger, Tam (eds), *Transgender Identities: Towards a Social Analysis of Gender Diversity* (London: Routledge, 2014), pp. 106–26.

DeFranza, Megan K., Arel, Stephanie N. and Stockly, Kate, 'Sex on the margins: centering intersex, transgender, and sexually fluid voices in religious and scientific discourse', *Theology & Sexuality*, 24, 2 (2018), pp. 65–71, https://doi.org/10.1080/13558358.2018.1463636 (accessed 10 March 2022).

Denshire, Sally, 'On Auto-ethnography', *Current Sociology Review*, 62, 6 (2014), pp. 831–50, http://dx.doi.org/10.1177/0011392114533339 (accessed 10 March 2022).

Derouen, Sister Luisa, 'Proclaiming the Truth of God's Transgender People', *CrossCurrents*, 68, 4 (2018), pp. 561–8, https://doi.org/10.1111/cros.12343 (accessed 10 March 2022).

Dille, Sarah J., *Mixing Metaphors: God as Mother and Father in Deutero-Isaiah* (London: T & T Clark International, 2004).

Dowd, Chris and Beardsley, Christina, *Trans Affirming Churches: How to Celebrate Gender-Variant People and Their Loved Ones* (London: Jessica Kingsley, 2020).

Dowd, Chris, Beardsley, Christina and Tanis, Justin, *Transfaith: A Transgender Pastoral Resource* (London: Darton, Longman & Todd, 2018).

Marie Draz, 'Realness as Resistance: Queer Feminism, Neoliberalism, and Early Trans Critiques of Butler', *Hypatia*, 37, 2 (2022).

Dussel, Enrique, *Ethics of Liberation in the Age of Globalization and Exclusion* (Durham, NC: Duke University Press, 2013).

Edmonson, Tess, '*The Argonauts*: Review', *International Contemporary Art*, 127 (2015), p. 68, https://www.proquest.com/docview/1722627548/1FA3FC7DD6AE48B1PQ/2?sourcetype=Magazines (accessed 10 March 2022).

Ekins, Richard and King, Dave, 'The Emergence of New Transgendering Identities in the Age of the Internet', in Hines, Sally and Sanger, Tam (eds) *Transgender Identities: Towards a Social Analysis of Gender Diversity* (Abingdon: Routledge, 2010), pp. 25–42.

Ellis, Carolyn, *The Ethnographic I: A Methodological Novel About Autoethnography* (Walnut Creek, CA: AltaMira Press, 2004).

Ellis, Carolyn, Adams, Tony E. and Bochner, Arthur P., 'Autoethnography: An Overview', *Forum: Qualitative Social Research*, 12, 1 (2011), pp. 1–19, https://www.qualitative-research.net/index.php/fqs/article/view/1589/3095 (accessed 10 March 2022).

Emezi, Akwaeke, 'Biography' (2019), https://www.akwaeke.com/biography (accessed 10 March 2022).

Emezi, Akwaeke, *Freshwater* (London: Faber & Faber, 2018).

Engdahl, Ulrica, 'Wrong Body', *TSQ: Transgender Studies Quarterly*, 1,

1–2 (2014), pp. 267–9, https://doi.org/10.1215/23289252-2400226 (accessed 23 December 2021).

Espinoza, Roberto Che, 'Transing Religion: Moving Beyond the Logic of the (Hetero)Norm of Binaries', *Journal of Feminist Studies in Religion*, 34, 1 (2018), pp. 88–92, http://dx.doi.org/10.2979/jfemi studreli.34.1.13 (accessed 10 March 2022).

Faith Survey (2021), https://faithsurvey.co.uk/uk-christianity.html (accessed 10 March 2022).

Fiorenza, Elisabeth Schüssler, *But She Said: Feminist Practices of Biblical Interpretation* (Boston, MA: Beacon Press, 1992).

Foltz, Tanice G. and Griffin, Wendy, 'She Changes Everything She Touches: Ethnographic Journeys of Self-Discovery' in Ellis, Carolyn and Bochner, Arthur P. (eds), *Composing Ethnography: Alternative Forms of Qualitative Writing* (London: AltaMira Press, 1996), pp. 263–85.

Foster, Kirk A., Bowland, Sharon E. and Vosler, Anne Nancy, 'All the Pain Along with All the Joy: Spiritual Resilience in Lesbian and Gay Christians', *American Journal of Community Psychology*, 55, 1–2 (2015), pp. 191–201, https://doi.org/10.1007/s10464-015-9704-4 (accessed 10 March 2022).

Foucault, Michel, tr. Sheridan, Alan, *Discipline and Punish* (New York: Pantheon Books, 1977).

Frymer-Kensky, Tikva, *In the Wake of the Goddesses: Women, Culture and the Biblical Transformation of Pagan Myth* (New York: Ballantine Books, 1992).

Funk, Jaydi, Funk, Steven S. and Whelan, Sylvia, 'Trans*+ and Intersex Representation and Pathologization: An Interdisciplinary Argument for Increased Medical Privacy', *Berkeley Journal of Gender, Law & Justice*, 34, 1 (2019), pp. 117–47, https://doi.org/10.15779/Z380C4S K4F (accessed 10 March 2022).

Furey, Constance M., 'Eros and the Argonauts', *Theology and Sexuality*, 22, 3 (2016), pp. 155–64, https://doi.org/10.1080/13558358.201 7.1329812 (accessed 10 March 2022).

Gans, Herbert J., 'Participant observation in the era of "ethnography"', *Journal of Contemporary Ethnography*, 28, 5 (1999), pp. 540–8, https://doi.org/10.1177/089124199129023532 (accessed 10 March 2022).

Gherovici, Patricia, 'Depathologizing Trans: From Symptom to Sinthome', *TSQ: Transgender Studies Quarterly*, 4, 3–4 (2017), pp. 534–55, https://doi.org/10.1215/23289252-4189956 (accessed 10 March 2022).

Glaser, Barney G. and Strauss, Anselm L., *The Discovery of Grounded Theory* (Chicago, IL: Aldine Publishing Company, 1967).

Glaser, Barney G., *Basics of Grounded Theory Analysis: Emergence vs. Forcing* (Mill Valley, CA: Sociology Press, 1992).

Gleeson, Jules, 'Judith Butler: "We need to rethink the category of woman"', *The Guardian* (7 September 2021), available at, https://www.theguardian.com/lifeandstyle/2021/sep/07/judith-butler-interview-gender (accessed 24 March 2023).

Good Law Project, 'The NHS must fulfil its duty to young people', 2020, https://goodlawproject.org/update/nhs-duty-to-young-people/ (accessed 11 March 2022).

Gozlan, Oren, *Transsexuality and the Art of Transitioning: A Lacanian Approach* (New York and London: Routledge, 2014).

Graham, Elaine L., *Making the Difference: Gender, Personhood and Theology* (London: Bloomsbury Publishing, 1995).

Graham, Elaine, Walton, Heather and Ward, Frances, *Theological Reflection: Methods* (London: SCM Press, 2005).

Gray, Sarah A. O., Carter, Alice S. and Levitt, Heidi, 'A Critical Review of Assumptions about Gender Variant Children in Psychological Research, *Journal of Gay & Lesbian Mental Health*, 16, 1 (2012), pp. 4–30, https://doi.org/10.1080/19359705.2012.634719 (accessed 11 March 2022).

Green, Marcus E., 'Rethinking the Subaltern and the Question of Censorship in Gramsci's Prison Notebooks', *Postcolonial Studies*, 14, 4 (2011) pp. 385–402.

Greenough, Chris, *Queer Theologies* (London: Routledge, 2020).

Greer, Germaine, *The Whole Woman* (London: Transworld Books, 2014).

Grue, Jan, 'The problem with inspiration porn: a tentative definition and a provisional critique', *Disability & Society*, 31, 6 (2016), pp. 838–49, https://doi.org/10.1080/09687599.2016.1205473 (accessed 10 March 2022).

Gutiérrez, Gustavo, *A Theology of Liberation: History, Politics, and Salvation* (2nd edn) (New York: Orbis, 1988).

Hall, Wendy A. and Callery, Peter, 'Enhancing the rigor of grounded theory: Incorporating reflexivity and relationality', *Qualitative Health Research*, 11, 2 (2001), pp. 257–72.

Halperin, David, 'The Normalization of Queer Theory', *Journal of Homosexuality*, 45, 2–4 (2003), pp. 339–44, https://www.researchgate.net/publication/23555352_The_Normalization_of_Queer_Theory (accessed 10 March 2022).

Haraway, Donna, 'Situated Knowledges: The Science Question in Feminism and the Privilege of Partial Perspective', in Harding, Sandra (ed.), *The Feminist Standpoint Theory Reader: Intellectual and Political Controversies* (London: Routledge, 2004), pp. 81–102.

Harding, S., 'A Socially Relevant Philosophy of Science? Resources from Standpoint Theory's Controversiality', *Hypatia*, 19, 1 (2004), pp. 25–47, https://www.jstor.org/stable/3810930 (accessed 17 March 2022).

Harding, Sandra, 'Introduction: Standpoint Theory as a Site of Political, Philosophic, and Scientific Debate', in Harding, Sandra (ed.), *The Feminist Standpoint Theory Reader: Intellectual and Political Controversies* (London: Routledge, 2004), pp. 1–16.

Harding, Sandra, 'Rethinking Standpoint Epistemology: What is "Strong Objectivity"?', in Harding, Sandra (ed.), *The Feminist Standpoint Theory Reader: Intellectual and Political Controversies* (London: Routledge, 2004), pp. 127–40.

Harrison-Quintana, Jack, Grant, Jaime M. and Rivera, Ignacio G., 'Boxes of Our Own Creation: A Trans Data Collection Wo/Manifesto', *Making Transgender Count: Transgender Studies Quarterly*, 2, 1 (2015), pp. 166–74, https://doi.org/10.1215/23289252-2848949 (accessed 10 March 2022).

Hartke, Austen, *Transforming: The Bible and the Lives of Transgender Christians* (Louisville, KY: Westminster John Knox Press, 2018).

Hartman, Ann, 'Many ways of knowing', *Social Work*, 35, 1 (1990), pp. 3–4.

Hayano, David M., 'Auto-Ethnography: Paradigms, Problems, and Prospects', *Human Organization*, 38, 1 (1979), pp. 99–105.

Herman, Didi, *The Anti-Gay Agenda: Orthodox Vision and the Christian Right* (Chicago, IL: University of Chicago Press, 1997).

Hesse-Biber, Sharlene Nagy, *Feminist Research Practice: A Primer* (Thousand Oaks, CA: Sage Publications, 2014).

Heyes, Cressida J., *Self-Transformations: Foucault, Ethics, and Normalized Bodies* (Oxford: Oxford University Press, 2007).

Hines, Sally, *TransForming Gender: Transgender Practices of Identity, Intimacy and Care* (Bristol: Policy Press, 2007).

Hines, Sally, 'Introduction', in Hines, Sally and Sanger, Tam (eds), *Transgender Identities: Towards a Social Analysis of Gender Diversity* (Abingdon: Routledge, 2010), pp. 1–24.

Hines, Sally, 'Recognising Diversity? The Gender Recognition Act and Transgender Citizenship', in Hines, Sally and Sanger, Tam (eds), *Transgender Identities: Towards a Social Analysis of Gender Diversity* (London: Routledge, 2014), pp. 87–105.

Hird, Myra J., 'Gender's nature: Intersexuality, transsexualism and the "sex"/"gender" binary', *Feminist Theory*, 1, 3 (2000), pp. 347–64, https://doi.org/10.1177/14647001000100305 (accessed 10 March 2022).

Holman Jones, Stacy and Adams, Tony E., 'Autoethnography is a Queer Method', in Browne, Kath and Nash, Catherine J. (eds), *Queer Methods and Methodologies: Intersecting Queer Theories and Social Science Research* (Abingdon: Routledge, 2010), pp. 195–214.

Hood, Jane C., 'Orthodoxy vs Power: The Defining Traits of Grounded Theory', in Bryant, Antony and Charmaz, Kathleen M. (eds), *The*

Sage Handbook of Grounded Theory (Thousand Oaks, CA: Sage Publications, 2007), pp. 151–64.

hooks, bell, 'Choosing the Margin as a Space of Radical Openness', in Harding, Sandra (ed.), *The Feminist Standpoint Theory Reader: Intellectual and Political Controversies* (London: Routledge, 2004), pp. 153–60.

Hughto Jaclyn M. W., Pletta, David R., Gordon, Lily, Cahill, Sean, Mimiaga, Matthew J. and Reisner, Sari L., 'Negative Transgender-Related Media Messages are Associated with Adverse Mental Health Outcomes in a Multistate Study of Transgender Adults', *LGBT Health*, 8, 1 (2021), pp. 32–42, https://doi.org/10.1089/lgbt.2020.0279 (accessed 11 March 2022).

Humphrey, Rhianna, '"I think journalists sometimes forget that we're just people": Analysing the effects of UK trans media representation on trans audiences', *Gender Forum*, 56, 1 (2016), https://www-proquest-com.ezproxye.bham.ac.uk/scholarly-journals/i-think-journalists-sometimes-forget-that-were/docview/1759000383/se-2 (accessed 2 April 2022).

Hunt, Ruth, *The Book of Queer Prophets: 24 Writers on Sexuality and Religion* (London: William Collins, 2020).

Isherwood, Lisa and McPhillips, Kathleen (eds), *Post-Christian Feminisms: A Critical Approach* (London: Routledge, 2016).

Isherwood, Lisa and Stuart, Elizabeth, *Introducing Body Theology* (Sheffield: Sheffield Academic Press, 1998).

Jeffreys, Sheila, 'They Know It When They See It: The UK Gender Recognition Act 2004', *The British Journal of Politics and International Relations*, 10, 2 (2008), pp. 328–45, https://doi.org/10.1111/j.1467-856x.2007.00293.x (accessed 10 March 2022).

Jeffreys, Sheila, 'Transgender Activism', *Journal of Lesbian Studies*, 1, 3–4 (1997), pp. 55–74, https://doi.org/10.1300/J155v01n03_03 (accessed 10 March 2022).

Jensen, Robert, 'Is the ideology of the transgender movement open to debate?', *Feminist Current* (2016), https://www.feministcurrent.com/2016/06/27/ideology-transgender-movement-open-debate/ (accessed 15 August 2019).

Johnson, Jeffrey Alan, 'Information Systems and the Translation of Transgender', *Making Transgender Count: Transgender Studies Quarterly*, 2, 1 (2015), pp. 160–5, https://doi.org/10.1215/23289252-2848940 (accessed 10 March 2022).

Kelly, Siobhan M., 'Multiplicity and Contradiction: A Literature Review of Trans* Studies in Religion', *Journal of Feminist Studies in Religion*, 34, 1 (2018) pp. 7–23, http://dx.doi.org/10.2979/jfemistudreli.34.1.03 (accessed 10 March 2022).

Kelso, Tony, 'Still Trapped in the U.S. Media's Closet: Representations of Gender-Variant, Pre-Adolescent Children', *Journal of Homosexu-*

ality, 62, 8 (2015), pp. 1058–97, https://doi.org/10.1080/00918369. 2015.1021634 (accessed 10 March 2022).

Kim, Annabel L., 'The Politics of Citation', *Diacritics*, 48, 3 (2020), pp. 4–97.

Koch-Rein, Anson, PhD Thesis: 'Mirrors, Monsters, Metaphors: Transgender Rhetorics and Dysphoria Knowledge', Atlanta, GA: Emory University, 2014), https://etd.library.emory.edu/concern/etds/0v838 098q (accessed 11 March 2022).

Koch-Rein, Anson, Haschemi, Elahe Haschemi and Verlinden, Jasper J., 'Representing trans: visibility and its discontents', *European Journal of English Studies*, 24, 1 (2020), pp. 1–12, https://doi.org/10.108 0/13825577.2020.1730040 (accessed 10 March 2022).

Labuski, Christine and Keo-Meier, Colton, 'The (Mis)Measure of Trans', *Making Transgender Count: Transgender Studies Quarterly*, 2, 1 (2015), pp. 13–33, https://doi.org/10.1215/23289252-2848868 (accessed 10 March 2022).

Ladin, Joy, 'In the Image of God, God Created Them: Toward Trans Theology', *Journal of Feminist Studies in Religion*, 34, 1 (2018), pp. 53–8, https://doi.org/10.2979/jfemistudreli.34.1.06 (accessed 10 March 2022).

LaMothe, Ryan, 'A Modest Proposal: A Pastoral Political Theology', *Pastoral Psychology*, 63, 4 (2014), pp. 375–91, https://doi.org/10.1007/s11089-013-0557-1 (accessed 11 March 2022).

LaMothe, Ryan, 'Discerning a Theological Orientation for Pastoral Psychologies of Care: Theologies of Subjugation and Theologies of Vulnerability', *Pastoral Psychology*, 69, 4 (2020), pp. 405–21, https://doi.org/10.1007/s11089-020-00916-3 (accessed 11 March 2022).

Leach, Jane, 'Pastoral Theology as Attention', *Practical Theology*, 153, 1 (2007), pp. 19–32, https://doi.org/10.1080/13520806.2007.11759 074 (accessed 10 March 2022).

Lefevor, G. Tyler, Sprague, Brianna M., Boyd-Rogers, Caroline C. and Smack, Abigail C.P., 'How well do various types of support buffer psychological distress among transgender and gender nonconforming students?', *International Journal of Transgenderism*, 20, 1 (2019), pp. 39–48, https://doi.org/10.1080/15532739.2018.14521 72 (accessed 10 March 2022).

Levy, Denise L. and Lo, Jessica R., 'Transgender, Transsexual, and Gender Queer Individuals with a Christian Upbringing: The Process of Resolving Conflict Between Gender Identity and Faith', *Journal of Religion & Spirituality in Social Work: Social Thought*, 32, 1 (2013), pp. 60–83, https://doi.org/10.1080/15426432.2013.749079 (accessed 11 March 2022).

Loughlin, Gerard (ed.), *Queer Theology: Rethinking the Western Body* (Oxford: Blackwell, 2007).

Lowe, Mary Elise, 'From the Same Spirit: Receiving the Theological

Gifts of Transgender Christians', *Dialog*, 56, 1 (2017), pp. 28–37, https://doi.org/10.1111/dial.12293 (accessed 11 March 2022).

Lucas, Grace, 'Gut thinking: the gut microbiome and mental health beyond the head', *Microbial Ecology in Health and Disease*, 29, 2 (2018), https://doi.org/10.1080/16512235.2018.1548250 (accessed 10 March 2022).

Lui, P. Priscilla and Quezada, Lucia, 'Associations Between Micro-aggression and Adjustment Outcomes: A Meta-Analytic and Narrative Review', *Psychological Bulletin*, 145, 1 (2019), pp. 45–78, https://doi.org/10.1037/bul0000172 (accessed 11 March 2022).

Maddix, Mark A., 'Embracing Postcolonialism: The Future of Christian Education', *Christian Education Journal*, 15, 3 (2018), pp. 479–90, https://doi.org/10.1177/0739891318809209 (accessed 2 December 2021).

Makhoul, Marwan (2019), اين أمي ISBN: 9786144254721, tr. @dia lectichiphop, Twitter, https://twitter.com/dialectichiphop/status/155 7049741610999808 (accessed 6 September 2022).

Mann, Rachel, *Dazzling Darkness* (2nd edn) (Glasgow: Wild Goose Publications, 2020).

Mayeda, Graham, 'Who Do You Think You Are? When Should the Law Let You Be Who You Want to Be?', in Shrage, Laurie (ed.), *You've Changed: Sex Reassignment and Personal Identity* (Oxford: Oxford University Press, 2009), pp. 194–216.

McAdams, Dan P., 'Narrative Identity', in Schwartz, S. J., Luyckx, K. and Vignoles, V. L. (eds), *Handbook of Identity Theory and Research* (London: Springer, 2011), pp. 99–115.

McFadyen, Alistair I., *The Call to Personhood: A Christian Theory of the Individual in Social Relationships* (Cambridge: Cambridge University Press, 1990).

McLean, Craig, 'The Growth of the Anti-Transgender Movement in the United Kingdom: The Silent Radicalization of the British Electorate', *International Journal of Sociology*, 55, 6 (2021), pp. 473–82, https://doi.org/10.1080/00207659.2021.1939946 (accessed 10 March 2022).

McQueen, Paddy, 'Feminist and Trans Perspectives on Identity and the UK Gender Recognition Act', *The British Journal of Politics and International Relations*, 18, 3 (2016), pp. 671–87, https://doi.org/10.1177/1369148116637998 (accessed 11 March 2022).

Mollenkott, Virginia R., *Omnigender: A Trans-Religious Approach* (Cleveland, OH: Pilgrim Press, 2001).

Moltmann, Jürgen, *The Crucified God* (Minneapolis, MN: Fortress Press, 2015).

Moreira-Almeida, Alexandra and Santana Santos, Franklin, *Mindfulness in Behavioural Health: Exploring Frontiers of the Mind-Brain Relationship* (London: Springer, 2012).

Morris, Jan, *Conundrum* (New York: Henry Holt, 1986).

Mullhall, Anne, 'Queer Narrative', in Somerville, Siobhan, B. (ed.), *The Cambridge Companion to Queer Studies* (Cambridge: Cambridge University Press, 2020).

Mullins, R. T., *The End of the Timeless God* (Oxford: Oxford University Press, 2016).

Nadal, Kevin L., Davidoff, Kristin C., Davis, Lindsay S. and Wong, Yinglee, 'Emotional, Behavioral, and Cognitive Reactions to Microaggressions: Transgender Perspectives', *Psychology of Sexual Orientation and Gender Diversity*, 1, 1 (2014), pp. 72–81, https://doi.org/10.1037/sgd0000011 (accessed 11 March 2022).

Nagel, Thomas, *The View from Nowhere* (Oxford: Oxford University Press, 1986).

Nagoshi, Julie L., Nagoshi, Craig T. and Brzuzy, Stephan/ie, *Gender and Sexual Identity: Transcending Feminist and Queer Theory* (London: Springer, 2014).

Naples, Nancy A. and Gurr, Barbara, 'Feminist Empiricism and Standpoint Theory: Approaches to Understanding the Social World', in Hesse-Biber, Sharlene N. (ed.), *Feminist Research Practice: A Primer* (Thousand Oaks, CA: Sage Publications, 2014), pp. 14–41.

National Health Service, 'Overview: Gender Dysphoria' (NHS, 2020), https://www.nhs.uk/conditions/gender-dysphoria/ (accessed 17 January 2022).

Nelson, Maggie, *The Argonauts* (London: Melville House UK, 2015).

Norwood, Kristen, 'Meaning Matters: Framing Trans Identity in the Context of Family Relationships', *Journal of GLBT Family Studies*, 9, 2 (2013), pp. 152–78, https://doi.org/10.1080/1550428X.2013.765262 (accessed 3 April 2022).

Nye, William, 'GS. 2071B: Welcoming Transgender People: A note from the Secretary General' (2017), https://www.churchofengland.org/sites/default/files/2017-11/gs-2071b-welcoming-transgender-people-a-note-from-the-secretary-general.pdf (accessed 23 December 2021).

Nyssa, Gregory of, Schaff, Philip (ed.), *Great Catechism: Nicene and Post-Nicene Fathers series ii, Vol. 1*, http://www.ccel.org/ccel/schaff/npnf205 (accessed 10 March 2022).

O'Brien, Michelle and Beardsley, Christina, 'The Sibyls' Gender, Sexuality and Spirituality Workshop', in O'Brien, Michelle and Beardsley, Christina (eds), *This is My Body: Hearing the Theology of Transgender Christians* (London: Darton, Longman & Todd, 2016), pp. 11–22.

O'Donovan, Oliver, *Transsexualism: Issues and Argument* (Cambridge: Grove Books, 1982).

Oakley, Lisa, Kinmond, Kathryn and Humphreys, Justin, 'Spiritual abuse in Christian faith settings: definition, policy and practice guidance', *The Journal of Adult Protection*, 20, 3–4 (2018), pp. 144–54, https://doi.org/10.1108/JAP-03-2018-0005 (accessed 11 March 2022).

Omeje, Sade, 'Review: *Freshwater* by Akwaeke Emezi', *The Mancunian* (2018), https://mancunion.com/2018/11/22/review-freshwater-by-akwaeke-emezi/ (accessed 11 March 2022).

Oort, Johannes van, 'The holy spirit as feminine: Early Christian testimonies and their interpretation', *Hervormde Teologiese Studies*, 72, 1 (2016), pp. 1–6, https://hdl.handle.net/10520/EJC196161 (accessed 1 December 2021).

Outler, Albert C., 'The Wesleyan Quadrilateral in Wesley', *Wesleyan Theological Journal*, 20, 1 (1985), pp. 7–18, http://wesley.nnu.edu/fileadmin/imported_site/wesleyjournal/1985-wtj-20-1.pdf (accessed 28 May 2022).

Ozanne, Jayne, '"Conversion therapy", spiritual abuse and human rights', *European Human Rights Law Review*, 3 (June 2021), pp. 241–9.

Partridge, Cameron, '"Scotch-Taped Together": Anti-"Androgyny" Rhetoric, Transmisogyny, and the Transing of Religious Studies', *Journal of Feminist Studies in Religion*, 34, 1 (2018), pp. 68–75, https://doi.org/10.2979/jfemistudreli.34.1.09 (accessed 11 March 2022).

Paton, Stephen, 'They Do Not Speak for Us: Feminists Hit Back at Trans-Exclusionary Activists in Open Letter', *The National* (3 March 2019), https://www.thenational.scot/news/17472564.they-do-not-speak-for-us-feminists-hit-back-at-trans-exclusionary-activists-in-open-letter/ (accessed 22 July 2019).

Pearl, Monica B., 'Theory and the Everyday', *Angelaki: Journal of the Theoretical Humanities*, 23, 1 (2018), pp. 199–203, https://doi.org/10.1080/0969725X.2018.1435401 (11 March 2022).

Pels, Dick, 'Strange Standpoints, or How to Define the Situation for Situated Knowledge', in Harding, Sandra (ed.), *The Feminist Standpoint Theory Reader: Intellectual and Political Controversies* (London: Routledge, 2004), pp. 273–90.

Perrone, Pierre, 'Obituaries: Coccinelle', *The Independent* (16 October 2006), https://www.independent.co.uk/news/obituaries/coccinelle-6230828.html (accessed 23 December 2021).

Plaskow, Judith, 'Transing and Gendering Religious Studies', *Journal of Feminist Studies in Religion*, 34, 1 (2018), pp. 75–80, https://doi.org/10.2979/jfemistudreli.34.1.10 (accessed 11 March 2022).

Plato, tr. John Burnet, *Platonis Opera* (Oxford: Oxford University Press, 385–70 BC/1903 CE), para. 172a.

Ploder, Andrea and Stadlbauer, Johanna, 'Strong Reflexivity and its Critics: Responses to Autoethnography in the German-Speaking Cultural and Social Sciences', *Qualitative Inquiry*, 22, 9 (2016), pp. 753–65, https://doi.org/10.1177/1077800416658067 (accessed 11 March 2022).

Prosser, Jay, *Second Skins: The Body Narratives of Transsexuality* (New York: Columbia University Press, 1998).

Pugh, Ben, *Atonement Theories: A Way Through the Maze* (Cambridge: James Clarke and Co., 2014).

Rainbow, Jonathan H., *The Will of God and the Cross: An Historical and Theological Study of John Calvin's Doctrine of Limited Redemption* (San Jose, CA: Pickwick, 1990).

Raymond, Janice G., *The Transsexual Empire: The Making of the She-Male* (London: The Women's Press, 1980).

Reed, Terry, 'Good practice guidelines for the assessment and treatment of adults with gender dysphoria' (London: Royal College of Psychiatrists, 2013), https://www.rcpsych.ac.uk/docs/default-source/improving-care/better-mh-policy/college-reports/cr181-good-practice-guidelines-for-the-assessment-and-treatment-of-adults-with-gender-dysphoria.pdf (accessed 23 December 2021).

Reinsmith-Jones, Kelly, 'Transsexualism as a Model of Spiritual Transformation: Implications', *Journal of GLBT Family Studies*, 9, 1 (2013), pp. 65–99, https://doi.org/10.1080/1550428X.2013.748509 (accessed 11 March 2022).

Rogers, Carl, 'A theory of therapy, personality, and interpersonal relationships as developed in the client-centred framework', in Koch, S. (ed.), *Psychology: A Study of Science, vol. 3: Formulation of the Person and the Social Context* (New York: McGraw Hill, 1959), pp. 184–256, at p. 209.

Rood, Brian A., Reisner, Sari L., Puckett, Jae A., Surace, Francisco I., Berman, Ariel K. and Pantalone, David W., 'Internalized transphobia: Exploring perceptions of social messages in transgender and gender-nonconforming adults', *International Journal of Transgenderism*, 18, 4 (2017), pp. 411–26, https://doi.org/10.1080/15532739.2017.1329048 (accessed 3 April 2022).

Rooke, Alison, 'Telling Trans Stories: (Un)doing the Science of Sex', in Hines, Sally and Sanger, Tam (eds), *Transgender Identities: Towards a Social Analysis of Gender Diversity* (Abingdon: Routledge, 2010), pp. 64–85.

Rubano, Craig, 'Where do the Mermaids Stand? Toward a "Gender-Creative" Pastoral Sensitivity', *Pastoral Psychology*, 65, 6 (2016), pp. 821–34, https://doi.org/10.1007/s11089-015-0680-2 (accessed 11 March 2022).

Sandercock, Tom, 'Transing the small screen: loving and hating transgender youth in Glee and Degrassi', *Journal of Gender Studies*, 24, 4, pp. 436–52, http://dx.doi.org/10.1080/09589236.2015.1021307 (accessed 10 March 2022).

Savage, Helen, 'Changing sex?: transsexuality and Christian theology' (Doctoral thesis. Durham: Durham University, 2006), http://etheses.dur.ac.uk/3364 (accessed 11 January 2021).

Schafer, Peter, *Mirror of His Beauty: Feminine Images of God from the Bible to the Early Kabbalah* (Princeton, NJ: Princeton University Press, 2002).

Schneider, Laurel C., 'Homosexuality, Queer Theory, and Christian Theology', *Religious Studies Review*, 26, 1 (2000), pp. 3–12.

Schwartzmann, Julia, 'Gender Concepts of Medieval Jewish Thinkers and the Book of Proverbs', *Jewish Studies Quarterly*, 7, 3 (2000), pp. 183–202.

Sherwood, Harriet, 'Less than half of Britons expected to tick "Christian" in UK census', *The Observer* (20 March 2021), https://www.theguardian.com/uk-news/2021/mar/20/less-that-half-of-britons-expected-to-tick-christian-in-uk-census (accessed 2 November 2021).

Sklar, Julia, 'Zoom fatigue is taxing the brain. Here's why that happens', *National Geographic* (24 April 2020), https://www.nationalgeographic.com/science/2020/04/coronavirus-zoom-fatigue-is-taxing-the-brain-here-is-why-that-happens/ (accessed 13 November 2020).

Smith, Brett, 'Narrative inquiry and Autoethnography', in Silk, Michael, Andrews, David and Thorpe, Holly (eds), *The Routledge Handbook of Physical Cultural Studies* (Abingdon: Routledge, 2017), pp. 505–14.

Smith, Dorothy E., 'Women's Perspective as a Radical Critique of Sociology', in Harding, Sandra (ed.), *The Feminist Standpoint Theory Reader: Intellectual and Political Controversies* (London: Routledge, 2004), pp. 21–35.

Soskice, Janet Martin, *The Kindness of God: Metaphor, Gender, and Religious Language* (Oxford: Oxford University Press, 2008), p. 86.

Stewart, Raedorah C., 'Loop, Hook, Pull: Disabled by Design — Creating a Narrative Theology of Disability', *Theology Today*, 77, 2 (2020), pp. 179–85, https://doi.org/10.1177/0040573620920673 (accessed 11 March 2022).

Stop Hate UK, 'Transgender Hate', https://www.stophateuk.org/about-hate-crime/transgender-hate/, (accessed 7 November 2022).

Strachan, Owen, Yarhouse, Mark A., Sadusky, Julia, DeFranza, Megan K. and Sabia-Tanis, Justin, *Understanding Transgender Identities: Four Views* (Grand Rapids, MI: Baker Academic, 2019).

Strassfeld, Max, 'Transing Religious Studies', *Journal of Feminist Studies in Religion*, 34, 1 (2018), pp. 37–53, https://doi.org/10.2979/jfemistudreli.34.1.05 (accessed 11 March 2022).

Stuart, Elizabeth, 'Sacramental Flesh', in Loughlin, Gerard (ed.), *Queer Theology: Rethinking the Western Body* (Oxford: Blackwell, 2007), pp. 65–76.

Sumerau, J. E., Mathers, Lain A. B. and Lampe, Nik, 'Learning from the Religious Experiences of Bi+ Trans People', *Symbolic Interaction*, 42, 2 (2018), pp. 179–201, https://doi.org/10.1002/symb.387 (accessed 11 March 2022).

Szalai, Jennifer, 'Maggie Nelson's *The Argonauts*', *The New York Times* (7 May 2015), https://www.nytimes.com/2015/05/10/books/review/maggie-nelsons-the-argonauts.html (accessed 3 October 2020).

Thatcher, Adrian, *Gender and Christian Ethics* (Cambridge: Cambridge University Press, 2020).

The Church of England, 'What We Believe', https://www.churchof england.org/our-faith/what-we-believe/apostles-creed#na (accessed 3 January 2022.

The General Assembly of the United Reformed Church, 'Inclusive and Expansive Language' (London: The United Reformed Church, 2014), https://urc.org.uk/images/Global_and_Intercultural/Good_Practice/Inclusive-and-Expansive-Language.pdf (accessed 2 December 2021).

The House of Bishops, *Living in Love and Faith* (London: The Church of England, 2020).

The United Reformed Church, 'The Manual', 17, https://urc.org.uk/images/the_manual/A_The_Basis_of_union.pdf (accessed 3 January 2022).

Thorn, Rachael, 'Why Toilets are a Battle Ground for Transgender Rights', BBC (8 June 2016), https://www.bbc.co.uk/news/uk-england-36395646 (accessed 15 November 2019).

Trans Media Watch, 'How Transgender People Experience the Media: Conclusions from Research', *TMW* (April 2010), https://transmedia watch.org/wp-content/uploads/2020/09/How-Transgender-People-Experience-the-Media.pdf (accessed 10 March 2022).

Transrespect Versus Transphobia Worldwide (TVT), 'TMM Update Trans Day of Remembrance 2021' (11 November 2021), https://trans respect.org/en/tmm-update-tdor-2021/ (accessed 11 March 2022).

UK Government, 'Gender Recognition Act' (2004), http://www.legis-lation.gov.uk/ukpga/2004/7/contents (accessed 15 November 2019).

UK Government, 'Human Rights Act' (2010), http://www.legislation.gov.uk/ukpga/2010/15/ (accessed 22 July 2019).

United Reformed Church Equal Opportunities Committee, 'E3: Discussion on Inclusive Language and Expansive Language' (November 2013), p. 3, https://urc.org.uk/images/MissionCouncil/November_2013/Paper_E3_MC_November_2013.pdf (accessed 3 April 2021).

United Reformed Church, 'Statement of Faith' (1972), https://urc.org.uk/images/Free-Ebooks/WB2_Statements_of_Faith.pdf (accessed 10 March 2022).

United Reformed Church, 'A Brief History of the United Reformed Church: part of an introduction course on the United Reformed Church for those training as Elders, Lay Preachers, Local Leaders, Ministers of Word and Sacraments and Church Related Community Workers' (London: The United Reformed Church, 2011), https://www.augustine.org.uk/wp-content/uploads/2018/12/URC-History-Course-History.pdf (accessed 2 December 2021).

United Reformed Church, 'Assembly Executive round-up: 22–24 November 2021' (London: The United Reformed Church, 2021), https://urc.org.uk/latest-news/3982-assembly-executive-round-up-22-24-november-2021.html (accessed 2 December 2021).

United Reformed Church, 'Basis of Union' (London: The United Reformed Church, 1972/2021), https://urc.org.uk/images/the_manu al/A_The_Basis_of_union.pdf (accessed 2 December 2021).

United Reformed Church, 'Pastoral Cycle' (2021), https://urc.org.uk/ images/WalkingtheWay/documents/Pastoral_Cycle_Summary.pdf (accessed 10 March 2022).

Urban Dictionary (2021), 'Headcanon', https://www.urbandictionary. com/define.php?term=headcanon (accessed 11 March 2022).

Wall, Sarah Stahlke, 'Toward a Moderate Autoethnography', *International Journal of Qualitative Methods*, 15, 1 (2016), pp. 1–9, https:// doi.org/10.1177/1609406916674966 (accessed 11 March 2022).

Walton, Heather, 'Making Meaning: Being Spiritual in Social Research', *Reconsidering Methods and Methodologies in Theology Event* (Manchester: Lincoln Theological Institute, 5 February 2021) (conference paper).

Weekley, David E., 'Becoming Grateful Allies: An Interview with Dr Virginia Ramey Mollenkott', *Journal of Feminist Studies in Religion*, 34, 1 (2018) pp. 25–36, https://doi.org/10.2979/jfemistudreli.34.1.04 (accessed 11 March 2022).

Weiman-Kelman, Zohar, 'Transing Back the Texts, Queering Jewish Prayer', *Journal of Feminist Studies in Religion*, 34, 1 (2018), pp. 80–4, https://doi.org/10.2979/jfemistudreli.34.1.11 (accessed 11 March 2022).

Weissler, Chava, *Voices of the Matriarchs: Listening to the Prayers of Early Modern Jewish Women* (Boston, MA: Beacon Press, 1998).

Westbrook, Laurel, 'Becoming Knowably Gendered', in Hines, Sally and Sanger, Tam (eds), *Transgender Identities: Towards a Social Analysis of Gender Diversity* (Abingdon: Routledge, 2010), pp. 43–64.

Whitehead, James, D. and Whitehead, Evelyn Eaton, 'Transgender Lives: From Bewilderment to God's Extravagance', *Pastoral Psychology*, 63, 2 (2014), pp. 171–84, https://doi.org/10.1007/s11089-013-0543-7 (accessed 11 March 2022).

Wilcox, Melissa M., 'Religion is Already Transed; Religious Studies is Not (Yet) Listening', *Journal of Feminist Studies in Religion*, 34, 1 (2018), pp. 84–8, https://doi.org/10.2979/jfemistudreli.34.1.12 (accessed 11 March 2022).

Wolff, Joshua R., Kay, Theresa Stueland, Himes, H. L. and Alquijay, Jennifer, 'Transgender and Gender-Nonconforming Student Experiences in Christian Higher Education: A Qualitative Exploration',

Christian Higher Education, 16, 5 (2017), pp. 319–38, http://dx.doi. org/10.1080/15363759.2017.1310065 (accessed 11 March 2022).

Wolff, Michelle, 'A diptych reading of Christ's transfiguration: trans and intersex aesthetics reveal baptismal identity', *Theology & Sexuality*, 25, 1–2 (2019) pp. 98–110, https://doi.org/10.1080/13558358.2019. 1636173 (accessed 11 March 2022).

Wolfson, Elliot R., *Circle in the Square: Studies in the Use of Gender in Kabbalistic Symbolism* (Albany, NY: State University of New York Press, 1995).

World Council of Churches, *Baptism, Eucharist and Ministry* (Geneva: World Council of Churches, 1982).

Wylie, Alison, 'Why Standpoint Matters', in Harding, Sandra (ed.), *The Feminist Standpoint Theory Reader: Intellectual and Political Controversies* (London: Routledge, 2004), pp. 339–54.

Yarhouse, Mark, A., *Understanding Gender Dysphoria: Navigating Transgender Issues in a Changing Culture* (Downers Grove, IL: IVP Academic, 2015).

Yarhouse, Mark A. and Carrs, Trista L., 'MTF Transgender Christians' Experiences: A Qualitative Study', *Journal of LGBT Issues in Counseling*, 6, 1 (2012), pp. 18–33, https://doi.org/10.1080/15538605.20 12.649405 (accessed 11 March 2022).

Zoubaa, Sarah, Dial, Brandon, Ryan-Jones, Lindsey, Shah, Virakti and Yanos, Philip T., 'On the relationship between experienced microaggressions and mental health stigma among members of marginalized groups', *Counselling Psychology Quarterly*, 35, 4 (2021), https://doi. org/10.1080/09515070.2021.1968795 (accessed 11 March 2022).

Index of Bible References

Page numbers in *italics* indicate an implied biblical passage for which no reference is given on the page.

Index of Names and Subjects

incarnation 16–18, 141, 143,
  154–5, 160, 188–90
individualism ('selfishness') trope
  27–8
individuality of experience and
  insight 18–19, 25–6, 56–8,
  115–16, 179–80, 181–4,
  196–8, 203
intersectionality 47–8, 73–4,
  128, 129
interview technique 46–7, 48,
  56–7, 60–2

Jack (research participant) 7–8,
  72–5, 91–3
  on Christ 157
  creative practices 92–3, 124,
    129
  on God 74–5, 148, 149, 150,
    159, 168
  his identity and lived
    experience 72–6, 91–3, 113,
    116–17, 125–6, 130, 176,
    179
  on mirroring God 124
  personal qualities 128, 130
Jesus
  as Christ 154–8
  as example and role model
    155–7, 164
  female imagery and language
    for 36, 74, 142
  fleshiness of 167–8
  gender of 34–5, 130, 142, 158,
    188
  suffering of 83, 125–6, 143,
    154–5
John of the Cross, St 122, 125
Johnson, Jeffrey Alan 58
joy 98–104, 115, 157 *see also*
  euphoria
justice 128, 129–30, 157, 222

knowledge production *see*
  standpoint theory

kyriarchy, interruption of 66–7,
  70–1, 129–30

language
  for God 35, 74–5, 148–50,
    151–2, 153, 193
  for ourselves 130, 194
  as a place of struggle 22
  see also pronouns, use of
LGBTQ+ communities 93, 94,
  123, 132
Living in Love and Faith (Church
  of England) 69
love
  God's 5–6, 82, 161, 162
  human 140–1

Makhoul, Marwan 21
male privilege 46, 47, 86
marginalization 73–4, 87–8
marriage 41, 79, 87, 95 *see also*
  relationships
Mary Magdalene (biblical
  character) 99
Mayeda, Graham 76
McAdams, Dan P. 77
McFadyen, Alistair I. 119, 135
McLean, Craig 78
Meadows, Lucy 27
media representation of trans
  identities 77, 78, 88
medical ethics 209–10
mental health 80–1, 105, 118
Mike (research participant) 9,
  103–4, 219–23
  on deconstructing norms 177
  on God 145, 146, 147, 148,
    151, 152, 159, 160, 161, 177,
    183
  his identity and lived experience
    9, 103–4, 117, 118, 120–1,
    219–23
  on Jesus 156–7
  on mirroring 120–1
  personal qualities 128, 129–30

www.ingramcontent.com/pod-product-compliance
Lightning Source LLC
LaVergne TN
LVHW040605060125
800513LV00008B/35

* 9 7 8 0 3 3 4 0 6 6 0 0 2 *